THE

EVOLUTION
OF POLICY BEHIND
TAIWAN'S
DEVELOPMENT
SUCCESS

2nd Edition

THE
EVOLUTION
OF POLICY BEHIND
TAIWAN'S
DEVELOPMENT
SUCCESS

2nd Edition

Kuo-Ting Li

Introductory essays by
Gustav Ranis and John C.H. Fei

World Scientific
Singapore • New Jersey • London • Hong Kong

Published by

World Scientific Publishing Co. Pte. Ltd.

P O Box 128, Farrer Road, Singapore 9128

USA office: Suite 1B, 1060 Main Street, River Edge, NJ 07661

UK office: 57 Shelton Street, Covent Garden, London WC2H 9HE

*HC
430.5
L4725
1995*

Library of Congress Cataloging-in-Publication Data

Li, Kuo-ting, 1910–
    The evolution of policy behind Taiwan's development success / K.T.
Li ; introductory essays by Gustav Ranis and John C.H. Fei -- 2nd ed.
       p.   cm.
    Includes bibliographical references and index.
    ISBN 9810218389
    1. Taiwan--Economic policy -- 1945–   2. Taiwan -- Economic
conditions -- 1945–   I. Ranis, Gustav.   II. Fei, John C. H.
III. Title.
HC430.5.L4725   1995
338.95124'9--dc20
                                   94-39426
                                       CIP

British Library Cataloguing-in-Publication Data
A catalogue record for this book is available from the British Library.

Cover photographs reproduced with kind permission of the Government Information Office, ROC.

Printed in Singapore.

PROLOGUE

GUSTAV RANIS

There exists a lively interest today in the effort at transition growth, labeled development, in the third world, especially among the so-called newly industrializing countries (or NICs) and most especially with respect to probably its most successful member, Taiwan. The economic story of that success has already been told in several places, but the question of how and why it happened is still only imperfectly understood.

This book differs from many others on the subject of development at least in three ways: first, it focuses on the evolution of policy that lies below the surface of economic events; second, it records the recollections of a high-level practitioner of development; and third, it includes, in addition, introductory essays by two academicians concerned with development. Academicians look at the mystery of successful development quite differently; they may give advice to the government but essentially they enjoy the luxury of examining the process from a detached and dispassionate vantage point seeking to extract what is generalizable and transferable. Practitioners, on the other hand, although guided by a framework of ideas, are almost bound to be more problem- or crisis-oriented, with a sense of immediacy and practicality as they respond to urgent issues and constraints.

The armchair academician is prone to imagine that the world of action proceeds according to some well-thought-out master plan following some *a priori* theorizing. The practical policymaker (in this case a very high and influential official at the ministerial level), on the other hand, responds instinctively and often innovatively to the problem at hand. Only after some years do academicians, who must find a "system" and seek transferability, come up with an *ex post* rationalization of what must have happened in a consistent logical fashion to permit the Taiwan story to unfold as it did. The analysis of Taiwan's policy changes and development path is, in this sense, analogous to the experience with the New Deal of the 1930s. School children are taught how the major building blocks to get the United States out of the Depression were put in place carefully and selectively with one eye on Keynesian theory, which was just coming into vogue. But, in fact, it is well known that the New Deal emerged from the crucible of trial and error rather than from a theoretical blueprint. Much the same is true of the analysis of the liberalization path of Taiwan as seen by academicians and of the creative response to problems as seen by the practitioner. Policy analysis is often done after the fact while the design of policy must necessarily be done in advance. The historical record, nevertheless, is there for all to see, to analyze, and to benefit from in the best tradition of the social sciences.

Finally, a word on coverage. The academician naturally tends to see matters in a holistic fashion, endeavoring to look at the economy within a general equilibrium framework of interlocking parts. Jointly with Minister Li, John Fei and I have consequently prepared a policy matrix that lists important changes in the evolution of policy in a substantial number of sectors over time (see appendix). The practitioner, on the other hand, is most likely to focus on specific strategic issues or policy areas that he considers to constitute crucial bottlenecks to further forward motion. As a consequence, the main chapters of the book do not attempt to cover comprehensively policy changes in every single one of the economy's sectors or markets but focus on what Minister Li felt were the key strategic areas in which bottlenecks had to be broken to permit the economy to continue to move forward.

The practitioner is thus necessarily selective. I believe we are fortunate to have had one of the major participants in the evolution of policy on Taiwan available to give us his view on the important dimensions of that story.

Since World War II, econometrics, a methodology incorporating a combination of deductive theorizing and empirically observable statistical numbers (with or without a probabilistic formulation), has become a firmly entrenched academic tradition. By emphasizing policy formation and evolution, however, the authors of this volume hope to convey the message that in the study of the transition growth process of contemporary less developed countries there is a less quantifiable aspect of organizational (or institutional) change, which, though nebulous, is quite meaningful and essential. Nevertheless, in deference to the established method of economic analysis, the authors agree that a set of essential growth-related time series on Taiwan should be included in a statistical appendix. These vital statistics summarize the quantitative aspects of the unique transition growth phase of Taiwan (1950–90) that is quickly coming an end. Some readers may find this statistical record useful in their further investigations of the economic performance of Taiwan over these forty years.

1978

PREFACE

This is a rags-to-riches story. Within thirty years of its beginning as a war-damaged former colony, its population swollen by people evacuated from mainland China, the Republic of China on Taiwan was listed by the Organization for Economic Cooperation and Development (OECD) as one of ten newly industrialized countries (NICs). This book is a reflection on that growth—on how and why it happened and on what part of that how and why might be useful in helping other countries achieve economic growth and improved living standards. Broadly, then, this book is directed toward those interested in an overview of development in Taiwan and in the relationship between government policy and development.

Having assumed my current post of Minister without Portfolio, after earlier holding the Ministry of Economic Affairs (1965–69) and Ministry of Finance (1969–76) portfolios, I became convinced of the need to write about Taiwan's development, and I considered a descriptive study. However, there are several of those already available. My comparative advantage lay, it seemed, in concentrating on the evolution of government policy, where my involvement provided first-hand knowledge. Rather than simply looking back and recounting what happened in Taiwan, I wanted, in a sense, to look ahead by concentrating my discussion on features of Taiwan's development, particularly government economic policy formation, that could be instructive for the future of other developing countries.

Covering just the period from the late 1940s to the early 1980s, the writing of this book was encouraged and then supported by Gustav Ranis and John C. H. Fei. They devoted their time to writing introductory essays providing a simple model for understanding policy evolution and its links to Taiwan's development, respectively. The first chapter discusses some comparative studies of Taiwan's development and factors contributing to that development, including the island's geography, land reform, and United States aid, as well as providing overviews of aggregate growth and improvements in social welfare. Short chapters are then devoted to population, labor force, and export-processing zones. These are strategic areas in which I was particularly involved as a policymaker. Publicity surrounding the conference on population held in Mexico City in the summer of 1984 and the United States government's official position on birth control have again pushed into the news the discussion of problems that have been an ongoing concern in developing countries. Although Taiwan has already moved through the early stages of its demographic transition, this experience is not grounds for general optimism.

Policy changes are discussed in a largely chronological overview into which is woven an analysis of development policy generally and as it was effected in Taiwan. This section is as much an essay on Taiwan's development as it is a history of that growth. The book concludes with my feelings about the relevance to other developing countries of Taiwan's experience and the transferability of Taiwan's development policies.

As a government policymaker during this period, I have emphasized the government's role in the transformation, linking Taiwan's economic development and government policy and showing how they interacted and evolved with each other. This book tells what we did and tried to do as real-world planners and hands-on doers, few of us with formal training in economics. (Although since the early 1950s my career has been with the various agencies and ministries responsible for the economy, my education was in physics.) I write in the hope that other countries will be able to learn selectively from our experience, though it is not a blueprint for growth that other countries can follow directly.

Because details on Taiwan's development are available in a number of studies, I have limited the specifics to what I feel is necessary to put the discussion of policy evolution in context. For those interested in knowing more about various aspects of Taiwan's growth and development, three overviews of particular note are Kuo, Ranis, and Fei (1980) for general readers, Galenson (1979) for those seeking more detailed economic analysis, and Ho (1978) for a longer historical perspective.*

During the past thirty years I have given many speeches, presented many papers, and participated in many conferences and seminars. Three volumes of my speeches and papers (many done with the assistance of T. K. Tsui) have been published in English (1976, 1980, 1985).† Thus, my general views and lines of thinking on Taiwan's development are well known.

It remains for me to thank Professors Fei and Ranis for their encouragement, Professor Charles Kao for his assistance in preparing the initial draft, Wellington Y. Tsao for his administrative support, and Larry Meissner and T. K. Tsui for their editorial assistance.

K. T. Li
December 1987

---

*Shirley W. Y. Kuo, Gustav Ranis, and John C. H. Fei, *The Taiwan Success Story: Rapid Growth with Improved [Income] Distribution in the Republic of China, 1952–1979* (Boulder, Colo.: Westview, 1981); Walter Galenson, ed., *Economic Growth and Structural Change in Taiwan* (Ithaca: Cornell University Press, 1979); Samuel P. S. Ho, *Economic Development in Taiwan, 1860–1970* (New Haven: Yale University Press, 1978).

†K. T. Li, *The Experience of Dynamic Economic Growth on Taiwan* (Taipei: Mei Ya Publications, 1976); *My Views on Taiwan's Economic Development: A Collection of Essays from 1975 to 1980* (Taipei: Project on the Study of ROC Economic Development Strategy on Taiwan, 1980); and, *Prospects for Taiwan's Economic Development: A Collection of Essays from 1980 to 1984* (Taipei: Council for Economic Planning and Development, 1985).

WORDS ON THE SECOND EDITION

The first edition of this book was published in 1988, principally as a narrative portraying the evolution of Taiwan's economic development policy. To be brief, Taiwan successfully adopted the principle of the People's Livelihood, developing light industries first, then heavy industries, and later other related industries. As part of the process of development, the government encouraged savings and investments by the private sector, giving free rein to the market mechanism whenever possible but intervening to compensate for market inadequacies when necessary. In other words, the government sought to achieve a balance between market forces and planning, fostering the more desirable aspects of capitalism while avoiding its excesses. Policies were formulated or modified with a view to meeting the needs of successive stages of economic development, accommodating the legislative process, and winning public support.

As some readers of the first edition pointed out, aside from the development of agriculture, industry, and human resources, fiscal and monetary policies play a significant role in the process of economic development. With that in mind, two new chapters have been added to this edition to review the conduct of Taiwan's fiscal and monetary policies and their effects on the economy.

The government began to emphasize the importance of science and technology in economic development as early as 1965, when it launched the fourth four-year plan. Public involvement in research and development increased markedly through the 1980s, as special emphasis was given to the development of high-tech industries. These efforts, and their successful outcome, are the subject of a third new chapter.

The introduction by mainland China of economic reforms and an open-door policy over the last decade, as well as the gradual demise of its socialist system, has been of enormous significance worldwide. This transformation has permitted the rapid growth of investment in the mainland, especially by Taiwan firms and by foreign firms as well. Such investment has not only accelerated the pace of mainland China's industrial growth but also made it a power to be reckoned with in international trade. A fourth new chapter focuses attention on these developments and the burgeoning economic relations between the two sides of the Taiwan Straits.

I have tried to make the "Taiwan Experience"— Taiwan's unique achievement of rapid growth, price stability, and social equity—the unifying theme of the second edition of this book. All data and statistical tables, as well as relevant portions of the text, have been updated to 1991. It is my hope that this edition, like its predecessor, can serve as a useful guide to developing nations that are interested in following Taiwan's approach to economic development. Finally, I would like to express my deep gratitude to Professor John C. H. Fei and Messrs. T. K. Tsui, W. P. Chang, and N. H. Ma. Their constructive advice and many valuable suggestions helped make my task as a writer a pleasurable and rewarding experience.

K. T. Li
January 1994

CONTENTS

CONTENTS

THE EVOLUTION OF POLICY IN A COMPARATIVE PERSPECTIVE: AN INTRODUCTORY ESSAY

GUSTAV RANIS

Future historians will probably agree that the major economic and political event of the second half of the twentieth century was the transition to modern growth effort by the contemporary less developed countries (LDCs) after World War II. Viewed in a long-run historical perspective, trying to move their systems from a prewar condition of "colonial agrarianism" toward what Simon Kuznets has referred to as the epoch of modern economic growth (MEG) has constituted a monumental societal undertaking. This modern epoch is basically the *scientific epoch* that started with the Industrial Revolution in England in the latter part of the eighteenth century, that is, the routinized and institutionalized exploration of science and technology and its applications as an essential part of the art of production providing the primary growth-promoting force.

The impact of this new phenomenon on the speed of gains in material well-being as well as on the marked nature of the structural change away from agriculture (implying the urbanization of the population) has amounted to a profound change in the way of life as well as in the institutional environment that regulates economic activity. This new way of life has seemed both attractive and irresistible. Once started, the modern epoch spread geographically from England, in chronological order, to the Continent, the United States, Germany, Canada, and Japan in the nineteenth century, and to Eastern Europe as well as parts of Latin America during the early twentieth century. The development effort in most of the contemporary LDCs after World War II represents a further dispersal of that same modern epoch to Asia, the rest of Latin

1

America, and parts of the Middle East, with much of Africa still substantially behind the others.

It has become increasingly apparent in recent years that of all the contemporary LDCs making the transition growth effort, the so-called East Asian NICs (Taiwan, South Korea, Hong Kong and Singapore) have been most successful. The purpose of this book is to analyze the experience of one of this "Gang of Four", Taiwan, with the intention of determining whether an abstract set of ideas or conclusions can be generated from that experience that may prove useful to other situations similar in structure but not as far along in performance.

The authors are conscious of the fact that the Taiwan experience can, at best, be relevant only to a particular family of LDCs, though that family may be quite large—namely, the group of open dualistic economies characterized by the coexistence of a large agricultural and a smaller nonagricultural production sector internally and (given their size) by the relative importance of international trade and foreign capital externally. The conclusions of this book may, in other words, be less relevant for the oil-rich Middle Eastern countries or for many of the African countries (because of their educational and other infrastructural deficiencies) or to the very large countries of South Asia and China (because of the relatively smaller role of openness). It is therefore likely to be most relevant for the host of open dualistic economies of Latin America and of South and Southeast Asia, some of which seem to be continuously and often unsuccessfully struggling to effect their own transition while suffering from the maladies of the chronic import substitution policy syndrome—for example, excessive inflation, protection, overvalued domestic currencies, foreign exchange shortages, and slow growth.

As compared with the other LDCs, the common denominator of the East Asian NICs has been their relative shortage of natural resources, unless one considers the "location" of Singapore and Hong Kong as entrepôts as a natural resource. Since these four areas were not in a position to exploit something they did not possess, an inescapable conclusion must be that their overall success was due primarily to their ability to exploit something they did have: their human resources.

Inferentially, in other words, the secret of their success must be sought in the area of their policy experience through which each system's institutional environment was able to mobilize such significant creative energies of their populations as hard work, saving propensity, entrepreneurial strength, and the capacity to engage in risk-taking activities. The so-called Gang of Four apparently adopted policy measures outlining an environment or *institutional milieu* that turned out to be conducive to the effective mobilization of human resources in that broad sense. This is especially noteworthy because South Korea and Taiwan, at any rate, were viewed internationally as "hopeless basket cases" of development in the early 1950s. It must have been something largely within the system, then, that turned things around so dramatically.

Transition growth in all contemporary LDCs begins within the constraint of a certain set of initial conditions. For the East Asian NICs, these initial conditions are their relatively small size, their poor natural resources, and the high quality of their human resources as inherited from the historical past. Such cultural traits defined an initial social environment that undoubtedly proved especially conducive to modern growth. But it was policy changes over the past thirty years that built upon and modified that initially favorable environment. Thus, even though every other open dualistic system does not have the same initially favorable opportunities and cannot be expected to have the same type of performance, the policy experience of the East Asian cases can be instructive in substantially improving performance elsewhere and enhancing the chances for success in the transition growth effort.

A few additional words about the importance of the so-called special cultural traits are probably in order at the outset. It is quite clear that these human characteristics are part and parcel of a system's initial conditions. They were undoubtedly important and gave the East Asians an initial advantage but, unlike the case of initially favorable or unfavorable endowments of natural resources, such cultural conditions constitute advantages that are themselves subject to repair through human action over time.

INITIAL CONDITIONS

All policies (including economic policies) are formed within the context of a society's cultural environment. The authors of this volume have labeled the Chinese cultural background as one that is essentially pragmatic as a guiding principle for economic organization. Simon Kuznets, for example, commented as follows on the traits "associated with" or conducive to modern growth:

> The broad view associated with the modern economic epoch can be suggested by three terms: secularism, equalitarianism and nationalism. By secularism we mean concentration on life on earth, with a scale of priorities that assigns a high rank to economic attainment ... Equalitarianism means a denial of any inborn differences among human beings, unless and except as they are manifested in human economic activities... that makes man a full-fledged participant in the community of man... [bound together] by nationalism, the claim of the community of feeling grounded in a common historical past and its cultural heritage [on account of which] eqalitarianism is limited.[1]

Economic pragmatism, Chinese style, represents a mixture of these three elements that has much to do with the unleashing of human energies due to the equity of the reward system that encourages such efforts. In Tibet, for example, as in other agrarian societies, the priests pray while the peasants toil, a societal standard that meets none of the three precepts. As long as such initial conditions obtain, Tibet is unlikely to enter the modern epoch since it is constrained by such an entirely different set of values and principles of income distribution. It is, in effect, a system under which the merits of economic performance by individuals are neither valued nor calculated.

More precisely, secularism suggests a certain dedication to the materialism of secure "survival" rather than to other worthwhile, and perhaps even nobler, social, political, or moral causes. As Kuznets

---

[1] *Modern Economic Growth Speed: Structure and Spread* (New Haven: Yale University Press, 1966), pp.12–14.

also points out, Protestantism, as interpreted by Tawney and Weber, implies that even though a "secular people" also prays and meditates, it indulges in these nonenergy-consuming religious activities infrequently, in sharp contrast to the basic nonsecularism of medieval Christianity. Although a secular people can take to the streets to engage in energy-consuming demonstrations against issues that affect its own life only very indirectly (for example, to protest against racial discrimination, abortion, colonialism, dictatorship, or pollution), it does so rarely and somewhat half-heartedly. Historically, the Chinese are well known for their secular culture, leaving the pursuit of Buddhism as a full-time occupation to the small minority of the priestly class. What has been more sacred in much of the West (for example, God) was a relatively minor preoccupation in the East. The commonly held image of Eastern otherworldliness and Western pragmatism may indeed be reversed.

Equalitarianism in fact is equivalent to the modern term of income *distribution equity*. It suggests that social privileges like wealth and social status are expected to be awarded to all who choose to perform economic tasks with distinction. This, in turn, implies that the cardinal principle of equity, the *equalization of opportunity*, is realistically applicable to all; that is, that every person is made a full-fledged participant in the community of man. The award of medals to those who work hard on the production line may seem to run counter to such equalitarianism because the honor diminishes as the ranks of heroes swell. To achieve family honor and prosperity in the long run through toil and frugality (to climb up the social ladder from landless peasantry to landowning status, and from there to entry into the distinguished gentry class), on the other hand, was a realistic hope for all in traditional China. With its peculiar, competitive imperial exam and its land-tenure systems, traditional China indeed exhibited strong cultural traits along the lines of equalitarianism as it has been defined here.

Nationalism, by contrast, lends wisdom to the art of sharing by putting limits on equalitarianism, and it is acquired from an awareness of one's own history. The Chinese once again may be seen as unusually conscious of the continuity of their long, well-documented history of over 3,000 years, far exceeding that of, say, the Philippines or Brazil. Their instinct is that to continue to exist as a group, individual families must indeed share, but only moderately.[2] The extended family system, which put severe limits on equalitarianism in China as elsewhere, broke down gradually during the eighteenth century. From that time on, the Chinese increasingly came to believe that those who do not achieve through economic endeavor deserve to be relatively poor, notwithstanding a residual community obligation to provide them with minimal survival support to guarantee the opportunity to compete for survival. "To help in an emergency rather than in perpetuity" is an age-honored Chinese proverb.

This residual community of feelings under nationalism, moreover, implies an extension of the concern within a local community or village to a larger community when incomes are transferred by political forces among provinces. The feeling of concern for this larger community requires a careful assessment of the costs and benefits if equalitarianism is not to be too severely limited by this manifestation of nationalism. The difficulty is that the formation of reasonable—not too costly to equalitarianism—behavior rules on a national scale is slow to form even as nationalism usually has taken the population by storm in the postcolonial era. The trick is to translate a common consciousness of cultural heritage into behavioral rules that are conducive to the institution of a sequence of orderly reforms (for example, land reform and tax reform) that express calculated sympathy with other members of the community without endangering the underlying principle of equalitarianism.

It was this tradition of pragmatism, as translated into habits of family self-reliance coupled with the intuition that government patronage is neither necessary nor likely to be forthcoming, that the East Asian NICs were able to draw on in the early postwar era. It is no accident that all "Gang" members are geographically adjacent to mainland China

---

[2]Kuznets clearly recognized that there should be a limit on the interference with egalitarianism imposed by the "community of feelings" of nationalism when he wrote that "large incomes were justified because they were received by the economically efficient" while "the general rise in per capita economic product made the remaining inequality tolerable on rational ground" (*ibid.*, p. 14).

and inhabited by a people well known for their pragmatic culture. Ironically, it is also in this region that we have witnessed, over the course of the past thirty years, the wastage of human energies during the most violent social upheaval—the Cultural Revolution on the mainland, which focused on socialist redistribution in utter disregard of the basic equalitarian principle. The fact that the Communist regime seems to have recognized this problem and is seeking to rectify it by means of a drastic liberalization program testifies to the underlying pragmatic tradition that is now resurfacing after years of political suppression.

It does not stretch our imagination too far to see the significance of a pragmatic culture in the context of the transition growth effort, for economic pragmatism is clearly conducive to an increasingly market-oriented economy. The very notion of a market system, as narrowly defined by pure economic theory, marks off an area of human activity that is basically materialistic or secular. Clearly, a system that provides economic incentives also rewards distinguished economic performance. It assigns a progressively smaller role to the community of feelings as expressed by direct government intervention in the production process. Although the mainland regime will no doubt continue to emphasize its socialist objectives for political reasons, a free market solution, once started, appears to be irrevocable.

Taiwan has the same pragmatic cultural background, but in the absence of the political constraints of the Communist system, it has moved consistently in the direction of a market economy. This is what we have referred to in this book as a liberalization process. Alternatively and synonymously, one can view this as a process of the gradual depoliticization of the economic system, as the gradual withdrawal of political forces from the system that regulates economic activities. When one adds a time dimension one arrives at the notion of policy changes within an evolutionary perspective.

A major advantage of the type of economic pragmatism under discussion is the possibility of depoliticizing the economic system gradually, with economic agents devoting their energies increasingly to production, without the government, in spite of all rhetoric to the contrary,[3] really interfering too much in the name of income distribution equity. Given their cultural background, the populations of the East Asian NICs found it easier to accept the hierarchy of income and status related to economic achievement. This gave the policy liberalization process the rare dimension of linearity over time; that is, it was a process of change tending more or less consistently and irrevocably in the direction of a greater role for the market. Such linearity is observable in the series of small steps taken in that direction in all policy areas that affected the overall functioning of the system.

And such basic linearity, like good health, can really be appreciated only when it is missing. Secularism, equalitarianism, and restricted nationalism are not prominent features of the initial human resource conditions of most LDCs. For example, when LDC citizens have only a relatively short historical awareness of their own common cultural heritage, the feeling of community (nationalism) must often be hastily created. This usually involves rallying people through appeals to nobler, usually nonsecular causes (anticolonialism, welfare-statism, socialism, antimultinationalism, unionism) in which the visibility of government actions as a "partner" of the downtrodden is a key ingredient that fulfills an emotional need. Although people's awakening to the existence of a larger national identity covering strangers in far away places is in this way often readily achieved, the formation of orderly behavioral rules to implement an economic program to help the downtrodden ("who pays how much taxes to benefit which other parties" or "how has the government intervened directly to help whom by hurting whom") is an entirely different matter. In addition to the benefit side of the coin all government economic policies have a cost side that is usually underestimated, especially by politicians.

The high expectations that are aroused concerning the quick achievement of income equality through direct government action almost always lead to frustration. What usually follows in other LDCs is a series of erratic policy fluctuations without a clear trend, rather

---

[3]There are also posters on the walls in Taiwan swearing faithfulness to "income distribution equity", the same Sun Yat-sen principle as on the mainland.

than policy linearity in the direction of liberalization. Ironically, the consequence of this demand for equity is that it becomes more and more difficult to supply. In other words, once vocal demands are set in motion the tendency for helter-skelter, stop/go policy changes to be adopted becomes irresistible. Every change in the finance ministry, every foreign aid fad can lead to a new set of policies, sometimes liberalizing, more often directly interventionist in character. This is in sharp contrast, as we demonstrate, to the more or less linear trend of policies that permitted Taiwan to achieve growth and, incidentally, real equity as a consequence of an increasing reliance on markets over time.[4]

It may be especially appropriate in this context to note that Confucius also believed that social conflicts are due more to inequity than to poverty. Equity and income-distribution-related issues impinge on all socioeconomic controversies as well as on the central arguments of this book that are concerned with policy change. The usual tripartite ranking according to the relative importance attached by professional economists, moving from efficiency (microeconomic) through instability (macroeconomic) to equity, should be exactly reversed before it is of any use as a guideline for understanding the political process of policy formation in the transition growth process. Although equity, as we have defined it, is paramount, microeconomic Pareto optimality is almost irrelevant. Citizens agree readily on efficiency but have difficulty on what is meant by equity. Depoliticization, on which liberalization is based, constitutes a process of the discovery and acceptance of equitable rules of sharing (of the equalitarian variety) in the course of the modernization process.

THE EVOLUTION OF POLICY

In this book we have examined the dynamics of policy formation in Taiwan. This constitutes a new type of analysis that focuses on the

[4]See also Fei, Ranis, and Kuo, *Growth with Equity: The Taiwan Case* (Oxford: Oxford University Press, 1979).

importance of linearity in the evolution of economic policies by way
of two unconventional analytical inputs: the notion of subphases in
transition growth and the notion of a policy evolution matrix. The first
emphasizes the linearity or consistency of changes in the evolution of
the productive structure over time; that is, that it follows some sort of
orderly metamorphosis as it moves from agrarianism toward the
epoch of modern growth. The second deals with the question of an
evolving policy matrix that accommodates rather than obstructs such a
linear evolution in the organizational features of the system. The
juxtaposition of these two evolutions within the same framework of
reasoning constitutes, I believe, something of a useful methodological
innovation.

A unique feature of the transition growth experience of Taiwan is
that the thirty postwar years can be divided roughly into three main
subphases of transition growth: the initial, internally oriented, import
substitution subphase (1950–62), the externally oriented subphase
(1962–80),[5] and a technology-oriented subphase (after 1980). The
contrasting features of these subphases can be and have been well
documented[6] in terms of a system of macroeconomic variables (time
series for GNP, agricultural and nonagricultural output, total population,
agricultural and nonagricultural labor force, imports and exports,
savings, investment) that, when examined within an accounting framework, confirms the existence of such subphases. With the help of these
demarcations in the life cycle of the system one can trace the decline
of the relative importance of the agricultural sector and the growing
importance of international trade, as well as the shift in the composition
of exports. The emergence of a *technology sensitive* phase after 1980,
during which much R and D related activity came to the fore for the
first time, testifies to the near termination of the transition growth

[5]This subphase has, in fact, been further broken down into the 1962–70 period before the
system's unskilled labor surplus came to an end, and the 1970–80 period characterized by
the gradual shift to a more skill- and capital-intensive production and export mix after the
advent of unskilled labor shortage and substantially higher real wages.
[6]See Fei, Ohkawa, and Ranis in Ohkawa and Ranis, eds., *Japan and the Developing Countries*
(Oxford: Basil Blackwell, 1985). Here we note that a similar sequential order of subphases can
be detected for post-1950 South Korea as well as for historical Japan.

effort as the economy moves into modern growth marked by the routinized reliance on science and technology.

The essentially academic contribution of this book is perhaps best illustrated by our effort to classify development policies and to indicate their emergence over time with the help of a time axis (see appendix). Ten categories of policies are, in fact, identified in terms of their sectoral or market relevance. Accordingly, we note a division into Fiscal and Taxation Related Policies (I, II), Monetary and Foreign Exchange (III, IV, V), Government Enterprises (VI), Agriculture Policy (VII), Manpower and Education (VIII), Science and Technology (IX) and Economic Development Planning (X). By enclosing the years 1962–80 between vertical lines, we indicate the three main subphases of transition growth (from import substitution through external orientation to technology orientation) in order to show not only the timing (or the timely appearance) of a particular policy measure but also the more complex notion of the conformable evolution of policy that accompanied or accommodated the evolution of the economic system through the various subphases.

POLICY EVOLUTION AND INSTITUTIONAL CHANGE

Ever since the revival of interest in growth theory after the Second World War, economists have come to the conclusion that an understanding of the attempt at modernization in the less developed countries involves both economic analysis and institutional analysis. For example, more than twenty years ago Fei and Ranis stated the matter as follows:

> It is the purpose of this book to present a theory of development relevant to the typical labor surplus type of underdeveloped economy and to extract some policy conclusions from it. Our approach has been to seek a reasonable compromise between narrowly defined "economic analysis" emphasizing the logical precision of the relationships between measurable economic phenomena and broadly defined "organizational considerations" emphasizing the

importance for these measurable phenomena of the non-measurable
changes in the institutional milieu...[7]

Although much progress has, of course, been made since then,
especially in the economic analysis involving the measurables, the
nonmeasurable changes on the organizational, institutional, or political
economy side have proven to be more difficult and elusive.

The appearance in 1966 of Simon Kuznets's previously cited work
on "Modern Growth" provided the profession with a more historical
view, to the effect that growth in contemporary LDCs can be viewed
as passing through an organizational as well as an economic
metamorphosis. The organizational metamorphosis, at least in the mixed
economy case, can be seen as evolving in the direction of a more
market-oriented economy. This organizational metamorphosis is, in
turn, associated with a metamorphosis in the production structure that
becomes increasingly complex, both internally and externally. These
linked organizational and economic transitions can be viewed as
comparable to the physiological metamorphosis of a biological entity
(a butterfly) as it goes through various stages of life (silkworm, larva,
butterfly). In the evolution of human organizations, however, there is a
basic difference: the process is accompanied by an evolving system of
ideas, or ideologies. In the analysis of policy formation, however, I
believe an effort must be made to place such, often nebulous,
expressions as "institutional inertia", "vested interests", "vested ideas",
or "outmoded economic theories" into some sort of logical order. I
take this to be the central argument and novelty of this book.

Commonly, the terms *social organization* and *institution* tend to be
used interchangeably.[8] To an economist, a market with all its prices
represents a *coordinating mechanism* in which all the participants that
are being regulated may be assumed to be otherwise unrelated strangers.
This is an organizational view of the market. However, an economic/

---

[7]*Development of the Labor Surplus Economy: Theory and Policy* (Chicago, Ill.: Irwin Press,
1964), preface.

[8]According to Webster's dictionary, an *institution* is defined as the totality of "practices,
relationships and organizations in a society or culture." Notice that the term *system of ideas*
does not appear.

institutional framework differs from this mechanical/organizational view because the institution is also concerned with ideas. In particular, it takes into consideration the fact that institutional participants may not entirely be strangers. They are to some extent concerned for each other when, guided by the idea of the community of feeling or broader social relations, they decide to support each other either directly or indirectly, through the government. An institution is thus seen as the sum of the behavioral practices of an organization supported by certain ideas governing human relations, by a feeling of community concerning what is "right" or "wrong" with respect to members of that community. In the course of the transition growth process it is to be expected that as the economic system becomes more complex the arena of human activities in which people behave as arm's length strangers becomes relatively larger over time.

In all societies, it is the set of laws and regulations and their implementation that make up policies. They obviously constitute the most important component of institutions. Thus a policy evolution, as traced in the policy matrix here, is really tantamount to an evolution of institutions or of ideas on human relationships at least as they affect the most essential socioeconomic groups. This suggests that the elusive and nebulous topic of economic/institutional change can be pinned down by focusing on the income distribution implications of economic policy change. After all, the area of human activity in which citizens need not entirely disregard community is composed mainly of ideas related to income distribution. This is quite clear from the prominence attached to the provision of "taxation with consent" in the constitutions of Western democracies. Policy instruments (taxes, interest rates, and foreign exchange rates), whether used wisely or foolishly, always carry important income distribution implications, often tantamount to "taxation without consent." This is decidedly more true in the political processes of a developing country than in developed societies.

The liberalization and depoliticization of a mixed LDC economy does not necessarily imply that the government does less. In fact, as compared with the LDCs, the governments of the industrially advanced countries as a group usually spend a much higher percentage of national income, so in that sense the government does *more*. The crucial test for liberalization is the withdrawal of political forces from the market system—especially the domestic finance and international trade markets—where the *income transfer impact* of policies (for example, a manipulated foreign exchange rate or interest rate) on various social groups (labor, consumers, farmers, urban entrepreneurs) is not firmly backed up by the political consensus of a pluralistic society. Unfortunately, such a political consensus is hard to achieve because, on monetary matters, the income transfer impacts are not as well understood as outmoded macroeconomic theories, which usually emphasize Pareto optimality or problems of short-run instability in industrially advanced societies.

Even though all social institutions (including funeral procedures and fashions) are subject to change, the process must invariably overcome the resistance of vested interests (for example, that of the funeral profession or husbands) as well as of vested ideas (ancestor worship or notions of sex appeal). The fact that policy changes must go through a political process of enactment and implementation implies that such resistance is usually quite explicit and deliberate.

Although policy formation analysis cannot therefore avoid reference to systems of ideas and vested interests, taking a longer term perspective greatly simplifies matters. As Keynes admonished us,[9] the popular notion of the importance of vested interests (for example, the resistance of welfare recipients to government budget cuts in the United States, or the resistance to tariff reductions by domestic firms in Taiwan) is usually exaggerated. In the long run, what really counts in policy formation is the power of ideas. The United States Congress, for example, is currently keenly aware of the struggle of vested interests for entitlements under various welfare programs. Few, in a historical or reminiscent mood, would interpret the birth of the welfare state over the quarter century 1950–75 as the product of greed rather than "noble ideas." Yet, for the analysis of short-run policy fluctuations in LDCs, the role of vested interests may well be crucial. It is, however,

---

9. John Maynard Keynes, *General Theory*, final page.

the linearity of policy changes in Taiwan, seen in a long-run historical perspective, that is the main subject of this book. Whatever "resistance" by vested interest groups is put up is soon enough rendered oblivious by the force of "history." In this book, we have chosen not to put such vested interests at center stage in spite of their short-run journalistic appeal. Instead, we concentrate on institutional changes as an issue ideologically related to income distribution in the course of the transition growth process.

IDEAS AND POLICY INSTRUMENTS

The importance of ideas in policy formation is well illustrated by the treatment of Taiwan's import substitution subphase (1950–62) in this book. Two sets of issues are the focus. On the one hand, there is the issue of the preexisting economic structure and the underlying system of ideas culminating in the adoption of an import substitution strategy. On the other hand, there is the issue of the content of the various import substitution policies used to implement that strategy.

Most contemporary LDCs emerged after World War II sporting the economic structure of a primary export economy and the ideology of a postcolonial system. This ideology essentially has three ingredients that converge to form the so-called mixed economy, a politicized market system. The first relates to the adoption of an import substitution strategy in the effort to achieve a measure of autarky, or economic independence, to put alongside recently achieved political independence. The second relates to the deployment, to some degree, of centralized economic planning. The third is tied up with a strong sense of nationalism requiring the visible presence of the sovereign state in the economic arena.

In such a system there is unlikely to exist a clear delineation between those areas of human activity into which the government does or does not intrude. Almost every nontraditional activity involving social relations—from education to entertainment, from dress codes to hair codes—invites the possibility of government regulation. Such intrusions are not as much the fault of the vested interests of civil servants, who consequently acquire power, as of citizen demand for emotional fulfillment. Taiwan initially was no exception to the generalized adoption of such a politicized system. The subsequent trend toward depoliticization of its economy must be seen in that broader historical perspective of the earlier, omnipresent intrusion of government power.

During the period of initial or primary import substitution (1950–62), Taiwan adopted the familiar package of policies (overvaluation of the domestic currency, government deficits, restriction of imports, "low" interest rates, price inflation) used by many contemporary LDCs of the open dualistic variety to implement the import substitution strategy. Various policy instruments were deployed to help overcome the initial difficulties of autarky and underline the "omnipotence" (or imagined omnipotence) of civil servants. The most pronounced of these difficulties was the initial inexperience of the new entrepreneurs together with the educational deficiencies of the civil servants who were in charge of implementing such policy intrusions.

In the context of a pure economic approach the quantity of money (M), the interest rate (i), the exchange rate (r), the rate of import duties (t), and prices (p) are treated as instrumental variables in macro-model equations. Indeed they often represent policy instruments rather than market-determined equilibrium magnitudes in LDCs. In order to analyze policy formation in the political process, however, the variables (M, i, r, t, p) must be more closely linked to the underlying system of political ideas. Within the import substitution package, for example, the set (M, i, r, t, p) is deployed by the political powers who initiate and carry out an import substitution strategy in order to forcefully transfer income from one class of economic agents (for example, consumers or farmers producing an export crop) to another class (for example, industrialists or the treasury). Such *forced income transfers* are sanctioned by the current system of ideas (for example, anticolonial, socialist, or nationalist). Although we are certainly not unmindful of the impact of these variables on growth (within a more narrowly defined traditional economic analysis), we are even more interested in the basic question of what caused certain policies to be adopted in the first place.

In the typical contemporary LDC, civil servants, operating a small-sized government budget, may realistically be able to produce much less than is expected of them. Since total outputs are produced mainly by private citizens, as a consequence of which purchasing power is generated and circulated, the economic power of the civil servants lies primarily in their ability to transfer income from those who earn it to those who do not. Although by these acts the fundamental principle of economic pragmatism—rewards for those who perform—is violated, whether these transfers are accomplished through the direct fiscal tools of taxation and expenditure or through the indirect tools of price controls and exchange rates may make a substantial difference for the performance of the system. In fact, there exists the even more powerful alternative of money creation (dM/dt), which may prove most costly of all. What makes this a feasible tool in the developing countries is that the private sector cannot avoid the use of money (M) as a medium of exchange that, while circulating, also serves as the *unit of account* for economic rewards within the market system. Unearned income or purchasing power manufactured by money creation thus becomes a perfect substitute for earned purchasing power in commanding goods and services in the marketplace. The power of money creation is indeed limited only by the growing realization within the realm of ideas that it is likely to be harmful.

The record of wartime public finance shows that by using money creation (dM/dt) civil servants can acquire virtually unlimited amounts of goods and services, or wipe out any overhanging of government indebtedness, without resort to taxation. Civil servants can thus grant purchasing power to industrialists, at negative interest rates, without resort to voluntary savings. They can build up a stock of foreign exchange for their own use without resort to international borrowing. If resorted to by private citizens, this same set of actions would certainly be condemned as counterfeiting. In the hands of public-spirited civil servants, however, the creation of money (dM/dt), when used in conjunction with policy variables such as taxation (t), the foreign exchange rate (*r*), the interest rate (*i*), international borrowing (*b*), and government expenditures (*e*), constitutes a legitimate (if silent) act of burglary. This is especially true where there exists neither the tradition of central bank autonomy nor near-autonomy, where, in effect, there is an inability to resist the political pressures for monetary expansion. There are few societies in which all transfers are "on the table" and openly debated within a pluralistic democratic system. It is always a matter of degree, but it is especially difficult to restore monetary and fiscal responsibility where these traditions did not exist even in colonial times.

Monetary and fiscal responsibility thus constitutes a crucial ingredient of economic pragmatism. A government loan enacted to save a troubled Chrysler Corporation in the United States was indeed preceded by prolonged legislative deliberations on the costs to the taxpayers versus the benefits to Chrysler stockholders and workers. In the typical developing country such an action can be mandated as an executive decision simply by means of monetary expansion implying a "benefit without cost".[10] In other words, in most advanced industrial countries the cost-benefit calculation is more likely to be subject to a political process beforehand, whereas in most LDCs the cost or the benefit is implicitly apportioned to unidentified parties after the fact—usually with a considerable time lag between money creation and price inflation. Economic pragmatism implies moving toward the calculation of contributions and rewards for people as market participants. Monetary and fiscal restraint imply a similar meticulous calculation of the costs and benefits for citizens as participants in the political process. Taxation with representation becomes meaningless when money creation is used routinely to solve problems.

The popularity of an expansionary monetary policy and the permanence of price inflation (as in some Latin American countries) is partly due to political ideology—for example, where there is a short tradition of democracy or a long tradition of military dictatorship, all types of economic problems tend to be "solved" conveniently through

[10]In the case of Taiwan, it should be noted, the practice of lending to industries in distress or lending to strategic industries was discontinued at the end of the 1970s.

the avoidance of cost-benefit calculations embedded within the political process. A substantial part of the blame, of course, is the mysterious way in which monetary matters work themselves out under the table—"in a way not one in a million understands" (Keynes). When money is viewed as a liquid asset and when the linkage between money creation and desirable inflation is severed by a large time lag, people entertain the notion that money creation can, in the long run, also accomplish the "good things" that it appears to be able to do in the short run. Civil servants in developing societies are at times especially easy victims of this view. The reason we may "all be dead in the long run" can sometimes be traced to the illusory solutions we seek in the short run.

THE COMPLETION OF THE LIFE CYCLE

As is well known, the success of transition growth in Taiwan has been due in large part to the gradual abandonment of the import substitution strategy in the early 1960s. The accumulation of policy-related data over more than twenty years (1962–84) provides convincing inductive evidence to support the central thesis of this book, namely that this is a case of policy evolution moving linearly in the liberalization direction. Depoliticization of the economic system occurred on all fronts but not simultaneously, as is shown along the horizontal axis of our policy matrix.

Although Taiwan's institutional transformation is, of course, not yet quite complete, at present the system is almost ready to behave like an industrially advanced country immersed in modern growth. Of all the contemporary open dualistic economies, Taiwan is undoubtedly the first to have "graduated," in effect almost to have completed its life cycle of transition growth. This central thesis could not have been supported by inductive evidence much earlier. The appearance of this book is thus extremely timely.

The linearity of the policy evolution in Taiwan can be seen from the fact that the liberalization movement gained momentum through time in small cumulative steps rather than by the large leaps and bounds that often imply reversal and policy fluctuation. For a particular policy, such as devaluation, to take root, it must be a "step" in the "life" of the policy adjustment process. Usually an *ad hoc* first small step is followed by a bigger step a few years later, one that has more of an ideological appeal. Obviously the only way to portray institutional change is through the fact that thoughts and practices change concurrently. A good example is provided by the evolution of the fiscal policies indicated on the axis in the policy matrix, in which one can note the sequence of tax reform measures (income tax, 1955; tax reform, 1970; introduction of a value added tax, 1983) adopted in order to broaden the tax base in response to threats of a budget deficit. The pragmatic government never had the illusion that a fiscally responsible treasury could avoid the unpleasantness of having to confront the pain of political compromise. Moreover, as we point out, although the aversion to deficits represented the initial motive for tax reform, once carried out such reforms in turn led to new ideas.

To cite another example, the *ad hoc* liberalization of import controls via several small steps by 1971 subsequently gained momentum so that, by 1983, it could take on an entirely new and unprecedentedly ideological appeal by accepting the principle of the survival of the fittest and the discipline of international competition in the domestic market—a far cry from the xenophobia and autarkic appeal of the early import substitution era. Many previously sacred cows (public enterprises and/or the automobile industry) are now faced with scheduled tariff reductions and threatened with the prospect of virtual extinction through the competition of imports.

In short, the chorus for liberalization in the Taiwan newspapers of 1983–84 certainly would have shocked those awakened from their early 1950s sleep. This manifestation of a new self-confidence to meet and win in fair competition with foreigners in the domestic market is itself, of course, the culmination of success in competing in foreign markets during the earlier years. Policy formation at any moment in time clearly cannot be understood in a flashbulb vacuum, independently of what transpired in earlier phases of transition growth, either in the realm of the evolution of ideology, consequent changes in policy, or related changes in performance.

The small-step approach to policy change advocated in this book is really quite natural because vested ideas are seldom abandoned over-night. As Keynes pointed out "those who are thirty-five or over do not give up their belief readily." The introduction of a new tax system in Taiwan was, for example, heralded over a long period by the propagation of the "ideology" of the necessity of never-popular new taxes. The bill for a value added tax (1983) was prepared, studied, discussed, and propagated for at least ten years before it could be enacted. In fact, the enactment of a value added tax that is least distortionary in terms of relative prices was viewed as complementary to the scheduled substantial reduction of tariffs (1983). Thus, to keep the budget in balance and simultaneously to free up relative prices were the twin objectives consistent with the liberalization movement of the early 1980s.

Seen in this long-run, historical perspective, 1986 may well turn out to have been a significant landmark in the evolution of the institutions of Taiwan. Even though economic liberalization constitutes the central theme of the evolution of economic policy described here, the reader should also be aware of the fact that this process in the economic arena has, in fact, been accompanied by a gradual process of democratization in the political sphere. An acceleration of the pace of both the liberalization and democratization process in 1986 was then manifested in the formulation of new ideas that continue to be debated on the island. It is our unconditional prediction that the maturing of these new ideas will ultimately usher in another new subphase of policy once these tendencies are translated into new policy and/or legislative measures and that this will occur in the not too distant future.

In the economic arena, the implementation of a value-added tax (1986, category I of our matrix) as a government response to the emergence of a small prior budget deficit (1982), testifies to the persistent resistance to government deficits and inflation. The introduction of a new customs valuation system (1986, category II) constitutes a further liberalization measure in that the assessment of import duties based on a tariff schedule calculated to discriminate against imports was replaced by import duties based on actual values. With respect to interest rate policies, the introduction of a prime rate system (1985, category III) moved the financial system one step closer to the free market end of the spectrum, with borrowers stratified by credit-worthiness rather than by political connections. Another event of major importance that occurred in 1986 was that the national currency was permitted to appreciate, persistently and significantly (1986, category IV), itself an indication that the system's political structure had entered a new phase of maturity in coming to terms with the persistent export surpluses that began to emerge after 1982. The resulting accumulation of very large foreign exchange reserves (more than US$70 billion by the end of 1987) is increasingly seen as a problem, replacing the traditional mercantilist view of seeing it as an undisguised blessing, not only in terms of Taiwan's international economic relations (especially with the United States), but also in terms of Taiwan's domestic economy.

It is our firm prediction that further economic policy changes in at least four areas will find their way into the policy matrix in the near future. The proposed further tariff reductions (1983, category II) will be implemented, and the current effort at the liberalization of capital markets (1983, category V) will be accelerated to integrate the Taiwan economy more fully with that of the rest of the world and to make it compatible with the demands of global, market-oriented efficiency.

Such liberalization of trade and capital movements signifies a further reduction of the penetration of the market by political forces in terms of the selection of specific directions of investment and even specific projects. Another significant continuing change in the institutional framework governing Taiwan's international economic relations is the partial dismantling of its centralized foreign exchange reserve system under which the government has traditionally monopolized the holding of foreign exchange reserves as it first monopolized the power of monetary expansion in order to acquire its huge stockpile of reserves. The system will undoubtedly evolve in a direction that allows the nonbank public to hold a portion of Taiwan's foreign exchange reserves so that, subject to private choice, some of the holdings can be converted into foreign assets including real estate or capital investments.

All liberalization movements are, of course, not necessarily the result of temporary foreign exchange affluence or temporary pressures from the United States that relate to its own trade deficit, pressures which might be viewed as short run and transitory. Far more important is the long-run process of liberalization I have been describing, of which the anticipated organizational changes in the years ahead simply represent logical extensions.

In the political arena, the democratization process brought with it during 1986 institutionalization of a polity characterized by competitive parties. This was followed not only by the elimination of martial law but also the permission for the publication of additional newspapers, the depoliticization of institutions of higher education, and greater tolerance generally, ranging from religious cults to teenage hair styles. In its broadest sense such parallel liberalization efforts imply the gradual atrophying of the government's authoritarian power in both the economic and political spheres. Government can be expected gradually to abandon its position as the one legitimate and uninhibited moralizing center. What is significant in the liberalization process in Taiwan is that this gradual transition is likely to be accomplished in the context of an atmosphere of accommodation and orderliness. The traditional Chinese cultural value of pragmatism may have much to do with this peaceful evolution that has brought Taiwan into an epoch of modern economic growth characterized by the coexistence of pluralistic interest groups that compete with each other in both the economic and political spheres, as is the case in the industrially advanced mixed economies.

TRANSFERABILITY OF POLICY EXPERIENCE

There is little need for yet another volume to catalogue the set of "wise" policy measures that have been adopted in Taiwan over the past thirty years. These policies, moreover, have more recently become part of the *conditionality* discourse among the experts of the

International Monetary Fund, the World Bank, bilateral donors, and many contemporary LDCs: how to balance the budget, to devalue, to control inflation, to liberalize imports. Nevertheless, the fact that such "wise" advice is given repeatedly also implies that it is often ignored, or that it is tried and subsequently abandoned. What one often observes, consequently, are policy fluctuations with or without a steady trend. In recognition of this fact and as one by-product of our examination of policy evolution in Taiwan, we briefly consider the transferability of this experience. By recognizing that there may be some historical logic to the evolution of systems and the adoption of certain policies in transition growth, we have been able to distinguish between policies that, in the short run, accommodate from those that obstruct that evolution.

For LDC spokesmen and analysis who sometimes argue that the policies of Taiwan, as good as they may be, are irrelevant for them since they are "not yet ready", or because Taiwan is a "special case", we responded that thirty years ago Taiwan was not ready. It started its own transition growth process with initial per capita GNP levels not much higher (US$159 in 1957) than those of India or those of Fukien Province on the mainland at the time. Today, Taiwan's per capita income exceeds that of India by 800% and that of Fukien by something like 700%. In fact, the many mixed economies of the third world more favorably endowed with natural resources than the "Gang of Four" might well take heart from the fact that their initial conditions are more favorable rather than less.

The important lesson for other mixed, open, dualistic economies, in fact, is that there is always time to start the cumulative process of linear policy change. The experience of Taiwan indicates that the requirement of good policy is in large part to move through time unmistakably in the general direction of liberalization. As Kuznets suggested, by the time countries enter the modern growth epoch their production structure is likely to converge in a common pattern. It would not stretch imaginations too far to suggest that the organizational features of mixed LDCs will also tend to converge in the use of a market-oriented system typical of the industrially advanced countries.

It is this sequential, gradual approach toward a clear objective that is likely to be more successful than following the all-or-nothing propositions of purist advisers. This idea of a sequential order of policies of course also entails the notion of policy priority in the liberalization process: that certain policies should be liberalized first, depending on the seriousness of various bottlenecks at each point in time. A good example is the relative importance of the efficiency of horizontal allocation of resources domestically relative to the extent of overvaluation of the exchange rate.

Government discretionary controls clearly bias the direction of private investment. In Taiwan the tariff protection and import controls of 1952 and the Statute for the Encouragement of Investment in 1960, all part of the import substitution era, caused substantial *resources allocation inefficiencies* that violated the principle of Pareto optimality sacred to the microtheorist. Rare indeed is policy advice offered by international agencies that will not include as a top priority the dismantling of such discretionary controls. And yet the Taiwan historical experience has shown that a country can live with some of these controls for a long while and still be quite successful in its transition growth effort. The Statute for the Encouragement of Investment, for example, is not scheduled to terminate until the late 1980s, while only relatively small steps in the direction of tariff reduction and import liberalization were taken in the 1960s and 1970s (see the policy matrix) as a prelude to a major push in 1983. Although effective rates of protection were relatively low by LDC standards, there has been no radical reduction in tariffs, such as occurred in Chile, until this day.[11] The message from Taiwan thus is that monetary restraint and a realistic foreign exchange rate are more important than the elimination of discretionary controls that can be tackled at a later point in this evolutionary policy perspective. This may come as a surprise to the pure economist, given his strong vested ideas concerning the importance of Pareto optimality, but the message nevertheless is valid for most LDCs endeavoring to move from fourth to third best situations.

The successful policy experience of the East Asian NICs is, in fact,

---

[11]Even after the 1983 tariff reductions, the maximum tariff rate is still a whopping 73%.

transferable to other open, dualistic, developing economies if, and only if, economic pragmatism is transferred as well. If what the country aspires to are such cultural values as income sharing through welfare programs to direct market-generated income from one social class to another, policy fluctuations and upheavals are likely to continue to stand in the way of economic progress. Since good economists can usually predict policy impacts with relative ease, the suitability of the policy experience of Taiwan is dictated by the transferability of its political economy decisions, especially the ability to gradually depoliticize the economic system, so that families are increasingly rewarded by their economic performance rather than by entitlement through political patronage.

It is only natural that a book on the formation of economic policy on Taiwan be the joint product of academic development theorists who have observed rather closely the historical path of development of Taiwan and a high-level government practitioner who has been one of the principal architects of economic policies on the island over the past thirty years. The book is thus a joint effort at reasoning with respect to development policies as well as with respect to the political processes underlying policy formation. The principal author, Minister K. T. Li, is a firm believer in the doctrine of the "Three People's Principles" of Dr. Sun Yat-sen (the principles of nationalism, democracy, and economic livelihood) . The fact is that these principles have consistently provided the guidelines for policy design through both the establishment and, later, the dismantling of the politicized system of import substitution. This strongly suggests that the success of these principles was largely due to the flexibility with which they were applied in the course of the transition growth process. The analysis of Taiwan's policy evolution embodied in this book thus leads us to the insight of the need for a compromise between granting economic actors the freedom of self-reliant participation and the mutual concern for citizen welfare. In fact, Fei and Ranis's earlier, related work on this issue indicated that an increasing emphasis on development through

---

[12]See *Growth with Equity: The Taiwan Case* (with Shirley Kuo).

market liberalization proves to be perfectly consistent with the equity of income distribution objective.[12]

A realistic, pragmatic liberalization effort, resolutely maintained, is thus much superior to the frequently encountered fluctuating policy patterns that alternate between periods of doctrinaire interventionism and periods of equally doctrinaire laissez-faire. This is the essential piece of transferable knowledge conveyed in this book's analysis of Taiwan's transition growth process. It is superior because it is likely to be more sensitive to both economic analysis, in terms of the sequence among sectors, and the recognition of economic actors' need for linearity in policy direction. It is superior also because it recognizes the realities of political economy in terms of who is helped and who is hurt by various policy changes and how, in recognition of all this, the required minimum consensus for action can be established and sustained.

1987

A BIRD'S EYE VIEW OF POLICY
EVOLUTION IN TAIWAN
AN INTRODUCTORY ESSAY

JOHN C. H. FEI

A large part of the world lives in LDCs. These countries are still in what is called the agrarian epoch, in contrast to what Simon Kuznets has termed the epoch of modern growth. The industrial revolution in the last quarter of the eighteenth century marked the beginning of the end of the agrarian epoch. Starting from England, the nineteenth and twentieth centuries have seen the geographical spread of modern growth. The years since World War II have been the transition period into the modern epoch for many LDCs. In this introduction I provide an overview of that process, and how it relates to government policies, using Taiwan as an example. The general characteristics of the modern growth epoch, the transition process, and the policy formulation are outlined in section one. These are expanded on and applied in section two, which outlines Taiwan's transition, and in section three, which relates government policy to the transition in Taiwan.

THE TRANSITION TO MODERN ECONOMIC GROWTH

The basic innovation in the modern growth epoch is the conscious, sustained, institutionalized application of science and technology to industrial production. Beyond that, Simon Kuznets has shown that, from a long-run historical perspective, for all industrialized countries, passage into the modern epoch is marked by four other observable characteristics. The first is accelerated population growth. The second is the growth rate of capital (embodying technology), and this growth rate is even greater, so per capita capital increases. This makes possible the third characteristic, increased labor productivity, through which per capita income and consumption are increased. The final feature is structural change. The most important structural shift is the relative decline of agriculture, in terms of the percentage of population employed as well as in the share of total output (that is, GNP or value added). Thus, to the extent that we expect contemporary LDCs to make the transition into the modern epoch, all four characteristics (accelerated population growth, capital deepening, labor productivity gains, and structural change) will appear in the long run.

Historically, the geographical spread of modern growth has been mainly a process of spreading technological ideas and practices. With a vast store of technology readily available from already-industrialized nations, countries making the transition in the postwar period have been able to achieve impressive growth without fully recognizing the importance of sustained technological and scientific innovation. This was true for Taiwan, where such awareness came in the late 1970s, almost thirty years after transition growth began.

Virtually every LDC has experienced rapid population growth, and many have seen the relative decline of agriculture, at least as an employer and if only because the capacity of the land to absorb labor is limited. Population growth has led to urbanization, particularly in countries with high population densities. In one sense, then, industrialization can be considered a process for providing urban employment opportunities using modern (imported) technology. Without a food surplus, however, migration of the rural population to the cities cannot be sustained. The key, then, is increasing agricultural productivity, and it has been a missing element in many parts of the developing world.

There are two features unique to transitions in the twentieth century. The agrarian epoch in many contemporary LDCs includes a colonial period, and the agrarian epoch and colonial period end more or less at the same time. In economic terms, this means these countries inherit an economic structure based on the export of primary products—natural resources that are extracted or grown. In addition, manufactured goods, including consumer products such as textiles, have traditionally been imported. Consequently, the lack of industry compared to the industrially advanced countries has been obvious. The so-called import substitution strategy used by LDCs in the postwar period related directly to this almost universal consciousness of backwardness in industrial development and the persistence of colonial trade patterns.

Transition Phases

Successively higher levels of economic development have prerequisites, so the transition growth process can be viewed as a metamorphosis characterized by phases occurring in a reasonably definite sequence. The phases provide the framework for discussing the process. In analyzing transition growth in contemporary LDCs, I draw an important distinction between exogenous and endogenous factors. There are three groups of exogenous factors affecting the transition: the world economic environment, economic geography, and cultural and historical background. In the postwar period, at least until the second oil crisis of the late 1970s, the environment was particularly favorable for growth and transition.

Primarily because of the exogenous conditions of economic geography and historical and cultural background, the exact duration and nature of phases are different from one LDC to another. For Taiwan, the conditions were a good-quality, educated labor force and adequate commercialized entrepreneurship, but with significant population pressure and a shortage of natural resources. For these reasons, Taiwan has had two clearly identifiable transition phases, import substitution (1950–62) and external orientation (1962–80). In the 1980s, Taiwan entered a technology-sensitive phase.

Although each country's experience is unique on one level, it is not *sui generis*. At the start of their transitions, South Korea and, to a lesser extent, Japan also had demographic and economic geography factors similar to those of Taiwan. In all three countries, roughly the same level of output could be maintained by a smaller labor force with some organizational reforms and very little additional investment, a situation called a labor surplus condition. All three have been open to foreign trade, at least in the sense that trade has been a key feature in the transitional growth story. The agricultural and industrial sectors have coexisted at quite different development levels, giving the economy a dualistic character. This set of conditions can be termed *labor surplus, natural resource poor*, and *open dualistic economy*. We expect all postwar LDCs having these characteristics to exhibit the same sequence of phases, as indeed is the case of Taiwan and South Korea.

Many LDCs do not belong to this family, so their transition phases are somewhat different. Examples of other types include, in contrast to the dualistic model, the monolithic city-states (Hong Kong and Singapore) that are too small to have any significant agricultural sector. Latin America is generally a rich natural resource region. Until at least the 1970s Communist bloc nations were not open to trade. It is difficult to name an LDC that did not at least start the transition with a labor surplus (however short the supply of skilled labor).

Government Policies

Government policy is defined here as intervention or involvement in the functioning of the market system. In addition to policies that address specific areas (such as interest rates or taxes), there are policies to coordinate policies, which is often called "planning." Policies frequently relate to the creation or functioning of institutions (such as central bank or planning agency).

Generally, policies have been adopted with the aim of achieving two purposes: to enhance the performance of the economy and to promote nationalism in the sense of economic welfare. Simon Kuznets has emphasized the obvious tendency toward unity, manifested as nationalism or at least anticolonialism, as a prerequisite for the modern growth process. Socialism's emphasis on mutual concern and unity relates to this nationalism and helps explain the attraction socialism has for LDCs. Most LDCs in the transition growth process have a so-called mixed economy—that is, a market economy with a substantial role played by the government, although the mix can vary.

The observed characteristics of modern growth have appeared in all industrialized countries quite independently of policies. Kuznets's research goes further: the forces of science and technology defining the epoch have been so pervasive that the other observable characteristics have occurred regardless of culture, economic geography, or mode of organization (capitalist or communist). This raises the question, "Does policy matter much in the transition process?"

There is a sharp distinction between epochal growth and transition growth. On the simplest level, epochs are long. The agrarian epoch lasted for centuries if not millennia, and the modern growth epoch is well into its second century in England. An epoch possesses distinctive characteristics that give it unity and differentiate it from other epochs. (The concept of epochal growth is associated with Kuznets.) In contrast, evolution during the transition growth process is rapid, as each phase lasts only ten to fifteen years, and the entire process, consisting of three or so major phases, covers just thirty to fifty years. During the transition, the rules change, and this relates directly to organizational features of the economy. Government policies address these changes, and thus policy analysis is an important part of understanding the transition process.

Having said that, I nonetheless argue in this essay that for a particular type of LDC, the path of economic evolution during transition growth must be understood as policy neutral as a first approximation. In other words, the general transition path is determined by the exogenous factors, and passage through successive phases of transition growth can be explained without ever using the word *policy*.

Transition Phases and Government Policy

Growth is a continuous process, so the demarcation of transition phases is not precise. Policy changes can be made more abruptly, and the implementation of a new set of policies is often a convenient way to mark phase changes. This can lead to the notion that the current set of policy changes is causing the phase to change. But even in so-called planned economies, the new policies are more likely simply to be responding to the same accumulated effects of previous policies and objective forces that have led to the phase change.

Although economic development theory speculates extensively about the economic aspects of the transition growth process, a corresponding theory of policy evolution has not developed. Part of the difficulty, at least for economists, is that policymaking is a political process and thus outside the bounds of traditional economic analysis. One purpose of this book is to explain policy evolution and its relation to transition phases. In the rest of this chapter I provide a theoretical framework of policy evolution, which has been developed in part from my experience studying the development of Taiwan and thus draws on it for examples.

THE PROCESS OF POLICY EVOLUTION

Two types of forces act on policy evolution: objective and subjective. Objective forces are predetermined conditions (such as economic geography) and problems originating outside the country (such as the world economic environment). Policies address these forces, which are policy-neutral in the sense that they are determined independently of policy. Subjective forces, on the other hand, include the consequences of previous policies (solutions to old problems create new problems) and the ideology of the policymakers.

Given the objective forces, vested interests and vested ideologies determine which policy packages are adopted. Keynes observed that the power of vested interests is vastly exaggerated compared with the gradual encroachment of ideas and that the world is ruled by little else than ideology. On this basis and to simplify the analysis of the political aspects of policymaking, in this book we concentrate on ideology, largely ignoring vested interests.

The premise that ideology guides the formation of policy at each phase of development raises these questions: What are these ideologies? How are they formed and changed? Ideology is used here synonymously with political doctrine. Professional economic knowledge, including common sense, however, is also recognized in this book as an ideology.

Also, people's memories of their experiences can be important in shaping their ideologies, and thus their policies.

Even though it helps to have professional economic knowledge when selecting economic policies, policymakers are invariably guided (or at least believe they are) by political doctrine (for example, socialism, nationalism). That is, they seek policies that are felt to be consistent with their ideology. Thus, policy-neutral conditions determine the type of problems confronted, while ideology (vested ideas) both determines the process of selecting the policies and limits the possible outcomes.

The effect a set of policies has is known only with hindsight (and even then agreement is not always possible), but any set of policies inevitably has undesirable side effects, if not some undesired direct consequences. Thus, policymaking is an ongoing undertaking. Policymakers must anticipate and respond to problems even when their previous decisions have been successful, and they must sell the public on their decisions.

Accumulated successes, as well as problems, account for the move from one phase to another. Rapid growth in one industry can make others look relatively less well-off, even if they have also been growing. The expectations of the population also change as they become better educated, better paid, and so forth. In short, the economy evolves, priorities change, and so does the focus of policy. As the focus changes, policies or combinations of policies adopted during a particular phase are abandoned and replaced by a new combination during the successive phase. Policy changes follow the contour of economic evolution with some rationality, but with somewhat less predictability.

Suppose that a policy package is adopted. When policy-neutral evolution moves the economy inevitably to the next stage, new economic issues emerge that cannot be solved by the old package. Awareness of these new issues, usually associated with a slowing of growth, motivates debate on what to do. New ideas emerge, modifying the vested ones. That is, the ideology also evolves and thus helps to determine the new policy package. In transition growth, policy evolution must ultimately accommodate the objective forces. A disastrous policy (such as the Cultural Revolution on mainland China), which is usually the product of political indoctrination, can effectively delay economic development only when implementation is dogmatic. And even then, such policies are abandoned sooner or later. This thesis implies that policies can be judged on the basis of whether or not they accommodated the requirements of development at the time. If, with historical hindsight, transition and growth seem to have been facilitated, then the package was right, because a wrong package would have retarded growth.

Taiwan's development has been very successful, though the right policy was not always adopted. What we have seen is a willingness to experiment, a manifestation of the pragmatic orientation of Chinese policymakers only loosely dedicated to political doctrine. Policies that did not work were abandoned. Most that did work, survived; a natural-selection process was in evidence.

TAIWAN'S TRANSITION

During its transition phase Taiwan had a labor-surplus, resource-poor, open dualistic economy with a colonial heritage. Post-colonial, policy-neutral evolution has been through an initial import substitution phase (accommodated by an expansion of agricultural production), which began in the early 1950s, to an external-orientation phase (involving the export of labor-intensive manufactured goods), which started in the early 1960s and lasted through the 1970s. In this chapter I contend that the transition was natural, in the sense of being unavoidable, mainly because of Taiwan's objective initial conditions. These conditions also explain the very rapid growth, with considerable equity in income distribution, that Taiwan has enjoyed.

In this section I provide definitions and a simple framework to help understand the transition process, using Taiwan as an example. Dualism refers to the coexistence of two domestic sectors, agricultural and nonagricultural, each containing households and engaged in production, but at different levels of development. A labor surplus exists when roughly the same level of output could be achieved with a smaller labor force with some organizational reforms and very little additional investment. Open means open to foreign trade.

No system (especially a small economy with limited resources such as Taiwan) can develop in isolation. The principal external factor from the end of World War II until the oil crises of the 1970s was general worldwide prosperity and growth. As an open economy, Taiwan benefited from this.

The operation of an open dualistic economy can be described briefly. During the colonial period, labor is employed mainly in agriculture, with output partly consumed domestically and partly exported. The foreign exchange earned from these exports pays for imports of manufactured consumer goods. Demand for such goods is satisfied by imports, so there is little or no domestic manufacturing of consumer goods, such as textiles. Income generated by agricultural production is paid to labor and to land, and it constitutes the purchasing power available in the domestic market for consumption. This simplified description is adequate for present purposes, and it applies to Taiwan during the fifty years of Japanese colonial rule (1895–1945). By definition, the industrial sector is relatively insignificant during the colonial agrarian epoch, and it is generally involved in activities closely related to agriculture.

Import substitution is a development strategy involving domestically manufactured consumer products that had been imported. Foreign exchange earned by continued export of primary-sector products is used to import not only consumer goods but also producer goods (machinery) and raw materials as inputs for the new import substituting industries. As employment opportunities are created in the new industries, labor shifts out of agriculture and becomes the industrial labor force. Operation of the economy becomes more complex during the import substitution phase as many activities are added to the industrial sector. The sector now produces consumer goods that compete with (and substitute for) imports. In addition to the importation of producer goods and raw materials for the new industries, there are also inputs, such as fertilizers, to enhance agricultural productivity. Industry's value added includes wage payments and property income (interest, profit, and rent) for the entrepreneurial class.

The Transition from Colonialism to Import Substitution

Although specific initial conditions have been different for each LDC, import substitution has been the initial pattern for industrialization, with only a few exceptions. It is a natural outgrowth of colonialism. There are several reasons for this. The usual economic base of colonialism has been the exporting of primary products. This is also the basis for import substitution. When the industrial sector is undeveloped, the primary-product sector is the only one producing significant savings and foreign exchange. Because modern technology is transmitted to LDCs mainly through imported producer goods, the primary-product exports provide the principal means for acquiring modern capital goods and technology.

Beyond that, importers have already identified and established domestic markets, reducing the risk to local entrepreneurs in starting industries to produce for those markets. Because a shortage of skilled industrial labor and entrepreneurs is a major development bottleneck in the early transition phase, this can be important. Moreover, these local manufacturers sometimes have a better understanding of how to modify the products for local needs.

Import substitution is also seen as a nationalistic act, a repudiation of the colonial dependency, so ideology fits economic expediency. The new industries are seen as a way of creating jobs so that population pressure on the land can be relieved. The pace of labor absorption, however, is limited by the availability of capital and of entrepreneurs, as well as the need to train workers.

Foreign aid can be another element in the import substitution phase, as it was in Taiwan. Aid allows the country to run an import surplus by providing foreign exchange to pay for it, and it supplements domestic savings, thereby allowing higher investment levels. Because manufacturing producer goods requires more advanced technology (including skilled labor) and capital than most LDCs have, importation of these goods represents a technological complementarity between the LDC and developed countries.

As the substitution process proceeds, problems emerge. For a natural-resource-poor country, foreign exchange earnings are inadequate for the desired level of imports. This is often attributed to "unfairly low" prices of the primary products being exported (that is, the terms of trade are perceived as unfair). The labor force is still not fully employed, generally because population growth continually exceeds industrial job creation. Infant domestic industries may have problems competing with imports, particularly on quality. There are also usually government deficits and inflation. Inflation has been nearly universal among LDCs during transition growth because governments have found it a convenient way to solve socioeconomic problems.

On the other hand, entrepreneurs mature. Although they operate in a sheltered market, many acquire technical as well as organizational ability, and thus can compete in world markets. The labor force becomes more skilled because of training and general education, and it also becomes acclimatized to the rigors of modern factory life.

The Role of Agriculture

For a country with a colonial heritage, the agricultural sector plays a particularly important, and active, role during the early transition period since it is the major production sector. Generally speaking, as transition growth proceeds, the sector declines and is ultimately reduced to being an appendage of the industrial sector. For Taiwan during the import substitution period, agriculture performed especially well. Indeed, few other LDCs have been so fortunate in this regard.

The agricultural sector plays three essential roles. The first is to produce sufficient food to feed the population, including city dwellers. Beyond that, during import substitution it must provide an exportable surplus to earn foreign exchange. Finally, it must do this while releasing labor to the industrial sector. Structurally, commodity surpluses correspond to the appearance of agricultural savings, which are channeled to finance investment in the industrial sector. Initially, agriculture is the only sector that can produce a surplus, and this is one of the reasons the sector is so important. Later, industry can generate its own savings.

The key to agriculture performing such a role is a sustained increase in agricultural labor productivity. This is brought about by incentives as well as by more and better physical inputs, including infrastructure (such as irrigation systems), improved crop varieties, and fertilizer. In Taiwan during the early import substitution phase, access to these physical inputs was part of the incentive package along with land reform and other institutional changes in agriculture. The Farmers Association helped both in effecting the reforms and in spreading knowledge of better techniques and crop varieties. In many LDCs, transition has been slowed or derailed by policy failures in agriculture.

The Transition to External Orientation

External orientation means the emergence of industries that produce manufactured goods competitive in world markets. External orientation can also be called export substitution because the comparative advantage of the country has shifted from exports based on natural resources to exports based on labor. In other words, labor-intensive exports from the industrial sector are added to agricultural exports. For places with a limited natural resource base, such as Taiwan and Korea, external orientation leads to faster growth. Indeed, it is virtually the only avenue for fast growth.

Two factors account for the transition to external orientation, one negative and one positive. Negatively, the import substitution process must end. This process has two components: substituting domestic production for imports, and allocating foreign exchange earnings to importing producer goods (instead of consumer goods). When all domestic consumption is domestically produced, and all foreign exchange is used for producer-goods imports, the substitution process has run its course. How long the process continues depends primarily on the ability to expand primary-product exports. For countries with abundant natural resources, such as those in Latin America, import substitution can go on for a long time. For resource-poor countries, the end is sooner. In Taiwan and Korea it was a matter of ten to fifteen years. The positive reason is based on the maturing of entrepreneurs and the availability of surplus (low-wage) labor. From a long-run perspective, import substitution can be viewed as a learning-by-doing period for both entrepreneurs and the rest of the labor force.

Contrasts Between Import Substitution and Export Orientation

There are sharp contrasts between import substitution and external orientation from both economic and social perspectives. GNP growth is much faster in the latter phase. There are three reasons for this. Maturity of entrepreneurs and a more skilled labor force have already been noted. The third reason is that manufactured exports have been labor-intensive. For a labor-surplus economy, realization of this opportunity means the country can employ labor more productively, and, by embodying labor in exports, the economy can earn foreign exchange from its principal resource.

The foreign exchange shortage characteristic of import substitution gives way to frequent surpluses. A corollary of this is the termination, or at least decline, in foreign aid because of both increased affluence and the appearance of foreign exchange surpluses. Foreign private capital replaces aid. This investment is usually targeted at specific export-oriented projects, with the foreign investor building a factory or helping a local manufacturer produce specifically for the investor's home market. The attraction is the low-cost labor.

Unemployment gives way to a shortage of skilled labor as a major issue. Skill shortages lead to implementation of training programs and improvements in education. The pace of movement by workers from agriculture into industry quickens. In Taiwan, this movement was as much a pulling of workers out of agriculture by industrial job opportunities as it was a pushing of labor out of an overmanned agricultural sector. The shift of workers contributes to a more equitable income distribution.

Over time the role of agriculture changes and declines in importance. Industry can provide its own savings and foreign exchange. Indeed, it is usually necessary to start channeling resources into agriculture again. An absolute decline in the agricultural labor force, which tends to increase real wages for those remaining, shifts the focus of productivity gains from fertilizer and crop varieties to mechanization. In Taiwan, this has led to the demand for another round of land reform, this time to consolidate the area under cultivation into larger units for better utilization of machinery and other economies of scale. In Taiwan, affluence has not been confined to urban areas, in part because the pattern of industrial location has provided rural households with nonagricultural employment opportunities.

The external orientation phase brings greater quality and efficiency consciousness into the industrial sector. No longer selling only in protected domestic markets, producers must be competitive internationally in both quality and price.

THE EVOLUTION OF ECONOMIC POLICY

In broad terms, policies in an open, dualistic society are directed either at the industrial sector or the agricultural sector. Policy focus and policy content in each phase appear to have been determined by the nature of growth at that stage. In other words, the type of economic development has determined the policy focus, and policy changes have accommodated the requirements of growth. Thus, the emergence and decay of policies have been based on the formation of new ideologies induced by the objective, policy-neutral evolutionary process.

As will be evident from the discussion in this book, the record of ideology formation in Taiwan takes on two somewhat conflicting characteristics. The first is the continued invocation of the teachings of Sun Yat-sen, the founding father of the Republic of China, and the second is the concentration on immediate problems and the search for pragmatic solutions.

The appeal to an overriding ideology is not uncommon, but China is one of the few places where the ideology was indiginously assembled, and then by one of the leading personalities associated with Chinese nationalism. The teachings of Dr. Sun, therefore, have been decisive in the sense of having determined that the basic organizational features of Taiwan's economy would be market-oriented. Appeals to the teachings of Dr. Sun were made mainly to defend a market economic system against Communist ideology and to foster a sense of nationalism. Moreover, policymakers and advisers invariably sought to slip professional economic knowledge into the policy formulation process through assurances that it was, if not explicit in Dr. Sun's teachings, then implicit, or at least consistent with those teachings. Such a synthesis has not been difficult because the writings of Dr. Sun (including the People's Livelihood Doctrine) allow a good deal of latitude in interpretation, a feature appropriate to a mixed economy. And, although a lot of lip service was paid to long-range vision and planning, the debates usually centered on how to overcome short-term manifestations of whatever problem was most pressing at the time, be it unemployment, inflation, slow growth, or something else. Moreover, there was a tendency to treat each year, if not each month, as the arrival of a turning point in the island's development.

The Republic of China (ROC) government established in Taiwan was quite concerned with inflation, with good reason. Rampant inflation during the war of resistance against Japan eroded not just purchasing power, but also support for the ROC government on the mainland, particularly among its urban, middle-class constituency. Thus, in the minds of nationalist leaders, there was a strong link between price stability and political stability. In the interest of the latter, economic policies were expected (or at least hoped) to be consistent with the former. Nonetheless, inflationary pressures were very strong in the 1950s, in part because of government policy.

Taiwan's success may give the impression that appropriate policies were invariably promulgated, but this was not so. Instead, the spirit of pragmatism and experimentalism among Chinese policymakers was sufficiently strong to replace policies that were not working. This, of course, means that the policymakers had a reasonably clear idea of what it meant for a policy to "work"—that is, there was a consensus as to goals, or at least as to the direction they wanted to go.

Policy Focus During Import Substitution (1950–1958)

During the import substitution phase the strategy centers on the growth of import substitution industries by definition. This is done by using political power to augment the profits of domestic industrialists. Profits generated in this way are artificial in that they are not commensurate with actual entrepreneurial efficiency. In other words, they are windfall profits. Because profits must come out of the current income stream, the windfall is squeezed from the income of two other groups, producers in the agricultural sector and consumers in general. There is an income transfer from agriculture and consumers to the domestic industrial entrepreneurial class, that is, to those who own the import-substitution industries. Governments implemented this profit transfer strategy through several policy instruments: taxation (mostly tariffs), foreign exchange controls, and interest rates.

Tariff policy has two components. As regards consumer goods, high protective tariffs provide a wall to shelter domestic producers from import competition. Import duties on producer goods are low or nonexistent, which lowers the cost of production for domestic entrepreneurs.

The domestic currency is overvalued, to the benefit of importers. Making foreign exchange artificially cheap creates disequilibrium in the foreign exchange market: everyone wants to buy, and no one wants to sell, foreign exchange at the official rate. Access to foreign currency must be controlled, with government allocations assigning producer goods high priority. Controls also require exporters to deliver foreign exchange at the official rate. Overvaluation amounts to a (hidden) tax on exporters, most of whom are in the primary-goods sector, and a subsidy for importers. Consumers pay higher prices for domestic manufactured goods, as the import duties provide a price umbrella for local producers.

Interest rates are maintained at artificially low levels by the monetary authorities. Because the interest rate is not an equilibrium (or natural) one, the low-rate policy can be maintained only by government (politically-determined) rationing of investment funds to borrowers or by increasing the supply of loanable funds by expanding the money supply (currency and bank credit), which contributes to inflation. Inflation, however, is consistent with the objective of helping infant entrepreneurs. This occurs in two ways. First, it reduces the real rate of interest on their borrowings. Second, there is an artificial appreciation of the foreign exchange rate, making imports more expensive. To illustrate the point, suppose the price level doubled in Taiwan, while remaining constant in the rest of the world; to maintain purchasing power parity, Taiwan's currency should be devalued 50 percent. Although there were devaluations, the currency remained overvalued throughout the 1950s.

Political power was used, more or less consciously, to redistribute income indirectly through policies causing price inflation. That inflation helped industrial entrepreneurs at the expense of bank depositors, exporters (the agricultural sector), and consumers in general. Inflation is commonly used as an income redistribution device, not just in LDCs but also in advanced countries.

In looking at Taiwan's experience, it becomes clear that the desire to promote investment during import substitution by using a low-interest policy, as well as the large government deficits of the early 1950s, contributed to inflationary pressure. The government's desire to maintain price stability thus had to be balanced against the inflationary impact of its other policies. And there was the painful memory of the high inflation levels of the 1940s on the mainland.

Under the influence of S. C. Tsiang, a Cornell University economist, in the 1950s, Taiwanese monetary authorities were aware of the inflationary impact of the low interest policy. Thus, on several occasions interest rates were in fact raised to relieve inflationary pressure. This was probably the first application of a high interest rate policy as a means of combating inflation, and it was an apparent success.

When transition growth begins, LDCs also face the task of creating the financial and other institutions of a modern economy. These institutions are designed and established as the economy and policies evolve. Because of lack of faith in the ability of private domestic entrepreneurs, and the nationalistic centrism already mentioned as characteristic of the import substitution phase, the resulting economic institutions have been marked by the amount of control assumed by the government.

In summary, during the import substitution phase, government policy (that is, intervention in the market economy) is aimed at providing infant entrepreneurs with windfall profit. This is done through low interest rates, an overvalued currency, and high tariffs on imports of goods that are produced domestically. The economic problems falling out of these policies include foreign exchange shortages and price inflation. Even when the intention is to be fair, the allocation of foreign exchange and investment funds by the government can only be arbitrary when demand exceeds supply at administered prices. Thus, public enterprises and large-scale private enterprises generally have priority in the allocation of investment funds. Typically, the subsidized new industries have only a limited capacity to absorb labor, at least relative to labor-force growth, so unemployment is also a problem.

Under a highly controlled system, the economy is oriented toward "visible accomplishment" rather than production efficiency. This outline characterizes Taiwan, and almost every other contemporary LDC that started transition growth with import substitution.

The Emergence of External Orientation (1958–1963)

Evolution of the economic structure from the import substitution to the external orientation phase necessitates a new policy package. Slow growth, as import substitution runs its course, is the cue for policymakers to seek new accommodations. With the exhaustion of the domestic market's ability to absorb manufactured goods, export markets are the natural alternative. Policies to gain access to these markets are formulated.

The focus of the new, externally oriented strategy is revision of the policies for foreign exchange, tariffs, and interest rates in ways that lessen government control and strengthen market forces. The currency is devalued to a more natural level. The tariff wall around domestic producers is lowered, partly to combat inflation, but exporters are given protection and rebates on import duties. These reforms require domestic entrepreneurs to be more cost-price and efficiency conscious. At the same time, programs to improve the environment for private investment are undertaken.

In Taiwan between 1958 and 1963 when these policy revisions were being made, there was no idea that the economy was moving into an entirely new, externally oriented growth phase, and only with hind-sight has the significance become obvious. The contemporary record of ideology-formation for the policy switches testifies to the fact that the reforms were based on limited thinking about the immediate problems of unemployment and foreign exchange shortages. The external orientation phase had been underway for some time before it was apparent a new phase, based on labor-intensive manufactured exports, had begun.

As the new phase progressed in Taiwan, new policy areas became government concerns. To help the economy adapt to international competition, tariff rebates and export-processing zones were offered. Foreign capital, including direct investment, was solicited to produce labor-intensive exports. Attention increasingly was given to education and training to create a labor force with the skills needed by the growing manufacturing sector. These are all examples of policies accommodating the new growth phase.

Providing tariffs and establishing export-processing zones are aimed at creating an environment for the export of labor-intensive manufactured goods. They are market-oriented not only in the sense of reducing direct government involvement, but also in the sense of allowing international input prices to prevail, which is the basic goal of trade liberalization. Textiles are a good example. In Taiwan, many of the inputs are imported, including cotton and dyes. Exempting the inputs from duty when the final product is being exported means that foreign buyers do not bear the tariff burden a domestic consumer does, which makes the products more competitive.

During this phase, increased market orientation is generally limited to the export sector. The domestic market remains sheltered behind high import duties, so a form of dualism emerges. As in the import substitution phase, consumers continue to subsidize producers, bearing the burden of import duties, while domestic entrepreneurs are protected from competition from imports. In Taiwan this was recognized and justified with the slogan "foster exports with the domestic market".

The retention of government controls is due, partly if not mainly, to the fact that tariffs are an important source of government revenue. One precondition for reduced government trade protection is the establishment of a tax system (such as an income tax) that is not as disruptive of the market price structure as tariffs are. Taiwan did establish a corporate income tax, and it became a new instrument for influencing development, as exemptions have been used to encourage investment in selected areas (originally, export industries).

In Taiwan during the 1960s, as the economy progressed through the external-orientation phase, the set of urgent social and economic problems changed. Concern over unemployment gave way to concern over increasing real wages and a shortage of skilled labor. The foreign exchange shortage was replaced first by balanced international payments, then an export surplus. Foreign aid ended; private capital flows picked up. Government deficits became surpluses. Competition increased and the horizons of entrepreneurs broadened. There has hardly been a period or place where so many economic changes occurred in just ten years.

Continuous External Orientation Phase (1963–1982)

In sharp contrast to the price inflation of the import substitution phase, during the external orientation phase, Taiwan enjoyed not only rapid growth but also substantial price stability, at least until 1973. The explosive output growth in the 1960s caused by export expansion contributed to price stability in several ways, but in particular by establishing a balance between real production and the money supply.

Tax revenue increased, which reduced government deficits, even with lower tax rates.

Increased prosperity also increased savings available to the commercial banking system. The monetary authorities no longer had to rely on money supply expansion to meet investment demand, since domestic savings and foreign investment provided the needed funds. This, together with the abandonment of the low-interest policy, decreased the inflationary pressure attributable to monetary policy during the 1960s.

Price stability during the early external orientation period also relates to an important external factor: Taiwan's major trading partners, particularly the United States, had stable prices. Thus worldwide price stability and moderate domestic money supply growth account for stable prices in Taiwan during the 1960s and early 1970s.

For reasons initially external to Taiwan, slower economic growth and inflationary pressure returned in the aftermath of the mid-1970s oil crises. The growth slowdown paralleled slower growth in the United States. In the 1970s the economic slogan most often heard was "growth with stability".

General worldwide inflation was transmitted to Taiwan by the exchange rate system, which, while floating in name, was fixed in practice. Although the exchange rate was intentionally overvalued during the import substitution phase, it has been generally undervalued since then. This undervaluation has contributed to monetary expansion. Domestically, the monetary authorities resorted to money supply expansion in the belief that it would stimulate investment and thus revive growth. This was also done by many industrially advanced countries. The result was inflation.

Experience has taught us that government cannot use monetary expansion to maintain low interest rates, and that it cannot devalue currency to stimulate exports when there is an export surplus. This is recognized in Taiwan, but the ideology of the early 1980s is still that such attempts are beneficial.

As the 1970s progressed, Taiwan's policymakers and private entrepreneurs sought to increase the quality and sophistication of the products made in Taiwan. The island has emerged as a major electronics manufacturer. Government policies have encouraged this step up the technology ladder directly and indirectly through such programs as science parks (the successor of export processing zones) and improved technical schools.

ONGOING POLICY AREAS

Most of the discussion so far has been about policies regulating the activities of entrepreneurs in a mixed economy. There are several additional policy areas that deserve mention, including development planning, public enterprises, and the provision of infrastructure.

Providing infrastructure—transportation facilities, the educational system, and the like—is almost universally considered an area of government responsibility. However, there is an ongoing debate about where to draw the line between public and private provision of some of these items, such as public versus private power, buses, trains. With few exceptions (Hong Kong, for one), for ideological reasons contemporary LDCs have opted for operating large parts of their economies through public enterprises. This also occurred in Taiwan.

During the import substitution phase in Taiwan, public enterprises were even less efficient than private industry. Efficiency was not a concern; serving the public interest was; hence the slogan "public enterprise must continue, despite the losses." As efficiency consciousness increased, both the public and the government reexamined this premise governing public enterprises. Then the slogan became "they need to be run in a business-like manner."

Many contemporary LDCs have a planning commission responsible for constructing five-(or whatever-) year plans. Plans usually have been frameworks for thinking about relationships between resource allocation and overall objectives, rather than detailed attempts to coordinate the allocations directly. This may be termed planning for policy, as distinguished from planning for resources (as a socialist state would). A planning commission concerned with policies has the role of an economic general staff, or "council of economic advisors" as such a group is now called in Taiwan (and in the United States).

I have argued that government policy should be viewed as accommodating or obstructing the basic forces underlying economic development. This may seem a strange way to introduce a book on government policymaking, but K. T. Li and I feel that there is some inevitability attached to much of what happens in the transition process. The "inevitable," however, is not necessarily easily or directly achieved. Our contention is that policies can help or hinder the development process. Presumably government planners and policymakers intend to promote growth, but they do not always succeed. Often this is because they attempt to divert growth from its natural course, rather than accommodate it. Taiwan is an example of a place where the policy choices were exceptionally "good" in the sense of helping to accommodate growth.

The initial conditions and problems of contemporary LDCs are different from those Taiwan faced, and they will not follow the same path as Taiwan. But some rules of the road emerge from Taiwan's experience. If there are universal lessons in this book, they are that pragmatism pays, and that transition growth at least historically can proceed rapidly when there are accommodating policies in place.

1

SOME
BACKGROUND
ON TAIWAN

Taiwan is a success story in the annals of economic development and it is enough to know that to read the rest of this book. For those who are not familiar with that story, however, this chapter provides a synopsis and cites a number of more detailed studies. The topics discussed include some comparative studies of Taiwan's development and factors contributing to that development, including land reform and United States aid, as well as overviews of aggregate growth, improvements in social welfare, and the island's geography.

THE NATURAL SETTING

Taiwan lies less than 150 kilometers southeast of mainland China. With its tiny satellite islands, it has an area of 36,000 square kilometers, and it is not quite three times as long (north-south) as it is wide. Taiwan is comparable in size to the combined area of Maryland and Delaware, or to Belgium, or to the Netherlands, but with much less arable land and far more people than any of them. Two-thirds of Taiwan is mountainous: almost all of the arable land, about one-fourth of the total area, is cultivated or urbanized. In 1991 the island supported a population of 20.6 million — more than two-and-a-half times that of 1950. However, population growth since the late 1970s has been below 2% compared to 3.3–3.7% in the 1950s. Density is over 500 people per square kilometer.

The area in agriculture in 1991 was 884,000 hectares, some 13,000 hectares more than in 1950. The soil is not inherently fertile, but has been made productive by the heavy use of chemical fertilizers.

Sugar and rice have been the principal crops; pineapple, mushrooms, and asparagus are important canned food exports. Sweet potatoes, tea, and bananas are also grown. Forests cover around 20,000 square kilometers, more than half the land area, but most of this is in the rugged mountains that run the length of the island. Logging has been curtailed because of soil erosion, and reforestation is underway.

The sea coast is about 1,600 kilometers long, and both warm and cold currents pass the island, making nearby fishing grounds historically fertile, but they are now fully exploited. Restructuring in the fishing industry has been taking place as larger vessels are built for deep-sea fishing. The raising of eel and shrimp in either fresh water or semisaline water developed very fast over the past decade in areas where the collection of ground water had caused land subsidence.

Taiwan is subject to an average of four typhoons a year. The rivers are short and swift, providing opportunities for hydroelectric power and irrigation, but also making flooding a problem.

There are few mineral resources — marble and small amount of poor quality coal. The marble has been extensively developed and is sold into world markets, mostly as finished products. Some natural gas is also available.

A CHRONOLOGY OF DEVELOPMENT

Under Japanese rule (1895—1945), agriculture was promoted and some infrastructure was built as part of making Taiwan a rice bowl for Japan. This included construction of power facilities as well as irrigation and transportation systems. There was also some light industry. During the Second World War, however, Allied bombing caused severe damage, and what escaped was in poor condition because of excessive use and lack of maintenance. Forests were overcut and agricultural output suffered from the halt in fertilizer imports.[1]

---

[1]For a fuller account of the period 1860—1970, see Samuel P. S. Ho, *Economic Development in Taiwan, 1860–1970* (New Haven: Yale University Press, 1978).

Improvement in economic conditions was slow from 1945 to 1949. The deteriorating situation on the mainland preoccupied the central government, and the island was in no position to begin any large-scale reconstruction on its own. Moreover, the mainland's rampant inflation reached Taiwan.

With the relocation of the Republic of China's government to Taipei in 1949 some 1.6 million people moved to Taiwan from the mainland, increasing the population by over one-fourth. With this influx and the natural increase, the population rose from about 6 million in 1945 to over 8 million (including soldiers) in 1951.

Inadequate production and government budget deficits led to inflation after 1949, and this was exacerbated by the general rise in world commodity prices following the outbreak of the Korean War in June 1950. With the war, however, the U.S. government changed its policy and later resumed both military and economic aid. The aid, along with new government policies to reduce inflation, helped stabilize prices and build confidence, which in turn stimulated business activity. Still, it was 1952 before total agricultural and industrial production exceeded the peak during the Japanese period, and not until later were those levels surpassed on a per capita basis. In the accompanying figure, growth since 1953 is summarized.

Between 1953 and 1962, Taiwan succeeded in laying the base for self-sustaining growth. The economy's growth rates were among the highest in the world, and inflation was moderate. However, a large part of the increase in output was offset by a rising population. The average annual rate of real growth was 3.8% per capita GNP, more than half the economy's 7.3% rate.

There was a shortage of investment capital, alleviated in part by United States aid. Aid accounted for some 40% of capital formation. Rapid growth created new employment opportunities, but not fast enough to keep pace with the population. Low economic growth and high population growth kept per capita GNP at around $165[2] throughout the 1950s.

---

[2]Unless otherwise specified, this unit of currency refers to U.S. dollars.

Low income levels restricted the government's ability to raise money through taxes, and with its heavy commitment to defense spending, there was a large deficit that was financed with bank borrowing and thus contributed to inflation. There was also a trade deficit, as Taiwan had to import not only capital equipment for industrial development, but also raw materials and food. United States aid financed 40% of this inflow.

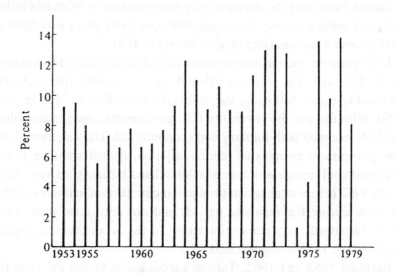

Fig. 1. Growth rates of Real GNP. 1953—1979.

Source: Shirley W. Y. Kuo, Gustav Ranis, and John C. H. Fei, *The Taiwan Success Story: Rapid Growth with Improved [Income] Distribution in the Republic of China, 1952– 1979* (Boulder, Colo.: Westview, 1981), p. 8.

In the government's first development plan (1953–56), emphasis was on fertilizer production, electric power, and textiles. Although industry developed during the 1950s, agriculture continued to be the more important sector, still accounting for one-third of net domestic product in 1960, compared to less than one-quarter for industry. (Services including the government with its large defense budget, accounted for the rest.) Over half of employment and exports were in the agricultural sector in 1962.

In the late 1950s a number of important economic, financial, and monetary measures were taken by the government:

1. The unification of foreign exchange rates, begun in April 1958, ended in 1960 when the N.T. dollar was fixed at a realistic unitary rate of NT$40 to US$1, providing a very important basis for export promotion.
2. The organization of Industrial Development and Investment Center (IDIC) was established to study and identify all the factors affecting the investment climate, and to propose the revision of taxation and land laws or regulations which retarded domestic capital formation and export promotion.
3. The approval of the nineteen-point economic reform program as a guideline for accelerated growth.
4. The drafting and final approval by the legislature of the Statute for the Encouragement of Investment in September 1960, which provided the legal basis for further economic growth and export expansion.

This changed rapidly as the 1960s progressed: industrial growth of 18.5% per year far outstripped agriculture's 4.3%. Population growth slowed, so even more of the gains flowed to consumers, even though the share of national consumption in gross domestic product dropped from 87.5% in 1962 to 67.9% in 1972. With increasing domestic savings, United States aid declined and finally ended in 1965.

Exports grew even faster—28% annually, for a nine-fold increase between 1963 ($332 million) and 1972 ($3 billion). Imports also increased. The role of trade in Taiwan's economy is illustrated by noting that in 1974 Taiwan, with a population of under 16 million, imported 40% more than India, with a population of almost 600 million, and 300% more than Pakistan, with 67 million. Since the late 1970s, over half of Taiwan's GNP has been exported.

The oil crisis of 1973–74 seriously upset Taiwan's long-term growth with price stability. Its impact on Taiwan's economy, which is heavily dependent on trade, was crippling. In an attempt to break inflationary expectations, in January 1974 the government instigated a contractionary monetary policy and significant price hikes (many prices were government controlled). The lowest output growth in the postwar period was recorded in 1974, but by 1978 a new high growth rate was achieved; GNP growth in real terms was 1.1% in 1974 and 13.9 in 1978, respectively.

Since the 1979 oil crisis, the world has been a more hostile one for Taiwan, both politically and for trade. Growth was successively lower in the years 1979–82. Nonetheless, the government has emphasized research and development, introduced a systematic program for the development of science and technology, and established a science-based industrial park in Hsinchu, with two technical universities and the Industrial Technology Research Institute providing support. Hence, development continued and the quality and sophistication of products improved, aided not only by foreign firms operating in Taiwan, but also by local entrepreneurs. Although inflation was in double-digit during 1979–81, the earnings of manufacturing employees kept pace.

In 1991, per capita GNP surpassed $8,910 (almost two-fifths the level in the United States). Trade was $139 billion in 1991, of which 38.2% was with the United States and 20.1% with Japan. Taiwan has had a large trade surplus with the United States, but a deficit with Japan. Textiles remained the largest category of exports until 1983 when electronics and electrical manufacturers took the lead.

IMPROVEMENTS IN THE QUALITY OF LIFE

Improving economic indicators such as the growth rate of GNP is easier than improving social indicators such as public health and housing. For the Chinese in Taiwan and their government, the understanding has been that economic growth should be pursued in conjunction with the pursuit of improved living standards. In this section I look at a variety of measures of well-being, including income and wealth distribution. I confine myself to improvements from the 1950s through to the 1970s, as that is the period of transition growth: the improvements have continued.[3]

---

[3]Unless otherwise noted, data are from the Council for Economic Planning and Development. *Social Welfare Indicators. Republic of China* (Taipei: CEPD, 1987).

The usual proxy for living standards is per capita consumption. From 1952 to 1991 this increased 7.7 times (at 1981 constant prices), from NT$13,930 to NT$107,617. Over the same period calorie intake rose from 2,078 to 3,035.6 per day, protein from 49 grams to 85.1 grams. Infant mortality declined from 44.7 to 6.6 per thousand, and life expectancy rose from 58.8 years to 73.4 years. The share of homes with city water increased from 28.8% to 79.1%. The share of homes with electricity grew from 45.2% in 1952 to 72.5% in 1960, and 99.7% in 1991. Housing floor area per person rose from 7.02 square meters in 1965 to 20.96 square meters in 1986.

Education has been made available to most of the population, as is discussed in a later chapter. Already in 1952, 84% of school-age children (ages 6–11) were enrolled in primary school; by 1991 the percentage was over 99.9 (ages 6–11). Strides at higher education levels are more impressive. While only one-third of primary school graduates went to middle school in 1952, 99.3% did in 1991. Less than 2% of young people (ages 18–21) went to college in the early 1950s; in 1991, over 34% did.

With growth has come a more equal income distribution. In a comprehensive study, Kuo found that between 1964 and 1972 the ratio of the income received by the top 10% to that received by the bottom 10% dropped from 8.6 to 6.8.[4] (This compares to the ratio of 19.3 in the United States in 1971.) Moreover, income inequality within occupations decreased.

The income equality achieved in Taiwan becomes more significant when compared to both developed and developing countries. Ahluwalia found that the average income share of the bottom 40% of households in developed countries was 16%, but only 12.5% in developing countries.[5] Taiwan's 20.4% in 1964 is comparable to Japan's.

[4]Shirley W. Y. Kuo, *Income Distribution by Size in (the) Taiwan Area: Changes and Causes*, mimeo. (Tokyo: Japan Economic Research Center, 1975).
[5]Montek S. Ahluwalia, "Income Inequality: Some Dimensions of the Problem," in Hollis B. Chenery, *et al.*, eds., *Redistribution with Growth* (London: Oxford University Press for the World Bank, 1974), p. 8.

To measure absolute poverty, Ahluwalia used per capita income levels of \$50 and \$75 (at 1971 constant prices).[6] For 1969, Taiwan had only 10.7% and 14.3% of its population below those levels, respectively, compared to the aggregate of 36.7% and 57.2% for the thirteen Asian nations in the study.

FACTORS AFFECTING GROWTH

Taiwan's success has attracted a good deal of scholarly attention, and in this work one can find a consensus on the more important factors contributing to the island's rapid growth:

1. The infrastructure and human resource foundation laid by Japan between 1895 and 1945.
2. The presence of a large group of trained and experienced professionals evacuated from the mainland.
3. The existence of the people who are willing to earn and to work hard.
4. Economic aid, primarily from the United States.
5. Early emphasis on agriculture, including land reform, the spreading of improvements in technology, and the increase of inputs, such as water, fertilizer, and pesticide.
6. Social stability.
7. General worldwide prosperity.
8. Openness of Taiwan and other countries to trade and transfers of technology.
9. Competence of the government.

I would like to stress three related forces I feel have been particularly influential in shaping the governments's policies, and thus in contributing to growth. These are Sun Yat-sen's teachings, the government's commitment to fulfilling social expectations (though cynics might say this has been only to retain political power), and a generally pragmatic approach.

[6] Ibid., p.12.

Although development policies have tended to be problem rather than ideology oriented, Dr. Sun's Principle of the People's Livelihood to satisfy the basic needs of the common people has been the guideline. This is explicitly required by Article 142 of the Republic of China's constitution. Particularly as to means, his work is general enough to allow a variety of interpretations, and conditions have been quite different to those where and when he wrote. But the basic needs would be the same throughout the world. We have nonetheless striven to follow the spirit of Dr. Sun, and to achieve his goal of improving the lot of the Chinese people.

This leads directly to the second element, the government's direct involvement in promoting socioeconomic development. Historically, the Chinese look to their government for certain things, and these expectations, combined with newer ones brought on by the Industrial Revolution, placed a great responsibility on us. Here, our pragmatism came into play. The government encouraged the private sector to develop consumer industries and concentrated its efforts on the building of infrastructural facilities for the entire economy. Government involvement does not always succeed, but because our commitment was more to the goal than to any specific means of achieving it, we have been more successful than those whose choices were narrowed by their ideology.

UNITED STATES AID

Over $4 billion was made available to the Chinese government in the form of grants, loans, and military equipment between 1951 and 1965. The nonmilitary $1.421 billion of this was equivalent to over 6% of GNP, and it financed some 40% of investment and imports during the period. Aid clearly played an important role in Taiwan's quest for self-sustaining growth. The government could not have sustained its level of defense preparedness without assistance, but this discussion excludes the $2.5 billion in supplies and equipment provided to the ROC armed forces under programs administered by various military agencies. In what follows, the word *aid* refers to the $1.5 billion made available through nonmilitary sources.

The annual level and composition of the $1.5 billion in total aid changed throughout the period, dropping from over 10% of GNP in 1951 to less than 2% of a much larger GNP in 1965, not counting the transfer of $250 million equivalent to the form of local currency counterpart fund in order to maintain the continuity of this program for social and economic development. In 1951–53, aid-financed imports of $150 million of basic foodstuffs and consumer goods helped break inflation and probably ensured the very survival of the Republic of China as an independent country.[7]

After this humanitarian aid, the emphasis shifted to explicitly defense-justified aid. This peaked in 1955–56, in the wake of the early 1950s Communist attack on an offshore island held by the ROC. Agricultural products were a larger part of aid after 1955, reflecting United States farm surpluses. Loans replaced outright grants as the period progressed. Only about one-eighth of the aid was justified to the United States Congress on development grounds. In form, aid originated as U.S. dollars or imports that were sold for NT dollars, with the local currency then being spent in Taiwan.

Assistance was classified into two programs, defense support and technical cooperation. Direct forces support, used for military construction and to purchase commodities and materials directly consumed by the military, constituted 8% ($124 million) of the aid, and ended in 1958. (This was in addition to the $2.5 billion in supplies provided through military channels.) The larger part of the defense program provided indirect assistance to the military. It funded either specific projects for a given time (such as construction of a road or power plant) or procurement of supplies for sale or use within Taiwan.

[7]See Neil H. Jacoby, *U.S. Aid to Taiwan: A Study of Foreign Aid, Self-Help, and Development* (New York: Praeger, 1966), pp. 118, 151, and 274. Jacoby, then dean of UCLA's Graduate School of Business Administration, was invited in 1964 by AID to write an evaluation of U.S. aid to the Republic of China. One of the conditions of his accepting was permission to publish it; this book is the result. See also Maurice Scott, "Foreign Trade," in Walter Galenson, ed., *Economic Growth and Structural Change in Taiwan* (Ithaca: Cornell University Press, 1979), pp. 368–81.

Imported items included food, raw materials such as cotton, wheat, machinery and tools, and lubricants. This represented 51% ($792 million) of the aid, and ended in 1961. Thus defense broadly construed accounted for 59% of the total aid.

Technical cooperation included sending U.S. specialists to the ROC and training Chinese technicians in different fields in the United States, and as such did not involve equipment or supplies beyond those used in teaching and demonstration. In other words, technical cooperation was primarily the salaries and expenses of American personnel assisting in land reform, agricultural extension services, civil aviation administration, public health, education, and other infrastructure projects.

Under the Agricultural Trade Development and Assistance Act (better known as PL 480, or Food for Peace), Taiwan received $349 million worth of surplus commodities, which was 23% of the total aid. Although the act was passed in 1954, shipments to Taiwan did not begin until 1957.

As a practical matter, aid was intended to help the government of Taiwan stabilize prices, rehabilitate and expand infrastructure, and increase productivity. Administration of the aid was vested in the Mutual Security Mission to China of the U.S. International Cooperation Administration (ICA), while coordination at the Chinese end rested with the Council for United States Aid of the Executive Yuan (CUSA).

Economic assistance wound down through the early 1960s, and although there was apprehension as to the consequences, in May 1964 the United States announced that, except for some direct military assistance and the sale of surplus agricultural commodities, aid would be discontinued by mid-1965.

After the Agency for International Development (AID, successor to the ICA) mission officially closed on June 30, 1965, a Sino-American Fund for Economic and Social Development was created by the ROC government to hold the local currency generated from sales of commodities, repayment of project loan, and other items previously provided under the AID program. Currently, the annual availability from this fund, that is, the net of the repayment of AID loans with

interest, is about U.S.$50 million. This fund underwrites projects not
unlike those previously financed by AID.[8]

In a chapter on the "Overall Performance of U.S. Economic Aid" in
the government-published 1965–66 *China Yearbook*, four effects of
this aid are presented.

1. Financing foreign exchange deficits. Between 1951 and 1964, 93%
   of the total deficit of $1.290 billion was made up by
   U.S. aid. As part of this, during the same period, U.S. aid arrivals of
   $1.150 billion accounted for 33% of total commodity imports
   of $3.540 billion.
2. Stabilizing prices. By providing NT$30 billion of U.S. aid
   commodities for sale in local currency, the aid helped remove
   otherwise excess purchasing power out of the economy.
3. Providing investment funds. Both U.S. dollars ($421 million)
   and local currency (NT$27 billion) were made available for
   development of electric power, transportation, communications,
   manufacturing, mining, and military projects.
4. Providing technical assistance. This included the training of some
   2,700 Chinese technical and managerial personnel.

United States government officials and others funded by U.S. aid
and counterpart funds consulted with the ROC government on policy
formulation. The ROC government occasionally invited Chinese
economists teaching in the United States, including T. C. Liu, S. C.
Tsiang, Anthony Koo, John Fei, and Gregory C. C. Chow for
consultation on policy or specific economic problems. These discussions
helped keep government officials abreast of thinking on development
issues.

Agricultural development was given an early and high priority.
Aid was concentrated in projects, mostly with aid-generated local
currency, selected by the Joint Commission on Rural Reconstruction
(JCRR), which was established, in the United States, under the 1948

---

[8]See Y. C. Chu, "Utilization of the Sino-American Fund for Economic and Social Development,"
Industry of Free China, Taipei, ROC, Sept. 1967, pp. 30–35.

China Aid Act.[9] Some aid was programed in the form of loans to government and was given directly to private enterprises, with CUSA acting as the clearing house for processing and screening. The absolute sums for the private sector were not large—under $20 million plus use of at least NT$283 million from the sale of aid imports. Between 1952 and 1958, U.S. aid was the source of 24% of private investment. Virtually every major firm received something, particularly those established during the first two development plans (1953–60).

Although the consensus is that aid played an important positive role in Taiwan's development, there are dissenters. Griffin argues that

> "Aid did indeed help to diminish the rate of inflation and improve the material conditions of the Taiwanese, but this was accomplished by permitting the level of consumption to rise, not investment. Foreign assistance deserves some credit for reducing hardship during the phase of reconstruction (early 1950s), but it does not deserve credit for the subsequent achievement of rapid growth."[10]

Aid to the Republic of China on Taiwan was at first largely justified as preventing the island's occupation by the Communists on the mainland. It is reasonable to assume that without the United States having made the commitment to support a strong Chinese armed forces to protect Taiwan, we could not now write about the successful development of the island. In at least that sense, aid was a necessary condition. Although it is less clear how crucial aid was after the mid-1950s, my feeling is that it certainly gave us a breathing space for shaping up and carrying out a policy for self-sustaining growth and provided a climate for outward-looking development. The fact is that

[9]The JCRR story is an interesting one, and I recommend Tsung-han Shen, *The Sino-American Joint Commission for Rural Reconstruction* (Ithaca: Cornell University Press, 1970); Joint Commission for Rural Reconstruction, *JCRR: Its Organization, Policies and Objectives, and Contribution to the Agricultural Development of Taiwan* (Taipei, 1973); and Samuel P.S. Ho, *Economic Development in Taiwan, 1860–1970* (New Haven: Yale University Press, 1978), chap. 9, to those wishing to know more. Shen was the doyen of Chinese agricultural studies in the 1960s.

[10]Keith B. Griffin, *Land Concentration and Rural Poverty* (London: Holmes and Meier, 1976), p. 262.

U.S. aid was phased out in mid-1965, sooner than expected by both Americans and Chinese. After 1965, the economy and exports grew much faster than expected, making self-sustained growth possible.

LAND REFORM

Agricultural output in 1946 was only slightly more than it had been in 1910, having fallen to about half the peak level reached in 1939. The irrigation system, fertilizer factories, and food processing facilities were damaged by bombing and lack of maintenance. Lacking fertilizer, soil fertility had declined. Preoccupied with the civil war on the mainland, the central government did not pay much attention, or offer much help, to Taiwan until the removal of the government to Taipei brought with it more professionals, managers, and entrepreneurs, supported with money and machinery.

The ROC government considered that ineffectiveness in alleviating extensive rural poverty and controlling runaway inflation, due largely to the Communist uprising after World War II, had much to do with its failure on the mainland. After retreating to Taiwan at the end of 1949, it thus quickly undertook a series of actions to gain the people's confidence and win international support. Land reform was part of this.

After the Sino-Japanese war, the Chinese government considered carrying out a land-reform program in keeping with Dr. Sun Yat-sen's teachings. A program was introduced on a trial basis only in part of Szechuan province, in western China. But because of the upheaval caused by the Chinese Communists, work was discontinued.

After moving to Taiwan, 60% of the population of which were farmers, the Chinese government in 1949 decided to carry out a thorough land reform program. Faced with the threat of a Communist takeover of the island, the local landlords were very cooperative. The reform was a success due largely to the fact that government leaders had no vested interest in land, that the government was determined to raise farm production and income in the face of the Communist threat, and that the landlords received relatively fair treatment. The reform indeed helped establish the credibility of the government's concern for the welfare of the farmer, and also, in my judgment, was the foundation of agricultural and industrial development.

Thorbecke sees three interrelated policy elements as crucial in the 1949–53 period. These are the establishment of JCRR, which was the major institution helping to implement agricultural aid; United States aid, which was the major source of funds for JCRR; and the land reform measures. He concludes, "Clearly, this last element had, by far, the greatest impact on the growth and distribution of output. Yet the close complementarity among these three elements made the land reform as successful as it was."[11]

The individual who had the major responsibility for carrying out reform was Chen Cheng. Born in a small village in Chekiang province on the mainland, Chen had firsthand knowledge of what the life of Chinese farmers had been. His experiences in the poverty-stricken agricultural area of Chingtien county where he was raised did much to fashion his outlook. While still young, he became convinced that land problems are at the heart of China's poverty and other troubles.[12]

As the governor of Taiwan province in 1949, Chen surveyed the land situation. The results were disturbing. High rentals and insecure tenure were identified as the leading problems. At the time, over 60% of the total population was engaged in farming. Of those, 39% (20% of the population) were tenants, 25% had partial ownership interests, but only 36% owned all the land they cultivated. These were all generally small tracts—1.4 hectares was the average per farm family, which is less than the area of two-and-a-half football fields. Some farm families indeed owned land while at the same time working as tenants on other farms.

Under the traditional system, a deposit of two years' rent was required to secure a lease, and the rents were equivalent to more than half the total crop. Because no account was taken of crop failures and collection

[11]Erik Thorbecke, "Agricultural Development," in Walter Galenson, ed., *Economic Growth and Structural Change in Taiwan* (Ithaca: Cornell University Press, 1979), p. 172.
[12]For an account of Chen's life, see W. G. Goddard, *The Makers of Taiwan* (Taipei: China Publishing, 1963), pp. 125–63.

was usually before the harvest, effective rents were higher. A survey by a private research organization commissioned by the government in 1948 found rents to be an average of 57% of the crop, with a high of 70%. Only one lease in ten was written, and tenure could usually be terminated at the will of the landlord.

Land reform was aimed at making tenants into land owners, but it was a goal that could not, the government felt, be reached in a single step. Instead, it was done in three planned stages. First came the reduction of farm rents in 1949, then the 1951 sale of public farm land (taken over from the Japanese), and finally, in 1953, implementation of the land *to the tiller* program.

In January 1949 the government began to make arrangements to carry out rent reduction. Actual enforcement started in April and was concluded in September. The speed at which the work was completed and the smoothness with which it went were surprising. Rent was limited to 37.5% of the main crop of 1949. If the original rent exceeded that limit, it had to be reduced, but if it was less, it could not be increased. Tenancy could no longer be terminated at will: written leases for a minimum of six years were granted to tenants, and a lease had to be renewed if the tenant had not violated it. Landlord's interests were not totally disregarded. Leases could be terminated if the tenant was two years in arrears, and landlords were represented on the various tenancy committees charged with settling disputes.

Although it cannot be attributed entirely to the rent reduction, production of major crops showed a substantial increase in the program's wake.[13] The combined results of higher production and lower rent improved farmers' income by 81% between 1949 and 1952.[14] Of the increase, one-fourth was used by the tenants to better their living conditions, and three-fourths to boost production. With their new prosperity, farmers referred to newly-acquired oxen as "37.5% cattle", and even new wives as "37.5% brides".

During the Japanese colonial period, severe restrictions had been

[13]See Anthony U.C. Koo, *The Role of Land Reform in Economic Development: A Case Study of Taiwan* (New York: Praeger, 1968), chap. 9.
[14]Chen Cheng, *Land Reform in Taiwan* (Taipei: China Publishing, 1961), p. 309.

imposed on Taiwanese land ownership, while Japanese nationals and firms were encouraged and helped to acquire land. The result was that 175,000 hectares (21.44% of the land under cultivation in 1945) were held by the Japanese at the end of the war. The Chinese government took over this land. Although some of it was sold, at the end of 1948, 104,000 hectares were tilled by tenants.

In 1951 regulations were promulgated to pass ownership to the farmers. All public farm land administered by the government and government enterprises, with the exception of what was necessary for water and soil conservation or for productive use by public enterprises, was to be sold to the incumbent tenant-cultivator. If the tenant did not want to buy, the piece could be sold to another farmer, but with a limit of approximately three hectares for each.

Six sales were conducted between 1951 and 1954, transferring some 110,000 hectares to 210,000 families, or an average area of not much more than one football field per family. The area of land that could be purchased by a family was determined in part by what was deemed necessary to support a minimum living standard, including such factors as the tract's productive capability and the size of the family.

The sale price was fixed at 250% of the value of the annual main crop. This was to be amortized over ten years, with payment in rice or in cash, depending on the crop produced. The government sold the rice and other crops received, using the proceeds as a fund to help other tenants acquire land. The total price paid for the land was 330,000 metric tons of paddy rice plus 882,000 metric tons of sweet potatoes.

The most important stage of the reform was the land to the tiller program, which was promulgated in 1953. Its enactment was a rather involved process that was designed to achieve a consensus and support for the program. After a draft had been prepared by an interdepartmental committee, in July 1952 the provincial government submitted Regulations Governing the Establishment of Owner-Farmers in Taiwan to the provincial assembly. This draft was also presented to county and municipal assemblies for comment, and a number of *ad hoc* groups voiced their opinions and concerns.

At the end of August, the draft, with amendments and comments, was sent to the central government. (It should be noted that the central government was composed almost entirely of immigrants from the mainland, and most key positions in the Taiwan provincial government were also held by mainlanders.) The cabinet conducted its own studies. One conclusion was to change the name of the bill to "Land to the Tiller." In mid-November the cabinet approved the draft, and its was submitted to the Legislative Yuan (of the central government). After seven weeks of study and debate, the bill was passed on January 20, 1953.

The purpose of the bill is clear from the revised title. The means to achieve it involved the government first buying land owned by a landlord and tilled by tenants and then selling it to the tenants. This two-step procedure was intended to finance and standardize the transfers. It was also felt that tension would be eased if it was not necessary for landlords and tenants to deal directly with each other. Landowners were permitted to retain the equivalent of up to 3 hectares of medium grade paddy. This contributed to the leveling of wealth among farm households. Jointly owned land was purchased without regard to the size of the holding. It is estimated that the wealth transferred by land reform was the equivalent of 13% of Taiwan's GNP in 1952.

The government purchased 140,000 hectares in 1953, which was 58% of all tenanted land, and resold it to 195,000 farm families (representing 64% of the tenant population on private land). Tenant families fell from 36.08% of all farm families in 1948 to 14.51% in 1959.

Land was transferred at the same price the government had used in selling former Japanese land (250% of the annual main crop), but, while the Japanese land had simply been expropriated, Chinese landlords received the sale proceeds. There was no intention of completely dispossessing the landlord class, if only because that would become a source of political unrest and instability. Payment to landlords was 70% in government land commodity bonds and 30% in shares in government-owned enterprises. This was innovative in two ways: it did not impose a burden on the current government budget, and it provided an inflation hedge for the former landlords.[15]

---

[15]Thorbecke, "Agricultural Development," p. 201.

Purchasers were charged 4% interest and had ten years to pay. The purchase payments plus land taxes, water fees, and other such expenses were about equal to the 37.5% rent the farmer would have paid as a tenant. To make the land transfers stick, production loans were made to purchasers and an extensive network of farmers associations and extension services was created.

There have been a number of studies on the effects of Taiwan's land reform.[16] Though their emphasis may vary, their results are similar; that is, comparing 1949 and 1960, both the immediate and long term benefits of land reform can be seen. Reform led to smaller holdings, and the resulting farms are no longer economically efficient. There has thus been a land consolidation, starting in 1959 and gaining momentum after the 1970s. This is simply another example of the observation that even successes can create problems.

DEVELOPMENT PARADIGMS

In the 1960s and 1970s, a substantial literature appeared that sought, if not to prescribe development strategies, then at least to describe patterns of successful or unsuccessful development. The better of these used intercountry comparisons, applying a variety of statistical methods to find trends and elements that correlated. I intentionally use the word *patterns* in preference to *strategy* because for the most part the studies have been *ex post facto* constructs to explain empirical findings. One purpose of this book is to explain the evolution of development policy in Taiwan, and as one involved in that policy formulation and implementation, I know that we did not set out in the early 1950s with anything like what I would call a comprehensive strategy.

[16]Chen Cheng, *Land Reform in Taiwan*; Koo, *The Role of Land Reform*; Hui-sun Tang and S.C. Hsieh, "Land Reform and Agricultural Development in Taiwan," in Walter Froehlich, ed., *Land Tenure, Industrialization and Social Stability* (Milwaukee, Wisc.: Marquette University Press, 1961); Young-chi Tsui, "A Preliminary Assessment of the Impact of Agrarian Reform on Taiwan's Agricultural Economy," *Industry of Free China*, Taipei, ROC, Feb. 1965, pp. 118–37; and Martin M.C. Yang, *Socio-Economic Results of Land Reform in Taiwan* (Honolulu: East-West Center Press, 1970).

Three important intercountry studies that include Taiwan are by Bela Balassa, Hollis Chenery, and Chenery and Moises Syrquin.[17] Balassa was among the first to identify the concept of export orientation and its role in development. His first article outlines the concept, and the second looks at Taiwan and Korea as examples of outward-looking economies. Chenery's studies are concerned, among other issues, with sources of foreign exchange and investment capital, including the availability of natural resources for export and the availability of foreign aid or private capital flows. The absence of extensive natural resources for export clearly influenced Taiwan's development pattern, and aid was especially important in the early stages.

[17]Bela Balassa, "Growth Strategies in Semi-Industrial Countries," *The Quarterly of Economics*, 84(1970):24, idem, "Industrial Policies in Taiwan and Korea," *Weltwirtschaftliches Archiv*, 106:1(1971):44–77; Hollis Chenery, "Targets for Development," in *The Widening Gap*: *Development in the 1970's*, Barbara Ward, J. D. Rumalls, and Lenore D'Anjou, eds. (New York and London: Columbia University Press, 1971); Hollis Chenery and Moises Syrquin, *Patterns of Development, 1950–70* (New York: Oxford University Press, 1975).

2

EVOLUTION OF FISCAL POLICY

INTRODUCTION

Fiscal policy, the flexible adjustment of government revenues and expenditures to guide private economic activity in a desired direction, is a major policy instrument of government. Fiscal policy is particularly important in developing countries, where the private sector is not well-developed and the government's share of total economic resources is relatively high. In such cases, it can have a broad and pervasive effect on overall economic activity. But as a country develops and the private sector acquires a larger proportion of economic resources, the economic functions of government diminish and fiscal policy plays a less prominent role, serving mainly as a stabilizing and equilibrating mechanism to counterbalance fluctuations in private economic behavior.

The evolution of fiscal policy in Taiwan has followed the same progression described above, with government intervention diminishing as the economy moved steadily in the direction of liberalization. Though there may be some disagreement over the effectiveness of fiscal policy, there is a broad consensus that changes in real fiscal variables (such as tax rates) do have an impact on economic activity. In fact, the fiscal policies adopted by the ROC government over the past forty years have had a profound influence on the economy. More important, regulations governing taxes and expenditures have been revised and updated whenever changes in the economic environment have so warranted. As a result, the evolution of fiscal policy in Taiwan has closely mirrored the process by which policy-led economic development has given way to development-induced economic liberalization. During this period, the government has undertaken four sweeping fiscal reforms to accommodate the needs of a changing economic environment.

Included in the last two reforms have been revisions of the Custom Duties Rebates on Exports and of regulations concerning import restraints and protective tariffs.

In retrospect, it appears that there has been a close relationship between fiscal reform and changes in internal and external economic conditions. For a better understanding of the evolution of fiscal policy, this divides the process into three phases: the so-called import substitution phase of 1950–1962; the export orientation phase of 1962–1980; and the science and technology orientation phase (also known as the period of accelerated liberalization), beginning in 1980.

IMPORT SUBSTITUTION PERIOD (1950–1962)

At the close of World War II, Taiwan's economy lay in ruins, the inflow from the mainland of large numbers of servicemen and civil servants, as well as their dependents, added to the central government's already heavy fiscal burden. At the same time, severe inflation, high unemployment, and a shortage of foreign exchange placed strict limits on the amount of revenue the government could raise by increasing taxes, issuing bonds, or borrowing. As a result, in addition to developing labor-intensive, import substitution industries, increasing the supply of consumer goods, and creating employment opportunities, stabilizing the government budget was a critical concern.

To achieve these goals and augment tax revenues, the government implemented the Statute for Integrated Tax Collection and the Uniform Invoice System in 1951. The Statute for the Encouragement of Investment was proposed in 1958 as a means of stimulating investment through tax exemptions. In addition, highly protective tariffs and import regulations were adopted to realize the twin objectives of strengthening domestic infant industries and raising tax revenue. Meanwhile, exports were encouraged by offering tariff rebates on raw materials imported for the purpose of manufacturing export goods.

(I) Statute for Integrated Tax Collection

Implementation of the Statute for Integrated Tax Collection was a major milestone of the first tax reform. Key features of this legislation are described below.

1. A household tax, consolidated income tax, and categorical income tax were adopted as a package. With the household tax serving as the basic tax, the consolidated income tax system spread the incidence of taxation among all citizens.

2. A consolidated income tax, encompassing all sources of income, was imposed on all incomes above a specified level (initially NT$18,000 per year). Citizens with incomes below that amount paid only a household tax to local tax authorities. Those with incomes exceeding that amount paid not only a local household tax but also a national consolidated income tax.

3. Consolidated income taxes already paid on income from such categories as wages, salaries, and interest were deductible from the household tax liability. As a result, not only was the burden of taxation distributed equitably and progressively, but the problem of double taxation was avoided.

The collection of taxes on income according to category marked a major advance in tax reform and set the stage for the introduction of a direct tax system.

(II) Unitary Income Tax vs. Complex Income Tax

The "complex income tax system," comprising the household tax, consolidated income tax, and categorical income tax, was not without its merits. Nevertheless, as it was designed to accommodate the household tax of the time, and national taxes (i.e., consolidated income taxes) were collected as a surtax, the system was flawed by serious deficiencies. The Income Tax Law amended on December 23, 1955, made provision for only two categories of income tax: a consolidated income tax and a business income tax. The new system was designated a unitary income tax system to differentiate it from the complex income tax system it replaced.

The "unitary income tax" was enacted in 1956. Major features of this system included:

1. Individual income taxes were collected in conjunction with business income taxes.
2. The undistributed earnings of business firms were subject to only the business income tax, which imposed a lower rate of taxation on income than the individual income tax. This method of collection encouraged the formation and development of businesses. In addition, business losses incurred during the preceding four years were deductible from taxable income of the current year, and business firms were allowed to accelerate the depreciation of plant, machinery, and equipment for tax purposes. These provisions strengthened the incentive to invest.
3. The "pay as you go" method of tax collection was adopted. Under this method, the tax authority at the beginning of each year estimated an individual's tax obligation for that year on the basis of the previous year's income, with taxes paid as income was actually earned. If the actual tax obligation differed from the estimate, the proper adjustment was made.

The tax reform of 1956 set the direction for the future development of Taiwan's tax system. It also promoted economic development by simplifying tax collection and increasing tax revenue. When the "Statute for Integrated Tax Collection" was abolished on January 12, 1968, the integrated tax collection method was retained.

(III) Uniform Invoice System

Before 1951, each business firm issued its own form of invoice. As a result, sales, stamp, and business income taxes tended to be underpaid, their computation was inaccurate, and their collection was far less satisfactory than that of the land tax and household tax. To remedy this problem, beginning in 1951, business firms were required to purchase uniform invoice forms from the government. Under the new invoice system:

1. Regardless of the form of payment or delivery, upon the completion of each sales transaction a business was required to issue to the purchaser a uniform invoice showing the amount of the sale.
2. A business was required to issue a uniform invoice for all revenue-generating transactions, even those not involving the exchange of real goods.
3. A business was required to issue a separate uniform invoice each time the title to goods was transferred, with the invoice recording the market value of the goods.
4. An agent commissioned to sell goods on consignment was required to issue a uniform invoice to a purchaser each time a sale was transacted. A separate invoice was to be issued to the consignor, showing the amount of commission per sale.

Implementation of the uniform invoice system sharply increased government revenues from sales, income, stamp, and banquet taxes, with taxable sales transactions recorded in Taiwan Province rising from NT$760 million in 1950 to NT$6,567 million in 1951. Nevertheless, the profound impact of the system invited efforts to circumvent it, and a brisk trade in uniform invoices issued by paper companies gradually developed. Needless to say, this practice seriously compromised the effectiveness of tax collection. However, it should be noted that such defects were not inherent in the system itself but arose from a lack of sufficient regulation and the negligence of tax auditors. Had the system been more soundly administered, it would have made a greater contribution toward enhancing tax collection efficiency and equalizing the burden of taxation.

(IV) Statute for the Encouragement of Investment: Phase I (1960–1970)

Taiwan began the task of economic reconstruction in the early 1950s, when the economy was still hamstrung by a shortage of both domestic capital and foreign exchange. The Statute for the Encouragement of Foreign Investment and the Statute for the Encouragement of Overseas Chinese Investment were enacted in 1954 and 1955, respectively, in the hope of resolving these problems. The two statutes gave a big boost to the import substitution strategy then being pursued, helping to promote economic stability and fostering the development of labor-intensive industries with modest technological requirements and relatively low capital intensity.

As the domestic market for labor-intensive manufactures became increasingly saturated in the late 1950s, the government switched from an inward-oriented to an outward-led development strategy. The Ministry of Finance and the Taiwan Provincial Government in 1958 organized a Tax Research Committee, which was to study ways in which tax policy could be employed to promote the success of the new strategy. In June 1960 the committee proposed both the Outline for Accelerated Economic Development and a Nineteen-Point Economic and Fiscal Reform. Both of these proposals were incorporated in the Statute for the Encouragement of Investment, enacted in September of that year to improve the investment climate and accelerate the pace of economic development. The Statute comprised 35 clauses, including provisions for tax exemption, the acquisition of land for industrial use, and the accommodation of state-owned enterprises. The major tax exemptions were as follows:

1. Newly incorporated firms and firms undergoing capital expansion were exempted from the payment of corporate income tax for a period of five years.
2. The maximum amount of corporate income tax and surtax paid by a producer could not exceed 18% of its total annual income. Producers that complied with the requirements of the Statute were eligible for a 10% corporate income tax credit.
3. Producers that reinvested current-year retained earnings in the expansion of plant and equipment were eligible for a corporate income tax exemption of up to 25% of total income for the year.
4. Corporations were exempted from the payment of taxes on returns from investments they made in other domestic corporations that were not eligible for tax exemptions and deductions.
5. Income from corporate stock issued at above par value was exempted from the corporate income tax.

6. Income from stock transactions was exempted from taxation.
7. Interest on bonds and dividends on stocks issued by specified industries were deductible from taxable income.
8. Interest income earned on saving deposits with a maturity of two years was exempted from the consolidated income tax.
9. Income earned from exports was exempted from the sales tax.
10. Two percent of income earned from exports was exempt from the income tax.
11. Producers were exempted from the payment of custom duties on imported machinery and equipment.
12. Producers were allowed to accelerate the depreciation of plant and equipment for tax purposes.
13. Deed taxes on land purchased for use in direct production were reduced by 50%.
14. Those who built factories for rent in industrial zones were exempted from the payment of property taxes on those factories.

The major objectives of the tax exemptions and deductions contained in the Statute for the Encouragement of Investment were to stimulate investment in productive enterprises, promote exports, and encourage savings. As the domestic market for locally produced consumer goods became increasingly saturated, export sales had to be expanded in order to earn the foreign exchange needed for further development and to create new job opportunities. And saving was promoted in order to secure a domestic supply of funds needed for investment.

(V) *Rebate of Customs Duties*

Customs duties incurred in the importation of raw materials used in the production of export goods were rebated upon the exportation of the goods, encouraging exports.

1. *Method of rebate*

1) Cash rebate on duties paid in cash: An importer who paid a duty in cash upon the importation of raw materials used to produce export goods received a cash rebate upon the exportation of the finished goods.

2) Rebate offset against duty payable: A duty payable liability incurred by an importer at the time raw materials were imported was offset upon application by the importer if the finished goods were exported within a specified period.

3) Bonded factories (or warehouses). Raw materials to be used solely for the production of export goods were shipped under the supervision of a customs official from the port of entry directly to a factory which, under a bond agreement with the government, was not required to pay customs duties on the materials. The finished goods were shipped under the supervision of customs official directly from the factory to the port from which they were exported.

2. Applicable items

The rebate of customs duties in Taiwan dates back to 1951, when duty rebates were granted on imported raw materials for nested straw hats. In the light of the increase in applications for duty rebates and the shortage of foreign exchange, the Ministry of Finance in 1954 implemented the Bill for Rebating Customs Duties on Imported Raw Materials Used for the Production of Export Goods in order to encourage exports. Under the Bill, export goods were eligible for duty rebates if:

1) They met international standards for quality and packaging.

2) They had a large, or a potentially large, export market.

3) There were no raw materials available domestically at prices comparable to those of the imported raw materials used in the production of the goods.

4) The imported raw materials accounted for a major portion of the cost of producing the exported goods, and customs duties for more than 2.5% of the total value of production.

The Bill for the Rebate of Customs Duties on Imports of Raw Materials Used for the Production of Export Goods was applied to a broad variety of export goods, with no restrictions regarding categories or items. However, only the first two methods of rebate described above were employed initially. The Bill for the Rebate of Customs

Duties underwent many revisions. As part of the 1961 revision, trading agencies and banks were authorized to set up bonded warehouses and factories, and to administer the rebate of customs duties. The rebate of duties on imported raw materials encouraged the development of export processing zones, helped increase foreign exchange earnings, and stimulated the creation of many new domestic job opportunities.

(VI) Tariff Protection and Import Regulation

Tariff protection and import regulation are widely used in developing countries to protect domestic infant industries. Taiwan also made use of these strategies during the period of import substitution, protecting domestic industries from foreign competition through high import tariffs and strict import restraints. As a result, Taiwan was able to substantially increase both its earnings of foreign exchange and tariff revenue. And it was not until the late 1950s that those measures were relaxed.

1. Tariff protection

Generally speaking, import tariffs were quite high during the 1950s, although tariffs on some items were adjusted downward. When the Import Tariff Code was first introduced in 1948, 10.10% of all imports were subject to a tariff rate above 90%. This share rose to 11.26% in 1955, but declined to 8.08% when the code was revised in 1959. Over the same period, items that were subject to a tariff rate between 60% and 90% initially accounted for 8.10% of total imports, with their share dropping to 7.4% then rising to 7.45%. The share of items against which a tariff rate between 30% and 60% applied rose at first from 28.10% to 34.71%, before falling to 27.70%. The share of items to which a rate lower than 30% applied stood at 53.17% initially, then declined for a time before rising to 56.77%.

In general, tariffs on imports of consumer goods were higher than those on intermediate goods. For instance, in January 1955 tariff rates averaged 43.24% for cotton fabrics, 90.56% for woollen and worsted fabrics, and 140.83% for artificial, synthetic, and silk fabrics. The average tariff rate on foods, herbs, tobacco, and alcoholic beverages was 66.52%. By contrast, the tariff rate on metal and metal products was only 26.37%, while that on chemical products was 27.63%. Although tariff rates on some fabric products other than cotton and linen fabrics were later reduced, they remained much higher for consumer goods than for intermediate inputs. This difference was even greater if rebates of custom duties, to be discussed later, were taken into consideration.

2. Import regulation

In 1953, 41.5% of all industrial products were subject to some form of import restraint, while 55.2% were not. By 1956 the former share had climbed to 51.0% and the latter had fallen to 48.1%. Due to a considerable change in import regulations in 1961, the share of total items free of import restraints rose to 53.7%, while the share of prohibited items declined sharply to only 3.5%.

PERIOD OF EXPORT ORIENTATION (1962–1980)

The government implemented a series of four-year economic development plans beginning in 1953. Under the first two of these plans, the strategy of import substitution proved so successful that the domestic market became saturated with consumer goods produced as import substitutes. Under these circumstances, to reap the benefits of economies of scale and sustain economic development the government shifted to an export-oriented strategy. The Statute for the Encouragement of Investment, introduced in 1960, provided a major stimulus to export growth, as did the devaluation of the NT dollar from 36.38 to 40.00 to the US dollar, and the augmentation of the customs duties rebate system. With the take-off of exports in 1963, the economy was poised for a new round of development.

By 1968 Taiwan had completed four economic development plans with spectacular success. Measured at constant prices, GNP in 1969 was 3.7 times what it had been in 1953. Real economic growth averaged 7% during the first two four-year plans, 9.5% during the third plan, and as high as 10.5% in the following four-year period. Robust economic growth and strong domestic and foreign demand provided further impetus for development. Nevertheless, relatively backward infrastructure and an inadequate tax structure and tax collection system acted as a drag on further development, while both the Statute for the Encouragement of Investment and import regulations were in need of updating. To remedy these conditions, the Tax Reform Committee of the Executive Yuan was established in 1968 and a third round of tax reform was initiated. The committee's primary responsibilities were the revision of both the Statute for the Encouragement of Investment and the Income Tax Law, and the implementation of the Customs Duties Rebate system. Other tasks included the revision of tariff and import regulations, and the reform of tax administration. In addition, between 1966 and 1969, export processing zones were set up in Kaohsiung, Nantze, and Taichung to promote exports.

(*I*) *Statute for the Encouragement of Investment — Phase II (1971–80)*

1. *Objectives*

Phase I of the Statute for the Encouragement of Investment expired at the end of 1970, after the statute had been amended three times. This period had been marked by steady economic expansion and rapid growth in domestic and in foreign and overseas Chinese investment. To promote the continued growth of investment and exports, sustain rapid economic expansion, and support other objectives of the fifth four-year economic development plan, in 1971 the Statute for the Encouragement of Investment was extended for ten years. This extension marked the beginning of the statute's second phase.

2. *Highlights*

1) New manufacturing firms were given an option of a five-year tax holiday or accelerated depreciation.
2) Existing firms that underwent capital expansion were eligible for either a four-year tax holiday or accelerated depreciation on fixed investment.
3) New amendments were introduced to promote the development of the capital market.

4) An income tax deferral was granted on new shares issued as a result of the investment of retained earnings in capital expansion.
5) The maximum amount of tax-free interest income that could be earned annually on savings deposits was increased.
6) The Executive Yuan was given the authority to suspend taxes on security transactions and income derived from such transactions, if conditions so warranted.
7) Exemptions and deferrals of income, stamp, deed, and land value increment taxes were granted to encourage merger and acquisition activity.

3. *Amendments*

The Statute for the Encouragement of Investment was revised seven times between 1973 and 1979 in response to new financial and economic developments. It was amended in 1973 to meet the financial needs of the ten major projects, in 1974 to cope with the first oil crisis, and in 1977 to promote the development of the second stage of import substitution (i.e., the development of industries to produce domestic substitutes for imported intermediate goods). The 1977 revision also contained provisions to encourage the development of capital- and technology-intensive industries, capital diversification, corporate mergers and acquisitions, and corporate R&D.

(II) Revision of the Income Tax Law

The division of income taxes into a consolidated income tax and a business income tax under the tax reform of 1955 was a significant step forward for Taiwan's tax system. Although further revisions were made in 1963 to simplify tax collection, strengthen tax reporting, and increase the number of exemptions and deductions, the basic features of the income tax law remained intact. In 1968, noting the small proportion of income taxes in total tax revenue and continuing inequities in the distribution of the tax burden, the Tax Reform Committee proposed a measure for "strengthening the collection of the consolidated income tax," which was enacted into law at the end of the year. In the meantime, revisions of major provisions of the business income tax law laid the foundation for further tax reform. In pursuit of greater equality and rationality, the revised consolidated income tax law of 1968:

1) Allowed a standard deduction from taxable income for those taxpayers who were unable to itemize their deductions. This provision guaranteed a minimum standard deduction for low-income taxpayers.
2) Readjusted the range of progressive income tax rates from 3–52% upward to 6–60%.

In 1968, the year the Tax Reform Committee was established, income taxes (most of which consisted of business income taxes) accounted for only 7.5% of total tax revenue. Following the tax-law revisions of that year, however, income taxes grew steadily until they became the major source of tax revenue. As the share of income taxes in total revenue increased, so did the income elasticity of taxation, and the tax mechanism assumed the functions of an automatic stabilizer of economic activity. Furthermore, the adoption of a minimum standard deduction and the upward adjustment of progressive tax rates brought the income tax law into greater harmony with the principle of taxation according to ability.

(III) Amendment of the Customs Duties Rebate System

Following its inception in 1955, the rebate of customs duties on exports was extended from handicrafts to include industrial products. As the number of items eligible for rebates grew, so did the amount of rebates — from NT$41 million per year during 1955–58 to NT$3,138 million in fiscal year 1969. This rapid growth in customs rebates resulted in a considerable backlog of administrative work for customs officials. In view of this situation, in 1968 the Tax Reform Committee of the Ministry of Finance proposed a Draft Revision of the Customs Duties Rebate Law. This revision was aimed at:

1) Simplifying the review of duty rebate standards.
2) Simplifying the processing of duty rebates.

3) Using computers and electronic calculators for book-keeping functions.

Nevertheless, with as many as 20,000 different standards and criteria involved, and with a single finished product sometimes embodying as many as 1,000 different intermediate materials, against each of which a separate tariff rebate might be applied, the administration of the system remained incredibly complex. To reduce that complexity, a lump-sum tariff rebate method was adopted in 1969. Under this method, a specific duty rebate was established for each category of exports, based on the "duty-paying values" of the imported raw and intermediate materials used in their production and on the tariff rates applied against those materials for a period of half to one year before. Although the number of tariff rebate applications processed each month increased by 15,000 after the adoption of the lump-sum tariff rebate, the number of new cases grew even more rapidly. As a result, there was no significant decrease in the backlog of rebate applications pending.

(IV) Import Liberalization and Tariff Reduction
The main purposes of tariff protection and import regulation are to protect infant industries, conserve foreign exchange, and raise tax revenue. But as Taiwan began to accumulate budgetary surpluses in the 1960s and its trade account moved into the black in 1971, it became increasingly apparent that exchange in import tariff and regulatory policies was in order. In August 1971 Taiwan revised its import commodity classification system to accord with the Brussels Tariff Nomenclature (BTN), a system of classification used widely throughout the world. It also significantly reduced the number of imports subject to regulation, substituting higher tariffs in place of import restraints and incorporating the previously applied 30% import surcharge within the nominal tariff rate. As a result, the nominal tariff rate rose sharply, although the real tariff rate declined.

With regard to import deregulation, the share in total imports of those items allowed to be imported free of all restrictions increased from 57.1% in July 1970 to 82.1% two years later, while that of items still subject to regulation shrank from 41% to 17.9%. At the same time the share of prohibited items (those affecting national security, social stability, or public health) fell from 1.9% to 0.04%.

As for import tariffs, the share of those items with a tariff rate higher than 90% rose to 14.51% of total imports in August 1973; items with a tariff rate between 60% and 90% accounted for 11.62% of total imports; and that of items with a tariff rate between 30% and 60% was 34.02%. By contrast, items with a tariff rate lower than 30% shrank to 39.81% of the total, although the proportion of these items which were imported duty free had risen from 0.9% in 1948 to 3.23% in 1973. Since the upward adjustment of tariff rates took place as part of the process of tariffication (the substitution of tariffs for quantitative restraints), it should not be thought of as an increase in the level of protection. Indeed, since it allowed consumers greater freedom of choice than they would otherwise have had (albeit at a higher price than in some countries), it should be viewed as a significant step toward economic liberalization.

(V) Export Processing Zones (To be discussed in Chapter 6)

IV. PERIOD OF ACCELERATED LIBERALIZATION (1980–PRESENT)

Science and technology became a leading force in Taiwan's economy with the inauguration of the Science and Technology Development Program in May 1979. At that time the world economy was still reeling from the recessionary effects of the second oil crisis, while at home the completion of the Ten Major Projects greatly enhanced the nation's basic infrastructure. Under such conditions, development strategy emphasized the encouragement of private investment and the development of technology-intensive industries. Toward those ends, the government introduced phase three of the Statute for the Encouragement of Investment" in 1980, and "four measures to alleviate business difficulties in 1981.

The government accelerated the pace of import liberalization and tariff reduction in 1983, both to lower the cost of production and strengthen the competitiveness of domestically produced goods in the world market. As the world economy recovered, Taiwan experienced rapid economic and export growth, and by the latter half of the 1980s, persistent trade surpluses had swollen its accumulation of foreign reserves to an all-time high. This situation favored the development of capital- and technology-intensive industries, and helped advance the process of economic liberalization and the further opening of the domestic market. In addition, a value-added tax was implemented in 1986 to meet the needs of economic modernization and tax rationalization.

(I) Statute for the Encouragement of Investment — Phase III (1981–1990)

When the second phase of the Statute for the Encouragement of Investment expired in 1980, a stagnating world economy had depressed the growth of Taiwan's exports and industrial production, as well as willingness to invest in the domestic economy. In view of these conditions, the government decided to prolong the life of the Statute for ten more years, the so-called Phase III of the Statute for the Encouragement of Investment. Major priorities under Phase III included:

1. Strengthening the competitive advantage of exports and accelerating export growth.
2. Augmenting the supply of energy and natural resources.
3. Improving the industrial structure.
4. Strengthening R&D in support of industrial upgrading.
5. Protecting the natural environment.
6. Mitigating the severity of domestic business fluctuations.
7. Promoting an equitable distribution of income.

The Statute of the Encouragement of Investment — Phase III was revised three times during the eighties, in 1982, 1984, and 1987, primarily to encourage the development of capital- and technology-intensive industries. At the same time, outward investment and the formation of venture-capital firms to invest in high-tech industries were emphasized. This change in priorities reflected a shift from preoccupation with export-led growth to greater concern for technological innovation, industrial upgrading, and national well-being.

(II) Import Liberalization and Tariff Reduction
The 1980s saw a further easing of import restraints and sharp cuts in import tariffs.

1. Expanding import liberalization
With very few exceptions, import controls were practically eliminated by the 1980s. The share of total items that could be imported free of restraint had risen to as high as 98.45% by December 1988, although it declined slightly to 96.99% in January 1989 after the adoption of the new HS System of classification. By January 1992, following the introduction of several liberalization measures, items imported free of control accounted for 97.35% of all imports, with the remainder still subject to some form of regulation.

2. Import tariff reduction
During the 1980s, tariffs were cut sharply, with the ceiling tariff rate reduced in three increments from 75% in 1986 to 50% in 1988. Items with a tariff rate between 1% and 30% increased their share of total imports from 60.06% to 84.17%, while the share of items with a tariff rate higher than 30% declined from 21.25% to 5.71%. Meanwhile, duty-free items as a percentage of total imports rose steadily, amounting to 13.42% of all imports by 1992.

As a result of the successive tariff reductions described above, the average nominal tariff rate fell from 31.04% in 1982 to 8.89% in 1991, and the average effective rate for all imports declined from 7.61% to 4.97% in 1991.

(III) The Phasing-out of Customs Duties Rebates on Exports
By lowering the price of exports relative to that of goods produced for domestic consumption, the tariff rebate system made Taiwan's exports more competitive internationally and encouraged domestic saving. But

after years of rapid economic growth and successive rounds of tariff reduction, tariff rebates began to lose their economic value. Recognizing that import liberalization was the wave of the future, the government, as early as 1983, proposed that tariff rebates be phased out over a period of five years. Since then the number of export items for which rebates are granted has been steadily reduced, until today they apply to only a few goods that embody high-duty imports as raw or intermediate materials. After the rebates have been completely phased out, producers that still require the use of dutiable imports will be encouraged to join the network of bonded factories operated by the Customs Bureau.

(IV) Value-Added Tax

The business tax, which is levied at a fixed rate on domestic sales, is one of the most important of Taiwan's sales taxes. In addition to the business tax, sales taxes include customs duties levied on certain imported goods, a commodity tax, and a stamp tax. Given the number of different sales taxes and the broad tax base against which they are applied, sales taxes have accounted for a large share of total tax revenue since 1950. As an example, sales taxes in 1952 generated 37% of total tax revenue, of which import duties, business taxes, stamp taxes, and commodity taxes contributed 22, 6, 4.4, and 4.6 percentage points, respectively. The share of sales taxes in total tax revenue surged to 43.7% in 1982, of which its constituent taxes accounted for 16.2, 9.3, 4.1 and 14.2 percentage points, respectively.

The complexity of the sales tax system invited such problems as double taxation and tax surcharges, which became more serious as the number of transactions involving the same goods and services increased. Furthermore, since the sales tax was levied on capital goods as well as consumer goods, it pushed up the cost of production and imposed an extra burden on domestic consumers. Even though the commodity tax was levied on only a few goods, its high rate distorted relative costs and prices, resulting in a dead-weight loss of consumer welfare and a misallocation of scarce resources. The stamp tax is a certificate tax by nature. However, after 1978, when the stamp tax law was revised, about 80% of stamp taxes were paid along with other sales taxes upon receipt of a uniform invoice, without a stamp being issued. As a result, the stamp tax remained a certificate tax in name only and, in effect, became a surtax imposed on top of the business tax.

Revision of the business tax law had been considered as early as 1969. In 1973, the Tax Reform Committee produced a Draft Value-Added Business Tax, but it was not until November 1983 that the Ministry of Finance submitted a finalized draft to the Executive Yuan. After lengthy debate and discussion, the Legislative Yuan enacted the new value-added business tax into law on January 17, 1986.

The new tax imposed a levy of 5% to 10% (currently 5%) on the value added (i.e., the difference between the value of goods and services sold and the cost of materials and supplies used in producing them) of all goods and services sold in Taiwan. At one stroke, it eliminated such long-standing problems as double taxation and business surtaxes.

Prices have remained stable and tax revenue has grown rapidly since the new business tax was implemented. Since July 1, 1988, the new tax, instead of being computed separately on the basis of sale price at the retail level, has been included in the sale value of goods and services. In addition, the tax-filing period has been extended from one month to two months.

V. CONCLUSION

Over the past forty years, fiscal policy has played an important part in Taiwan's reconstruction, industrialization, and economic development. By adopting protective tariffs and tax incentives in the early 1950s, the government stimulated the growth of basic industry, expanded exports to provide a broader market for domestic manufactures, and promoted economies of scale in industrial production. Once the proper level of development had been attained, tariff rates were slashed and the domestic economy was opened to imports. As a consequence, Taiwan's market today is one of the freest, and its tariff rates among the lowest, in the world. In the meantime, continuing efforts to rationalize the tax system have produced new sources of revenue for government and ensured a more efficient allocation of resources.

A sound tax system and sustained economic growth have, over time, helped stabilize government finances. If revenue from the sale of bonds were included in government income, the government would have enjoyed a budgetary surplus after 1964. With bond revenue excluded, the government ran a deficit for the years before 1972, although the size of the deficit was never large enough to impair the government's credit standing. With the exception of only a few years, government finances were in the black after 1972. However, in 1989, as government spending on land procurement for national development projects increased and the economy turned sluggish, the growth of tax revenue slowed and a budgetary deficit was once again incurred. This situation is expected to be only temporary, and will be corrected by more robust economic growth and higher tax revenue following completion of the Six-Year National Development Plan.

3

MONETARY REFORM

INTRODUCTION

Definition and Content of Monetary Policies

In any contemporary developing country, there are three major types of growth promotion policies that involve the creation of money by the monetary authority. First, monetary expansion can be used to cover the public finance deficit shown as the budget gap between government income and expenditures. Second, purchasing power can be created to cover the investment finance deficit shown as the gap between investment demand and voluntary savings. Third and finally, monetary expansion can allow the monetary authority to acquire foreign exchange reserves when there is an export gap (i.e., when exports exceed imports) not accompanied by outward capital movement. The three types of monetary expansion correspond to fiscal policies, investment finance policies, and foreign exchange policies, respectively. Since the Central Bank exercises the ultimate political (i.e., the sovereign) power to create money, these policies are but different facets of broadly defined monetary policies.

We have, in a different chapter of this volume, dealt with the post-war experience of the ROC with regard to the evolution or reform of fiscal policies for which the Ministry of Finance was primarily responsible. It is the purpose of this chapter to trace the contours of evolution of the other components of monetary policies, i.e., investment finance policies and foreign exchange policies, the administration of which is the primary responsibility of the Central Bank. Thus, monetary policy is concerned basically with the art of central banking.

Since the interest rate and foreign exchange rate are crucially involved in investment finance and foreign trade activities, respectively, the relatedness of the so-called *three vital rates* (i.e., the interest rate, the foreign exchange rate and the money growth rate), in playing their growth promotional roles constitutes the heart of any technical analysis of the art of central banking.

The monetary experience of Taiwan in the post-war period has certain unique features that can be interpreted as valuable lessons to be shared by other contemporary less-developed countries in general and the socialist PRC on the mainland in particular. This introductory section serves as a guide to this chapter by pointing out these unique features of the monetary experience of Taiwan as it evolved in the post-war years.

Financial Institution Construction and Monetary Policy Reform

From an historical perspective, to the contemporary less-developed countries (including Taiwan), the post-war period was a transition period as these countries terminated their pre-war agrarian-colonial heritage and marched toward modernization.

Primarily for this reason, in analyzing the monetary experience of Taiwan, a distinction should be drawn between *monetary policy reform* and *financial institution construction* that are two different facets of economic modernization. In particular, the financial institutions that serve to channel savings funds into the multitude of alternative investment outlets gradually took on a modern outlook as it became functionally differentiated and specialized. For functional differentiation and specialization are, indeed, the central phenomena involved in any evolutionary process.

The evolution of financial institutions is a process centered in the gradual appearance of specialized financial markets (e.g., stock, bond or money markets), financial agents (e.g., commercial banks, trusts, cooperatives) and financial instruments (e.g., bonds, negotiable bills), to make the financial institutions of the ROC look more and more like those of the industrially advanced countries. From an historical perspective, the modernization of financial institution construction is a story of the perfection of the financial market that will be analyzed in the second part (Section II) of this chapter. This introduction is concerned primarily with the evolution of monetary policies that will be dealt with in the first part (Section I).

Liberalization: The Central Theme of Evolution Toward Modernization

Readers should be alerted to the fact that the two sections — on policy reform (Section I) and on institutional construction (Section II) — are not independent of each other. In fact, the two parts, together, tell a coherent story that constitutes the central theme of this chapter, namely, the post-war evolution of monetary institutions in the ROC has been guided by the cardinal principle of liberalization, defined, quite generally, as a gradual atrophy of the arbitrariness of the political force from interfering in the economic activities of private society.

The two parts of this chapter are complementary because the economic role of bureaucratic discretion in the exercise of monetary policies was gradually replaced (i.e., substituted) by the automatically adjusting market mechanism as the latter became perfected over time. This substitution can, indeed, be interpreted as the central theme of this chapter.

Since the formation of all economic policies involves a political process, economic liberalization (i.e., the replacement of bureaucratic discretion by the market) represents the maturing of the political culture of contemporary less developed countries in the post-war period. In the language of political scientists, economic liberalization changes the government-society relationship when command and control (with heavy bureaucratic entrenchment) is replaced by the market (where bureaucrats need not be involved at all).

To the vast majority of less developed countries, the post-war period has been an epoch of decolonization that carried, as a by-product, a new-found sense of nationalism. This nationalistic orientation found expression in the predilection for government command that penetrated all levels of private social-economic life.

Evolutionary Phases Toward Liberalization

Taiwan was no exception to this orientation toward command and planning in the early post-war period. Compared with other contemporary less developed countries, what was unique about the transitional growth of Taiwan was her story of economic liberalization as she went through three evolutionary phases:

i) import substitution phase or I.S. phase (1950–1962)
ii) external orientation phase or E.O. phase (1962–1980)
iii) technology sensitive phase or T.S. phase (1980–1992)

Toward the end of the last (T.S.) phase, it became increasingly clear that, in the economic as well as the political sense, the modernization of ROC is near completion. From the political standpoint, the arrival of the T.S. phase led directly to a new polity of constitutional democracy — reflecting a matured political culture that curbs the arbitrariness of the government using the legislature. The evolution of monetary policy in the direction of liberalization is but another manifestation of the same principle that renounces government arbitrariness in the economic arena — usually referred to as Central Bank autonomy or neutrality.

Direction-Neutral of Monetary Policies

With respect to monetary reforms that will be analyzed in this chapter, it is useful to stress the fact that, in a mature developed economy (e.g., the U.S.), the purpose of monetary expansion (i.e., the creation of monetary purchasing power) as a policy instrument is quite different from its growth promotion role as emphasized in the less developed countries. The Central Bank of an industrially advanced country is a specialized agent that manages the quantity of money in a strictly direction-neutral way.

This art of central banking in a contemporary less developed country (including the ROC during the I.S. and E.O. phases) is quite another story because monetary purchasing power was made available for investment expenditures in particular industries that produce particular products. The philosophy of such a *direction-specific monetary expansion policy* rests on two convictions. First, bureaucrats are enlightened to the extent that they know the appropriate direction of investment (e.g., the government can foretell which industries are "strategic"). Second, it is politically appropriate for the government to help a particular industry or firm make money via the very exercise of growth promotion policies.

The ROC finally abandoned direction-specific policies in the T.S. phase as, for a modern society, the industrial structure is too complex for the government to foretell the direction of investment. Furthermore, for the government to help a particular industrial firm make money clearly violates the basic principle of political neutrality under constitutional democracy.

Thus, from an evolutionary perspective, direction-neutral monetary policy was adopted for political and economic reasons in the T.S. phase. Monetary expansion was not allowed to influence the interest rate and or the foreign exchange rate that, in principle, are to be determined by economic forces prevailing the world market.

When a country relies upon monetary expansion to solve economic problems (be it the government budget gap, the investment-savings gap, or the import surplus gap — see above) earnestly and persistently, the growth rate of money can be significantly higher than the GNP growth rate. Price inflation will occur sooner or later. In the ROC, price inflation was caused by the government budget gap in the early fifties in the rehabilitation period. Inflation, induced by an investment-savings gap, again occurred in the 1970s in the E.O. phase. A truly significant monetary experience of the ROC was the employment of a deliberate policy of high interest rates to combat price inflation during these inflationary episodes. The ROC was the first country in the world to practice such a policy successfully.

**Growth With Stability: Management of the Money Growth
Rate and the Interest Rate as Growth Promotion Instruments**

To see the significance of this policy innovation, it is well known
that when sustained price inflation is anticipated (e.g., the double-digit
price inflation in the 1970s in the U.S.) the market rate of interest will
have to increase sufficiently to compensate for the inflationary effect
so that the real interest rate will not be negative. In a free market
economy, the market rate of interest can make these upward adjustments
automatically through the market. In contrast, in the case of the ROC
where the quantity of money was controlled by the Central Bank to
promote growth, the interest rate for savings deposits was raised
deliberately during times of price inflation to encourage domestic savers
to put their savings in the form of savings deposits, reviving their faith
in the domestic currency. When this occurs, purchasing power is partly
demobilized as the quantity of money (i.e., the so-called M1, including
demand deposits and currency in circulation) as well as the velocity of
circulation decreases. The ROC experience has shown that price
inflation can be brought under control quickly and effectively by such
a high interest policy.

For this high interest policy to be effective, it is obvious that the
money growth rate itself must be slowed down. In the E.O. phase in
the 1960s, monetary management via government control of the interest
rate was sloganized as the art of growth with stability. In this regard, it
is useful to think of a *management format* of alternation in the money
supply in two regimes of low and high interest rates:

*(i) Expansionary Regime: To Achieve Rapid Growth with Low Interest
    Rates*

To promote rapid growth, the money growth rate is accelerated to
suppress the market rate of interest below the equilibrium level. In the
absence of market clearance, the excess demand for money for
investment, created by a low interest policy, is curbed by a direction-
nonneutral policy of credit rationing. However, the accelerated money
growth rate leads to price inflation.

(ii) Contraction Regime: To Achieve Stability Through High Interest Rates

To curb price inflation, the money growth rate is decelerated. In order to hasten the process of inflation control, a low interest policy is introduced to accompany the slowing down of the money growth rate.

Thus, growth with stability was the result of using of a system of monetary and interest policies characterized by an administration orientation. In an expansionary regime, the government resorts to the convenience of monetary expansion to help private entrepreneurs make money (via a low interest rate). Under this regime, the variation of the structure of industries is influenced by government control of the direction of investment via the exercise of direction-nonneutral expansionary monetary policies. What is achieved under a contractionary regime is a restoration of the natural rate of interest that serves to guide the allocation of investment funds in an ideal marketized system.

Thus, growth with stability is seen to be a politicized growth promotion strategy with implications for both rapid growth and the flexibility of the *industrial structure*. The so-called high interest policy under a contractionary regime is but an attempt to restore the natural rate of interest disturbed by indulgence in the convenience of monetary expansion in the expansionary phase.

Growth With Structural Flexibility

Taiwan finally abandoned the above managed monetary system as it proved to be incompatible with the requirement of growth with structural flexibility demanded by a modern technological society. In the T.S. phase since 1980, the Central Bank has gradually learned the art of modern central banking by acting as a specialized agent to control the quantity of money with direction-neutrality.

Total economic reform since 1978 on mainland China has a short history of only 14 years. What constitutes the heart of urban reform (since 1985) has centered on:

i) construction of marketized financial institutions; and

ii) a gradual learning of the art of central banking in the management of money, investment and interest rates.

In a seven-year period (1986–1992), PRC managers have experienced the socialist price inflation problem characterized by alternation between an expansionary regime and contractionary regime quite similar to the experience of Taiwan. The financial institutions of the PRC will remain quite primitive compared to the ROC standard — as will be described in Section II. Given this underdeveloped financial market, the alternation between expansionary and contractionary regimes will be a permanent feature of the PRC in the years to come. It is quite obvious that the monetary experience of Taiwan, with regard to both perfection of financial institutions (Section II) and evolution of the art of central banking (Section I) can be transferred to help policymakers on the mainland.

Foundation of "Managed" Foreign Exchange System

The evolution of the foreign exchange system of Taiwan in the post-war period through the I.S., E.O., and T.S. phases has been a story quite consistent with the overall story of liberalization. The foreign exchange system was based on a highly politicized arrangement resting on two cornerstones:

i) *a central reserve system* under which the Central Bank legally monopolized the holding of foreign exchange reserves, and

ii) *a compulsory acquisition arrangement* under which all the foreign exchange earned by the exporter must be sold to the Central Bank at an official exchange rate that can be determined arbitrarily by the monetary authority.

Thus, the central reserve system and compulsory acquisition of foreign exchange at artificial rates constituted the backbone of a highly controlled foreign exchange institution. The cardinal principle that guided the evolution of the foreign exchange institution centered on liberalization of the command-oriented system as the ROC economy went through the three transitional growth phases.

In the I.S. phase, foreign exchange policy was exercised to implement an import substitution strategy based on:

i) an *overvaluation of the domestic currency* at the official rate in order to discriminate against primary product exporters in favor of import-substituting industries, and

ii) excess demand for foreign exchange (brought about by overvaluation) by importers was dealt with by a host of *direction-nonneutral policies*, including the import licensing system and multiple exchange rates.

A foreign exchange system characterized by direction-nonneutrality and pro-import bias was a typical pattern adopted by many contemporary less developed countries in the post-war period to deal with the problems of the shortage of foreign exchange. In the early post-war period, few government officials of less developed countries could appreciate the fact that this acute sense of shortage of foreign exchange was the direct result of overvaluation of the domestic currency at the official rate.

The external orientation phase (1962–80) in the ROC was ushered in, to the credit of the policymakers, with the unification of the foreign exchange rate and correction of the overvaluation of the domestic currency that occurred during the import substitution phase. During the external orientation phase, the most important political-economic culture that appeared was the societal consensus of the overwhelming importance of export trade that was politically fostered. A tendency toward overvaluation of the domestic currency at the official exchange rate during the import substitution period was substituted by a bias in the opposite direction. Undervaluation of the domestic currency to promote exports became the order of the day.

However, in spite of the pressure for undervaluation, the employment of the foreign exchange rate to promote exports was carried out with restraint and moderation as the NT dollar was buffeted with periodic appreciation during the 1970s. A significant landmark in the process of liberalization of the foreign exchange rate was the introduction of the notion of a floating exchange rate in 1978. However, a truly floating system is one under which the foreign exchange rate is to be determined by the demand and supply of foreign exchange in the market place and not as a policy instrument to favor imports or to promote exports. Such a direction-neutral system of foreign exchange management was realized in Taiwan only late in the T.S. phase (after 1986) when the political-economic culture was mature enough to recognize that the foreign exchange rate should not be a growth-promotion policy instrument.

Liberalization of the ROC Economy in the T.S. Phase (1980)

As the ROC entered its T.S. phase after 1980, the political-economic institutions embarked on a course oriented toward full liberalization. In the political arena, the arbitrariness of government power had been curbed by constitutional democracy. In the economic area, the arbitrary political power of the government was replaced by the automatic adjustment mechanism of the market. In fact, the liberalization movement in the T.S. phase carries an *openness orientation* as the economic life of the population of the ROC is integrated with that of the rest of the world and is regulated by the pervasive market forces prevailing in the world market.

It was in keeping with this movement toward internationalization that the foreign exchange institutions of the ROC were gradually liberalized in the T.S. phase. The backbone of the command system (i.e., the monopoly of foreign exchange holdings and the compulsory acquisition provision of the Central Bank) was finally broken. Before this occurred, all economic contacts between Taiwanese citizens and foreigners were effectively controlled by the government—because all transactions involving the use of foreign exchange had to be approved by the government. (For example, a Taiwan millionaire could not make a monetary donation legally to Yale University or to the overseas movement for Taiwan Independence in New York without government approval.)

Marketization of the forces that determine the interest rate and the foreign exchange rate completes the modernization of the monetary institutions. The Central Bank has finally learned to be concerned with management of the growth rate of money with direction-neutrality manifested by meticulous insensitivity to the magnitudes of both the interest and the foreign exchange rate. The Central Bank finally became a modern central bank as a result of liberalization.

FINANCIAL POLICY

Financial policy is defined here to mean that monetary authorities adopt various regulatory measures to fulfill desired economic goals. In Taiwan's economic development over more than four decades, the financial policy was aimed at accelerating economic growth with stability, so the order of growth and stability in the formation of desired goals would be interchangeable on the basis of general economic conditions to promote economic development in the midst of stability. Between 1946 and 1949, for instance, Taiwan experienced hyperinflation due to significant excess demand pressures. Hence, the major goal of financial stabilization measures was aimed at curbing extraordinary price fluctuation through the introduction of monetary reform, gold savings deposits and preferential interest rate savings deposits. To achieve the goal of fostering the primitive industrial sector set by the import substitution strategy, moreover, the monetary authorities on the one hand isolated the domestic economy with restrictive foreign exchange regulations, and on the other hand channeled limited credits into import substitution industries. In line with the adoption of the export promotion strategy in the 1960s and the 1970s, the aims of the financial policy were to facilitate economic growth with the introduction of a unitary exchange rate system and an export financing system, while mitigating inflationary pressures became the primary goal during the periods of two oil crises. In the 1980s when the economy grew steadily despite low willingness to invest, the monetary authorities carefully created an expansionary environment to stimulate private investment.

The Monetary Reform in 1949

Immediately after World War II, Taiwan's economy was slow-moving and experienced hyperinflation. There were several factors contributing to the stagflation, amongst which were:

(1) Severe economic destruction during World War II;
(2) Occurrence of large-scale government budget deficits due to economic reconstruction;
(3) Spill-over effect of rampant inflation originating from mainland China; and
(4) Influx of about 1.6 million people from mainland China between 1945 and 1949, which amounted to one-fourth of Taiwan's population in 1945.

As a result, excess demand pressures increased rapidly and significantly, and hence the price level rose at an average annual rate of 500% between 1946 and 1948 and even increased further to almost 3,000% in the first half of 1949.

To stabilize the economy, the government delicately introduced the monetary reform of June 15, 1949, aiming to bring rampant inflation to a halt. The Old Taiwan dollar was exchanged for the New Taiwan dollar at a rate of 40,000:1, and the latter was pegged to the US dollar at an exchange rate of 5:1. All issuance of the NT dollar was backed by 100% reserves composed of gold, silver, foreign exchange and other precious commodities, and there was a NT$200-million ceiling on the issuance of new currency. In spite of the fact that new currency issued reached NT$267 million in December 1950 due to large government budget deficits, the rapid inflation was eventually kept in check during the early 1950s, a process aided by the adoption of other stabilization measures, and further decelerated to an average annual rate of 1.9% during the 1960s.

Interest Rate Policy

Before July 1989 when Article 41, concerning interest rate regulation, of the Banking Law was repealed, the desired goals of the interest rate policy were achieved through changes in the rediscount rate as well as the ceilings of various deposits and loans rates by the Central Bank. Theoretically, the market interest rate reflects the cost of capital, determined by market forces, which will affect rational activities in savings and investment. Given that Taiwan's financial market was underdeveloped and that most financial firms were state-owned, however, the monetary authorities were able to firmly control movements in the interest rate in order to accelerate economic growth. Hence, the prevailing interest rate might always be below the equilibrium level, causing excess demands for capital and capital rationing, or the so-called financial depression which would distort capital allocation. As the economy continued to grow and the scale of the financial market got larger, there were some drawbacks with respect to the administration-oriented interest rate policy in the economy, despite its advantages in terms of policy orientation and convenience. In November 1980, therefore, the Central Bank promulgated Essentials of Interest Rate Adjustment to expand the bands of interest rate movements, starting the process of interest rate deregulation. Financial firms could not be allowed to set their own rates until the revision of the Banking Law in July 1989, and the interest rates have been determined by market forces since then.

As mentioned before, the primary goal of the interest rate policy was aimed at stabilizing drastic increases in the price level in the late 1940s. In line with the introduction of monetary reform and gold savings deposits, the government also implemented preferential interest rate savings deposits on March 25, 1950 to absorb excess liquidity in the economy. The feature of the new deposits was their high interest rate which reached 7% per month, equivalent to an annual rate of 125% on a compounded basis. Although such a high interest rate did not generate positive real interest rates due to higher inflation rate, the high interest rate policy was very effective in dampening the prevailing hyperinflation. At the start of 1950, for example, time deposits in all banks amounted to NT$2 million, which increased to NT$35 million at the end of that year, equivalent to 7% money supply. Since the banking sector had introduced longer-term savings deposits, the monetary authorities suspended the preferential interest rate savings deposits at the end of 1958. At that time, the interest rate was dropped to 0.85% per month on three-month time deposits and the amount of time deposits reached NT$1,500 million or 29% of the money supply. Between 1950 and 1958, the interest rate on these new deposits was gradually lowered and the monetary authorities relied heavily on the high interest rate policy to call in a tremendous amount of idle money, greatly contributing to stability of the economy in the early development stage. While combating rampant inflation, moreover, the government used preferential loan measures (a constellation of lower interest rates and credit rationing) to encourage private investments in some designated industries, and hence to achieve the policy goal of the import substitution strategy. During the second half of the 1950s, for example, most loans were concentrated in the industries of textiles, apparel and paper products, instead of food processing and commerce sectors. Meanwhile, preferential loans for imported capital goods were also offered to foster the primitive industrial sector.

In the 1960s, which has been called the golden age of Taiwan's economic development, the government shifted its development strategy from inward-looking import substitution to outward-looking export promotion, in order to accelerate economic growth. The economic performance in this decade was remarkable: high economic growth rate of 9.4% per annum and low CPI increase of 3.9%. The primary goal of the interest rate policy during that period was targeted at promotion of economic growth. Hence, various interest rates were gradually lowered in most of the period, such as the rate on credit loans decreasing from 20.4% in 1961 to 15% in 1969. There were two exceptions when the monetary authorities raised interest rates on various deposits in 1968 and 1969 to stabilize the rising inflation rate. Two major factors, among others, contributed to the higher inflation rates in 1968 (7.9%) and 1969 (5%); one was significant excess demand for consumption goods and the other was rapid monetary expansion due to a drastic increase in bank loans to private enterprises. Because of the high interest rate policy, the inflation rate dropped to 2.8% in 1971, showing that high interest rates were one of the most effective means to dampen inflation.

In the early 1970s, most countries adopted expansionary monetary policies to accelerate economic growth. Similarly, Taiwan also lowered various interest rates and injected more credit into the economy to resume a two-digit growth rate; in July 1972, for instance, interest rates on loans and deposits were on average adjusted downward by 0.75 and 0.5 percentage points, respectively. Given both that the world economy grew prosperously and that there were signs of over heating in Taiwan's economy at that time, however, such expansionary monetary measures undoubtedly generated substantial inflationary pressure and were also controversial. Apart from lowering interest rates, moreover, an exceptional trade surplus in 1972 also created a signal increase in money supply which would ignite inflation further.

In 1973 when the first oil crisis occurred and there was worldwide shortage of food and raw materials, the world economy faced the first major setback while enjoying post-war economic prosperity. In the meantime, the international monetary system was confronted with great challenges due to the unrest in the world financial market. Hence, significant inflation emerged all around the globe, and Taiwan also experienced much higher price increases through imported inflation than in the 1960s. Because the CPI drastically increased by an unexpected annual rate of 47.5%, the monetary authorities were forced to raise interest rates three times to slow down the price increase; among others, the rate on two-year or longer time deposits was increased from 9% to 15% and the secured loan rate from 11.25% to 16.5%. Due to the larger price increases, the smaller increases in interest rates could not prevent the real interest rate from being negative and the negativity became larger. Therefore, the various deposit rates were raised by 3.25 percentage points at one shot in order to curb inflation. Again, such a high interest rate policy was very effective in absorbing excess liquidity in the economy. The annual rate of increase in time deposit accelerated from 16.7% at the end of 1973 to 36.5% at the end of 1974, and the amount of that increase reached NT$41.2 billion.

In 1974 when the world economy slided into stagflation, Taiwan's export volume was slightly higher than the previous year, growing by 1.4% which had been the lowest increase rate since 1952. To resume rapid export expansion, the monetary authorities lowered the bank's interest rates eight times as well as the interest rate on export loans between September 1974 and May 1979 with a view to strengthening international competitiveness. As expected, the economy expanded at two-digit rates once again during the period between 1976 and 1978.

As the oil price rose again sharply in 1979 and 1980, domestic inflation also reached an annual rate of 19% in 1980 and 16.3% in 1981 and economic growth rate registered at 5.8% and 4.1%. The second oil shock did generate smaller impacts on the economy than the first one in 1973. Having accumulated the anti-inflation experience during the first oil embargo period, the economy could adjust itself gradually in the face of external shocks. After rapid price increases in March 1979, the real interest rates on time deposits declined drastically, creating more inflationary pressures on the economy. To absorb excess liquidity into the banking sector and hence to mitigate inflationary pressures, the monetary authorities did not hesitate in raising bank rates three times. Due to the tight monetary measures, the rate of price increases decelerated to 3% in 1982, and once again the economy experienced rapid growth with stability.

Although such a policy, characterized by controlled adjustment in interest rates, was rather effective in fulfilling the desired goal with its flexibility and convenience, it would undoubtedly affect the efficiency of capital allocation due to its bad timing and/or possible rate overadjustment. Because the Central Bank did not have enough financial instruments to initiate open market operation, moreover, the general price level used to fluctuate drastically in the face of external shocks. In May 1976, a money market was established with an expectation of generating market short-term interest rates. Through rate competition and arbitration between banks, the establishment of the money market was a catalyst in the liberalization of bank interest rates. To further relax rate restrictions, the Central Bank set up an interbank call loans market and promulgated Essentials of Interest Rate Adjustment in 1980, which allowed banks to set their own interest rates on negotiable CDs (Certificate of Deposit) and debentures as well as bill discount rates. Since then, the monetary authorities had gradually implemented policy measures concerning interest rate deregulation, including the adoption of the prime rate system in March 1985 and the reduction in the number of rate ceilings in January 1986 (see appendix for detailed liberalization policy measures). Despite the existence of rate ceilings at that time, there was no effect on market rates because of loose monetary conditions. As the banking system became increasingly matured, in 1981 the government repealed Article 41 of the Banking Law concerning interest rate restrictions. This brought to an end the history of the interest rate control.

During the period of gradual interest rate deregulation (between November 1980 and July 1989), the monetary authorities repeatedly triggered minute rate adjustments to cope with changing economic conditions. It totaled fifteen cases of interest rate lowering and four of upward adjustment. Based on the above analysis, therefore, the conclusion was drawn that, while promoting interest rate deregulation, the monetary authorities also emphasized the role of interest rate policy in accelerating economic growth, and changed its procedure of monetary management with more reliance on various traditional credit instruments, instead of administrative directives and moral persuasion.

Foreign Exchange Regulations

Immediately after World War II, Taiwan's economy was in the stage of reconstruction from serious war damages, and it badly needed a tremendous amount of imports to resume the normal functioning of the economy. Due to a significant shortage of foreign exchange, however, a limited amount of imports did not properly meet domestic demands. Under such critical conditions, the government was forced to adopt foreign exchange rationing for the most urgent imports. In addition, the government implemented strict foreign exchange regulations on export acquisitions to accumulate foreign exchange reserves.

On June 15, 1949 when monetary reform was announced, the NT dollar was pegged at the rate of US$1 to NT$5, and the system of exchange settlement certificates (ESCs) was put in effect. The foreign exchange earned by exporters had to be sold to the Bank of Taiwan (performing as the central bank), 20% of which was exchanged for NT dollars at the official rate and 80% for ESCs. The ESCs were freely negotiable on the market and could also be sold back to the Bank of Taiwan at the official rate (US$1 to NT$5). Because of continuous inflation and trade deficit, however, the official rate for ESCs was repeatedly devalued; it reached US$1 to NT$7.5 in February 1950 while the official rate for currency was still at the initial level (US$1 to NT$5). Because of the rate discrepancy between currency and ESCs as well as substantial devaluation of the NT dollar, a multiple exchange rate system was introduced. Under the new scheme, different sorts of imports and exports applied to different exchange rates. Soon before April 1958 when the multiple exchange rate system started to be revised, for example, machinery, raw materials and intermediate inputs imported by the private sector as well as general imports for the public sector and US aid were transacted at the rate of US$1 to NT$24.78, and other imports at NT$32.28 (essential goods imported by US aid had an even lower rate of NT$18.78). While a rate of NT$20.35 was applied to goods exported by the public sector, a higher rate (NT$26.35) was given to exports by the private sector. Also, inward and outward remittances were set at the rates of NT$29.05 (NT$24.78 for the public sector) and NT$24.78, respectively.

There were three major considerations leading to the adoption of the multiple exchange rate system at that time. First, since the speed and the degree of devaluation did not keep pace with those of inflation, the NT dollar was significantly overvalued and hence imports and applications for foreign exchange increased substantially. In addition, the sizable demands for imports needed for economic rehabilitation and reconstruction also made the existing limited foreign exchange reserves become more scarce. Under such strained conditions, the multiple rate system was called for in order to efficiently allocate limited foreign exchanges among various uses and effectively improve the balance-of-payment position. Second, due to the overvaluation of the NT dollar caused by rampant inflation, importing commodities became very profitable and hence the demand for foreign exchange surged substantially. Faced with a foreign exchange rationing system at that time, however, importers would incur much higher costs in applying for foreign exchange and this, in turn, would place inflationary pressures on the already rising price level. Therefore the government employed the multiple rate system to restrict unnecessary imports and to encourage agricultural exports with a view to accumulating foreign exchanges and reducing inflationary pressures caused by imports. Moreover, the multiple rate system might be adopted to achieve various goals merely with the application of different rates for exports and imports, rather than an adjustment of a single exchange rate for all goods which would undoubtedly disturb the price level. Finally, in order to increase fiscal revenue, all imports started to be subject to a defence surcharge from September 1953 of 20% above the existing exchange rate. The defence surcharge was also gradually extended to outward remittances. To reduce public expenditures, meanwhile, goods imported by the public sector were subject to lower exchange rates. All these policy considerations therefore contributed to the implementation of the multiple rate system before 1958.

However, exchange rates under the multiple rate system were intrinsically determined by the monetary authorities, rather than market forces, so there was no market mechanism to work in the foreign exchange market. The multiple rate system inevitably generated several drawbacks such as excess administrative burdens, retarding exportation and causing illegal activities, over consumption and abnormal industrial development. More importantly, the multiple rate system severely distorted resource allocation, and the huge trade deficit did not shrink as expected because of small elasticities of both the demand for exports and the supply of imports. Therefore, it became necessary and urgent to revise the multiple rate system.

The Executive Yuan passed a Programme for Foreign Exchange and International Trade on April 11, 1958, starting the three-phase revision of the multiple rate system with a view to mitigating its negative impact. First of all, the number of exchange rates was reduced from 10 to 2. One was a basic rate of US$1 to NT$24.78 which applied to type A commodities, including sugar, salt, rice, fertilizer, soybean, wheat, cotton, oil, machinery and government remittances. The other was set at a combination rate of the basic rate with the market price of ESCs, and other goods (or type B commodities) were subject to this exchange rate. In the meantime, the 20% defence surcharge was integrated into import duties to isolate it from the determination of the exchange rate.

Next, on November 21, 1958, the government announced that the exchange rate for type A commodities also needed to add up the official price of ESCs, which was equivalent to the devaluation of the NT dollar from NT$24.78 to NT$36.38 for US$1. Since the market price of ESCs was very close to its official price, a unitary exchange rate system had intrinsically existed. Later on, however, the rising market price of ESCs made the dual rate system prevail again. In the final phase which started on August 10, 1959, a simple exchange rate was formed by combining the basic rate (NT$24.78) and the official rate of ESCs (NT$11.60), equal to the rate of US$1 to NT$36.38. Apart from the exports of sugar and rice, all transactions of foreign exchange would have to rely on ESCs as a means of settlement, which would infinitely be supplied by Taiwan Sugar Company. To reconcile the difference in the official rates of currency and ESCs, the NT dollar was devalued from NT$36.38 to NT$40 in exchange for one US dollar on June 1, 1961. Hence, the unitary rate system was formally established, and the system of ESCs would not be abandoned until September 27, 1963.

In December 1970, the Statute of Foreign Exchange Regulation was put into effect. Based on the Statute, the central bank had to set the exchange value of the NT dollar and adopt a fixed exchange rate system, pegging the NT dollar to the US dollar. Not until July 1978 would the exchange rate system be transformed into a flexible one, and the Central Bank had no obligation to maintain the fixed exchange rate of the NT dollar. To emphasize the market mechanism of the exchange rate, a centralized foreign exchange market was set up in February 1979. In the market, there was only a brokerage institution, called Center for Foreign Exchange Transaction, composed of five authorized foreign exchange banks. The Center acted as the only broker in interbank transactions of foreign exchanges and also announced the central exchange rate daily. The spot exchange rate set by the Center could not exceed the limits of 0.5% higher or lower than the central rate on the previous business day, and the limit was expanded to 2.25%.

Under the central rate system, although rate adjustment could flexibly be made every day on the basis of market conditions, it merely reflected the demand for and the supply of foreign exchange on the previous business day, rather than the time when the transaction took place. It became apparent that the central rate system needed to be revised to cope with the fast-changing international financial environment. To remedy the weakness, therefore, a new exchange rate system based on free price negotiation was formed in April 1989. Under the new scheme, the former limits on daily fluctuations of the interbank rate were rescinded, and all transactions more than US$30,000 (reducing to US$10,000 on July 2, 1989) could be freely negotiated. For transactions less than US$30,000 (later US$10,000), the exchange rate was set within a band of NT$0.1 above or below the so-called foreign exchange settlement rate for small amounts, which was determined by the five major authorized banks on every business day. In December 1990, the exchange rate liberalization had gone a step further with the rescinding of the foreign exchange settlement rate for small amounts. As a result, banks in all bank-customer transactions have been able to freely set their own rate since then, and we thus now have a similar exchange rate system that is adopted in advanced countries.

Taiwan's forward foreign exchange market was first established in April 1972, including the British pound, Swiss franc and Deutschmark as well as the US dollar in July 1978. The primary objective of the forward market was to provide a hedging device only for underlying trade transactions, excluding capital account transactions. The setting of the forward exchange rate was limited within a band of 2.25% above or below the prevailing central rate. And the central bank would absorb either foreign exchange position of the authorized banks, resulting from all forward transactions. In other words, all foreign exchange risks involved with forward transactions would be transferred from banks to the Central Bank. Later, the Central Bank adjusted the proportion of banks' foreign exchange positions in order to affect the exchange rate in both spot and forward markets. Because of the strong expectation of NT dollar appreciation during the late 1980s, the forward market was technically closed by adopting a cash basis, rather than an accrual basis, in calculating banks' foreign exchange positions. On November 1, 1991, the forward market was re-established to provide a facility for exporters and importers to hedge their exchange risks. Likewise, transactions in the capital account were still not allowed to take advantage of the forward hedging in order to reduce the impact on the spot rate.

Foreign exchange regulations indicate all intervention measures on foreign exchange transactions, which include controls on exchange rate fluctuation and capital movement. Their primary objective is to stabilize exchange rate fluctuations and hence to make the foreign exchange market function smoothly. Before July 1987, when most foreign exchange controls were lifted, the monetary authorities always relied on affecting the supply-demand condition in the foreign exchange market (or quantitative restrictions) in order to stabilize exchange rate fluctuation, rather than directly controlling the exchange rate itself. Between the monetary reform in 1949 and the emergence of the foreign exchange market in 1979, for example, a foreign exchange concentration system was implemented to centralize foreign exchange management by the Central Bank, under which the authorized banks had to maintain zero foreign exchange positions every day through settlement with the Central Bank. With respect to the supply of foreign exchange, the exporters were required to surrender foreign exchange earnings at the official exchange rate. To prevent the NT dollar from overvaluation, the exporters' earnings were exchanged for ESCs or export credits negotiable freely on the market, rather than domestic currency. In addition, the monetary authorities took advantage of the application for export licensing to ensure full compliance with foreign exchange surrender. On the demand side, a foreign exchange rationing system was adopted during the 1950s, in line with the scheme of guarantee deposits for imports. All these measures of exchange control aimed to deal with a balance-of-payments problem caused mostly by the currency overvaluation. By initiating a devaluation-cum-liberalization package, the government gradually lifted part of its exchange controls.

After February 1979, when the foreign exchange market was established, no longer were exporters required to surrender all foreign exchange, part of which might be held in the form of foreign currency deposits in order to facilitate the buoyancy of the foreign exchange market. Hence, the monetary authorities abolished the foreign exchange centralized system which had been in effect for three decades. In May 1986, the monetary authorities rescinded the requirement of prior approval with respect to trade-related transactions of foreign exchange, which was replaced by a system of post application.

As the trade surplus continued at a significant level and foreign reserves accumulated at a rapid pace during the second half of the 1980s, the NT dollar appreciated so rapidly that the economic impact and consequences would have been unthinkable or even unfavorable. To stabilize the foreign exchange market, the monetary authorities made a sweeping change in the exchange controls by revising the Statute for Foreign Exchange Regulations in July 1987, giving an impetus to further financial liberalization and internationalization. In addition to foreign exchange transactions in the current account, the revision also deregulated foreign exchange controls in the capital account, and gave local residents freedom in holding and utilizing foreign exchange. To minimize the turbulent impacts on exchange rate fluctuations, meanwhile, there were annual maximum ceilings on inward and outward remittances of each individual or company, which were set at US$50,000 and US$5 million, respectively. At present, the ceilings has been adjusted to US$3 million for both sorts of remittances to ensure neutral impact on exchange rate fluctuations of capital movements. Below these ceilings, remitted funds are not subject to prior approval as well as restrictions on end use posed by the Central Bank. With such a high degree of freedom on capital movements, it is inevitable that changes in international interest rates are exerting an increasingly significant impact on the domestic rate. Therefore, the vigorous deregulation of capital account transactions has been a catalyst for the internalization of the domestic financial market.

FINANCIAL STRUCTURE AND INSTITUTIONS

A well-established financial institution will extract savings into the financial system and channel them into most productive investments. Thus, an excellent financial system can play an important role in accelerating capital formation, and consequently promoting economic development. Based on Taiwan's four-decade development experience, it is undeniable that the financial sector not only has provided an important impetus for economic growth, but has also helped to generate a stable environment. *Financial deepening* [Shaw (1973)], an indicator measuring the degree of financial development in a country, reflects the phenomenon that the speed of build-up of financial assets is faster than that of accumulation of non financial (or physical) assets. Taiwan's financial deepening may be represented by the ratio of the amount of financial assets to nominal GNP level. The ratio increased rapidly, from 0.96 in 1966 to 2.78 in 1991, even reaching a peak of 3.48 in 1989. It reflected the fact that Taiwan's financial development was very remarkable, though not keeping pace with economic development.

Soon after Taiwan's restoration to the ROC government in 1945, the Provincial Government of Taiwan took over the operation of all existing financial institutions, and the basic framework of the financial system under Japanese rule virtually remained intact till 1949 when the state-run Central Trust of China was re-established in Taiwan. The financial system was regulated too restrictively to provide ample and diversified financial services to the public. In addition to allowing local autonomy, the government authorized the Bank of Taiwan to issue the Taiwan Dollar in May 1946. Due to the vicious effect resulting from the mainland hyperinflation and substantial budget deficits, however, Taiwan experienced an unprecedented financial trauma which was depressed by the monetary reform of 1949 and concurrent stabilization policy measures.

Starting in 1949, five state-owned banks moved their headquarters from the mainland to Taipei one after another. These banks specialized in agricultural development, industrial project financing, foreign exchange trading and foreign trade financing. After integrating these national banks with existing financial institutions, the structure of Taiwan's financial system was that of a vertically organized pyramid under the firm control of financial authorities with strict regulations.

To ensure all financial institutions were performing in an orderly manner and complying with regulatory requirements, Taiwan's banking sector had been characterized by specialization in terms of operational activities. Based on Article 20 of the Banking Law, four classes of financial institutions constitute the intermediation market: commercial banks, savings banks, specialized banks and trust and investment companies. The specialized banks include bank focusing on financing activities in the areas of agricultural development, industrial projects, land mortgages, foreign trade, medium- and small-sized businesses and the private sector (not existing yet). In addition, other financial intermediaries governed by other laws and regulations are the postal savings system, credit cooperative unions, the cooperative and local financial system (composed of Cooperative Bank of Taiwan and Credit Departments of Farmers' Associations and Fishermen's Associations) and insurance companies.

The major advantage of such a financial structure is the capacity for enhancing managerial integrity, enforcing market discipline, ensuring financial order and hence generating a stable development environment. Through its operation of policy orientation, more importantly, the system might accelerate capital formation with credit rationing for strategic industries during the period of credit drought, and consequently achieve desired national goals. Thus, in line with other appropriate economic policies, the financial impetus also helped to provide a favorable environment for economic expansion, which in turn contributed to the healthy development of Taiwan's financial sector. Under tight regulatory controls and conservative administration, the financial industry expanded slowly and steadily between 1950 and 1965 to stabilize the frangible financial condition resulting from the hyperinflation during the late 1940s. It was apparent at that time that the first priority set by the financial authorities was to make supportive efforts to rehabilitate the economy with little regard to economic efficiency.

As the economy continued to expand rapidly after the outward-looking, export-oriented development strategy was adopted, the government took a positive step towards gradually liberalizing the financial market by issuing the licenses for establishing new financial institutions. To cope with the fast-growing demands for financial services and products, several financial institutions were allowed to enter the financial market. They were some national banks (Bank of Communications, Farmers' Bank of China and International Commercial Bank of China), Shanghai Commercial and Savings Bank, an overseas Chinese bank as well as a Japanese bank (Kangyo Bank), during the 1950s and the 1960s. As the financial structure tended to develop in a specialization-oriented way, the government permitted seven private trust and investment companies to enter the financial and insurance markets in the 1970s, in order to make the specialized financial system more complete and to introduce profit-driven free-market principles to the market. Furthermore, several new banks were also given the right to establish operations, such as United World Chinese Commercial Bank in 1975, Export-Import Bank of China in 1979 and City Bank of Kaohsiung in 1982. As a result of the revision of the Banking Law in 1989, the Ministry of Finance issued permissions of establishment to 17 new private banks to further relax the restrictions on the domestic rights of establishment.

The first opening of foreign bank branches in Taipei was Kangyo Bank of Japan in 1958. Since then, the government has allowed foreign banks to set up their branches or representative offices in Taiwan, in order to bring in innovative and dynamic financial services of the advanced economies and to facilitate international trade and investment through their operations. As of the end of 1991, there were local branches and representative offices of 36 foreign banks in Taiwan. Although some of them created confusion for the market and headaches for the financial authorities, it is undeniable that their advanced and sophisticated financial operations contribute to the internationalization of the financial sector.

Apart from major domestic banks and local branches of foreign banks, Taiwan's banking sector also includes 8 regional Medium

Business Banks, 74 Credit Cooperative Associations, 285 Credit Departments of Farmers' Associations and 23 Credit Departments of Fishermen's Associations. The regional Medium Business Banks are smaller than the major domestic banks, and designed to meet the funding needs of small- and medium-sized corporations. The cooperative financial system is dominated and led by the Cooperative Bank of Taiwan, and its major objective is to provide basic financial services (deposits and loans activities) to members and hence to supply funds needed in specialized activities. Although, compared to the major domestic banks, they play a minor role in the flow of funds, these financial institutions provide a great contribution to the expansion of economic activities at the local level.

Like other financial systems, Taiwan's financial institutions can traditionally be categorized into two types: monetary and nonmonetary. The former has the ability to create deposit money and the latter does not. Thus, the nonmonetary financial institutions only absorb idle money into the financial system and transform it into active money; in other words, the existence of such financial institutions is merely to accelerate the speed of money circulation. The Postal Savings System, the most prominent nonmonetary institution, plays an important role in transferring funds from the private sector to the public sector. Due to its favorable tax treatment and the extensive network of its branch offices, the system creates savings deposits representing a large part of the prviate sector's financial assets. Postal savings funds are transferred via the Central Bank of China to a variety of public entities to strengthen infrastructure, such as electricity, transportation facilities, water resources, and so on. In addition to the Postal Savings System, the nonmonetary institutions also include trust and investment companies and life and property insurance companies. The trust and investment companies specialize in long-term lending and financial management, and obtain funds from trust accounts. Given their higher capital cost than the banking sector, they are experiencing the worsening competitive situation in providing long-term credits. Hence, the financial authorities allowed one trust and investment company to be reorganized into a commercial bank in July 1992 to enhance its competitiveness.

Experiencing fast economic growth and rapid trade expansion during the last four decades, Taiwan's economy enjoyed unprecedented prosperity in Chinese history, but did not save more than it invested in only one year out of the last twenty. In spite of dramatic financial deepening, the huge accumulation of excess savings since the early 1980s has not been properly transformed into productive investments, which squandered its economic potential. Hence, more financial liberalization and internationalization are called for to keep the financial development in pace with its enviable economic development.

With the aim of liberalizing Taiwan's financial system, the government has relaxed controls on the establishment of financial institutions, and also deregulated the restrictions on financial operations by revising the Banking Law. Although the financial system is characterized by specialization in financial activities and credit provision, its recent development tends to be directed toward universal banking. Hence, all banks can not only deal with basic financial activities (deposits and loans), but also provide other services, such as brokerage, underwriting and investing in stocks and bills. Besides, there are no longer the restrictions on interest rate settings, providing banks more operational and managerial autonomy. In addition to efforts to liberalize the financial sector, the financial authorities also boldly promoted its internationalization by allowing foreign banks to enter the domestic market, permitting the establishment of offshore banking units in late 1983 and encouraging domestic banks to set up branches or subsidiaries in major international financial centers. It is enthusiastically hoped that, with a highly liberalized and stable financial environment, Taipei will be emerging as a major world financial center in the Western Pacific.

With regards financial markets, Taiwan now has three major ones: the foreign exchange market, money market and capital market. Since the foreign exchange market has been discussed above, the other two markets will be the subject in this section.

Taiwan's official money market was first set up in 1976 with the purpose of starting interest rate liberalization and channeling savings from the curb market to the organized market. To achieve such goals, interest rates in the market are not subject to rate ceiling restrictions and can fluctuate more freely. Besides, its establishment and operation were expected to provide the Central Bank more financial instruments in credit management, after the first oil crisis hit the economy with rampant inflation in 1973 and 1974. The market instruments primarily consist of commercial paper, bankers' acceptances, trade acceptances, negotiable CDs, and treasury bills. Since 1984, the market has also included such financial instruments as government bonds, cooperative bonds and bank debentures with maturity shorter than one year, in order to enrich the sorts of instruments and to promote the buoyancy of the secondary market of such financial assets. Since its establishment, the money market has expanded remarkably in terms of amounts of transactions and issuance; for instance, the issuance amount increased from NT$12.3 billion in 1976 to NT$4,475.2 billion in 1991. Because of free rate fluctuation and rapid market expansion, the existence of the market has been a catalyst for interest rate liberalization. Furthermore, the financial authorities allowed domestic banks to engage in bill financing activities in 1992, breaking down the oligopolistic market conditions dominated by 3 bill financing companies. Even so, however, there are still conceivable improvements in the market in terms of both market scale and management techniques.

Financial instruments in Taiwan's capital market include government bonds, cooperative bonds and bank debentures with maturity longer than one year. Due to government integrity and the strict restrictions on corporative bond issuance, however, the capital market had been dominated by stock transactions. And because the banking sector extracted most government bond issues, which went straight into its vaults, there did not exist a secondary market for government paper. Hence, the stock market was the most important pillar of Taiwan's capital market, and here we will concentrate on it.

Although Taiwan's stock tradings started in 1953, shortly after the Land Reform, the official centralized stock market was set up in 1962. As the economy continues to grow, the size of enterprises becomes larger and private savings increase significantly, the width, depth and resilience of the stock market are also improving. In the primary market, the number of listed stock companies increased from 18 in 1962 to 221 in 1991, and the face value of listed stocks also grew from NT$5.5 billion to NT$616.7 billion during the same period. In the secondary market, similarly, the transaction volume even showed exponential expansion, from NT$0.5 billion to NT$9,682.7 billion during the last three decades and even reaching NT$25,407.9 billion in 1989. In spite of its substantial expansion, however, Taiwan's stock market still needs some sort of reform and deregulation in order to get rid of the image that it is closer to a casino than to an organized first-class stock exchange. Starting in 1983, hence, the government gradually adopted a series of liberalization and internationalization measures. First of all, foreign residents were allowed to indirectly invest in the stock market by purchasing shares in four Taiwan Funds, which was the first phase of a three-phase plan permitting foreign capital to enter Taiwan's equity market. Presently, we are in the second phase in which foreign institutional investors are allowed to directly participate in it, and shortly foreign residents will be directly engaged in Taiwan's stock tradings. With regard to outward portfolio investment, on the other hand, since 1991 foreign residents have been allowed to indirectly invest in foreign equities through the purchase of Taiwan Depository Receipts. Furthermore, the Security and Exchange Commission fully lifted the restrictions on the establishment of new security firms in 1988, which greatly contributed to the buoyancy of the stock market. Later on, it also allowed foreign security firms to set up local branches in Taiwan, along with other measures, to accelerate the pace of stock internationalization.

Finally, it is worthy to note that, like other developing countries, Taiwan has a significant proportion of financial activities undertaken through an unorganized market, along with the operation of the organized market. Such coexistence of an officially regulated market and an unregulated curb market in a financial system is *financial dualism*, which is the prominent feature of Taiwan's financial system. For example, surveys in the mid-1980s showed that 45% of all lending was done through the curb market. Basically, the major factors resulting in the existence of a curb market include a highly regulated, formal financial sector, interest rate controls, and inefficient financial markets. Due to the lack of legal protection and inherently uncertain risks, informal financial arrangements are typically of short-term credit so that the curb market is effectively a bill-financing market. In most developing countries, such as Taiwan, medium- and small-sized enterprises account for a large share of economic activity, which do not usually maintain adequate income statement and balance sheets and have significantly differentiating demands for financial services. As a result, the formally organized financial sector does not meet their specific demands, and the unorganized sector serves as their major supplier of financial services. It is undeniable, therefore, that the informal financial sector has generated a great contribution to Taiwan's economic success. Nevertheless, there are some economic disadvantages caused by the existence of the unregulated financial sector. First, given the relatively high interest rates of the informal financial sector to the formal one, the higher capital cost will blunt the competitive edge of medium- and small-sized enterprises which have been the pillar of Taiwan's economic development. Second, since the activities in the informal sector are not under the supervision of the authorities, its market expansion will create substantial tax evasion. Third, due to the lack of strict regulations on financial operation and arrangements in the informal sector, it is inevitable that there will exist illegal financial transactions and loss of market discipline, endangering financial stability. Finally, the rapid expansion of the curb market will inevitably impair the desired effect of monetary policy on economic activity, because of the inherent change in money velocity. It is expected that Taiwan's recent financial deregulation will shrink the scale of the curb market and hence minimize its negative economic consequences elaborated above.

CONCLUSION: LIBERALIZING THE FINANCIAL SYSTEM

From the point of view of the history of Taiwan's development, its rapid economic growth and trade expansion has been accompanied by changing patterns of financial development. Before the 1970s, the government employed strict regulations and administrative directives to ensure that limited resources were allocated in line with its development strategy and thereby achieve national goals. And the results were very encouraging. As the level of economic development got closer to the developed one, however, such an interventionist approach seemed less successful in accelerating the pace of development, but even squandering the economic potential. Therefore, when several factors promoted financial reform during the 1980s, the government took steps to liberalize its financial system. During the last decade, a number of countries, both developed and developing, adopted more liberalized financial policy measures than before to emphasize the market mechanism. Next, great progress in information processing and telecommunications spurred financial innovation and promoted closer integration among financial markets. This made it harder for financial authorities to regulate the financial sector. Third, rapid economic development placed greater demands on various financial services which could not be provided by a financial system handicapped by long-term ignorance of the government. Hence, it was urgent and desirable to call for financial liberalization and internationalization in seeking further development. Moreover, when Taiwan's foreign reserves accumulated rapidly during the second half of the 1980s, and thereby its international investment position improved greatly, its segmented financial market and ragged financial system needed to be restructured towards greater liberalization and less regulation in order to expand its economic scope and scale. It is worthy to point out, finally, that Taiwan had unintentionally taken steps toward gradual liberalization in an appropriate sequence. And this might be the major factor contributing to the continuous improvements in Taiwan's economic structure, laying down a sound foundation for further economic development.

APPENDIX: LIBERALIZATION OF TAIWAN'S FINANCIAL SECTOR—CHRONOLOGIES

1. *Relaxation of Interest Rate Restrictions*

May 1967	Establishing the money market to generate market short-term interest rates
April 1980	Establishing the interbank call loans market
November 1980	Promulgating the Essentials of Interest Rate Adjustment to allow banks to set their own interest rates on negotiable CDs and debentures as well as bill discount rates
November 1984	Expanding the upper and lower limits on loan interest rates
March 1985	Requiring banks to set prime rates as their own reference loan rates
August 1985	Allowing banks to set their own rates on foreign currency deposits, and repealing the Statute for Managing Interest Rates to give them more flexibility on interest rate settings
January 1986	Reducing the number of deposit rate ceilings from 13 to 4
July 1986	Reducing the number of reference rates of issuing commercial papers from 9 to 5 with adjustment of the rate structure
May 1989	Extending the range of maximum/minimum rates in the interbank call loan market to that of 14%/3%
July 1989	Deleting Article 41 of the Banking Law, concerning interest rate restrictions
October 1991	Establishing a call loan market for financial institutions to increase the number of market participants, such as banks, insurance companies, bill finance companies, and investment and trust companies

2. *Liberalization in Exchange Rate Movement*

April 1958	Replacing a multiple exchange rate system with a unitary exchange rate system in three phases
July 1978	Introducing a floating exchange rate system
February 1979	Establishing a foreign exchange market to strengthen market mechanism
March 1980	Abolishing the upper and lower limits on the NT$/US$ rate
August 1981	Expanding the fluctuation limits of the central rate from 1% of the rate on the preceding business day to 2.25%
November 1982	Announcing the real effective exchange rate index of the NT dollar by the Center for Foreign Exchange Transactions
April 1984	Revising the Regulation Governing Foreign Exchange Banks on Forward Foreign Exchange Transactions to allow banks to set their own forward rate
April 1989	Abolishing the Central Rate System and establishing a system based on free price negotiation
December 1990	Abolishing the Regulation Governing Foreign Exchange Settlement Rates for Small Amounts to liberalize the transaction rates in the bank-customer market
November 1991	Reopening the forward foreign exchange market

3. *Liberalization in Capital Movements*

December 1985	Amending the Statute for Foreign Exchange Regulation to exclude gold and silver from the definition of foreign exchange control, gradually loosen restrictions on foreign exchange control, and require report of settlements only after trade activities instead of application for settlement before the activities

July 1987	Amending the Statute for Foreign Exchange Regulation again to substantially relax foreign exchange controls:

(1) lifting controls on current-account transactions, and allowing residents to freely hold and use foreign exchange

(2) allowing a company or an adult to make outward remittances of up to US$5 million each year without prior approval and restriction on the use

(3) limiting the amount of inward remittances of a company or an adult each year, which increased to US$200,000 in June 1989, US$1 million in November 1989, and US$2 million in July 1990

(4) adjusting the ceilings of both inward and outward remittances to US$3 million to neutralize the impact of capital movements on exchange-rate changes

August 1989	Establishing the Taipei Foreign Currency Call-loan Market to meet industrialists' demands for foreign exchange funds, and signing linkage agreements with international money brokerage houses based on Singapore, Hong Kong, and Tokyo in February and August 1991, and March 1992, respectively, to further expand the scope of international banking operations
August 1990	Increasing the maximum amount of foreign liabilities of the banking sector from US$19.8 billion to US$30 billion to augment capital inflows

4. Deregulation of Domestic Banking Activities

<u>Domestic Banks</u>

July 1977	Permitting the reorganization of District Mutual

	Loans and Savings Companies into District Medium Business Banks
January 1979	Establishing the specialized Export-Import Bank of China to promote international trade
December 1983	Enacting the Statute for International Financial Activities to allow financial institutions to set up divisions of international financial activities, with a view to promoting international financial activities hence making Taiwan a regional international financial center
April 1984	Increasing the number of new branches/ representative offices of every bank per year from 2 to 3 (the number will be increased to 5 in 1993)
June 1986	Permitting 4 commercial banks to introduce CDs denominated in foreign currencies
November 1987	Allowing 11 state-owned banks to engage in margin-buying and short-sale stock transactions
May 1988	Permitting 7 local banks to set up Divisions of Trust to engage in activities of stock transaction, trust and investment
August 1988	Relaxing the restrictions posed on the Credit Department of Farmers' and Fishermen's Associations in loan activities to enhance the capability of local financial institutions for fund management
November 1988	Lifting the restrictions on the number of overseas branches of domestic banks
July 1989	Revising the Banking Law to allow the entry of new private banks
April 1990	Promulgating the Criteria for Establishing Commercial Banks and accepting applications for establishing new commercial banks
January 1991	Allowing banks to set their own terms for CDs denominated in foreign currencies

June 1991	Mapping out the sale of stocks of state-owned financial institutions on the basis of the Statute for Privatizing Public Enterprises to accelerate the pace of privatization
July 1991	Permitting the establishment of 15 new private banks; permitting one additional private bank to be established in May 1992 and allowing the China Investment and Trust Company to reorganize into a new commercial bank in July 1992 to strengthen market competition
November 1991	Promoting the issuance of public shares in the Bank of Communications and the Farmers' Bank of China to accelerate the pace of privatization
July 1992	Allowing domestic banks to engage in bill finance

Foreign Banks

October 1986	Allowing foreign banks to set up the first two branches in Kaoshiung
April 1990	Allowing foreign banks to establish savings departments, accepting passbook savings deposits as well as time savings deposits, and trust departments as securities underwriters, brokers, and dealers

Insurance Companies

May 1988	Permitting foreign insurance companies to open branches or subsidiaries in Taiwan
June 1990	Extending the branch licence period of foreign insurance companies, and allowing more branches to set up in Taiwan
January 1992	Revising the Insurance Law to significantly alter the proportion of insurance funds in use, and to permit new entry

| June 1992 | Promulgating the Criteria for Establishing Insurance Companies and accepting the applications for the establishment of new insurance companies |

5. *Liberalization in the Capital Market*

August 1983	Allowing securities investment and trust companies to set up, and permitting the issuance of Taiwan Funds with a view to channeling foreign capital into Taiwan's capital market indirectly
June 1989	Allowing foreign securities houses to set up branches in Taiwan
July 1988	Permitting new private securities brokerage firms to establish
August 1989	Promoting transactions in over-the-counter markets
September 1989	Establishing the Taiwan Securities Central Depositary Company to promote the Centralized Stock-custodianship System
September 1990	Promulgating the Regulation Governing Securities Houses' Engagement in Margin Buying and Short Sale
September 1990	Allowing foreign institutional investors to directly invest in the local market by relaxing the restriction on both inward and outward remittance, to accelerate the internationalization of Taiwan's capital market
May 1991	Permitting Taiwan Depositary Receipts to be available on the local market in order to set up a specific channel for ROC residents to invest in foreign securities
December 1991	Granting permission for the establishment of close-end funds of government bonds to expand the scale of the bonds market

4

POPULATION POLICY
AND FAMILY PLANNING

The emergence and evolution of a population policy and family planning program illustrate the conflicts between lawmakers and economic planners, between a minority viewpoint and the action of the masses. It shows that a vocal, persistent minority can delay, if not stop, smooth implementation of an urgently needed policy. Efforts to curb population growth have been hindered by Chinese ethics, inertia, and ideological conflict.

Few developmental problems evoke as much emotion and pessimism as the rapid increase in population in developing countries. It is equally true that few developmental relationships are as obvious as that of population pressure on per capita income. Thus, economic development has been called a process of increasing the fertility of the soil and reducing the fertility of human beings. Many people feel, however, that if the food supply is adequate, population control and family planning are not important. This ignores such wider ramifications as the demand for education, health, shelter, transportation, and other social services, as well as the pressure on savings, foreign exchange, or job opportunities. Reality and economic theory clearly show that the higher the rate of population growth, and other things being equal, the more difficult is the task of raising per capita income and sustaining economic growth.

AN OVERVIEW OF TAIWAN'S POPULATION

In 1984 about 19 million people lived in Taiwan in an area about the combined size of Maryland and Delaware, the population of which two states is under 5 million. The first census, conducted in 1905, put the population at just over 3 million; in 1946 it was slightly more than 6 million. By 1964, it had doubled again. Although flight from the mainland around 1949 added some 1.6 million people to the population, the significant trend is the fact that Taiwan has entered the second stage of its demographic transition. Although the death rate has been falling—from 18.2 per thousand in 1947 to 4.8 in 1984—the birth rate, though declining gradually, has remained high—38.5 per thousand in 1947, 19.6 per thousand in 1984. In the 1970s the population growth rate fell below 2%, but since then it has not fallen as much as was expected or hoped. Until 1983, the growth rate steadily fell to the much lower lever of 1%.

Population pressure is seen in several ways. The standard of living and its rate of increase are considered the most telling. Other indicators include the sheer speed of increase, density (particularly in regard to farm land), and the dependency ratio (the number of people under age 15 and over 65 compared to the number of people between 15 and 65). Looking at the period 1952–63, Salter summarized the situation in Taiwan well:

> Although the industrial production of Taiwan has increased impressively in the past decade this increase has not been accompanied by sufficient creation of employment opportunities. Even with wage scales favorable to management, the number of new jobs opened in the industrial sector has been less than 200,000 since 1952. In the same period the population has increased by more than 3 million people.... For every 31 people employed, there are 69 people not economically active... [if we note] the past decade of economic progress has still not succeeded in utilizing a greater portion of this inactive segment, we can perhaps understand why it is valid to say that Taiwan has a surplus population.[1]

The picture has changed significantly during the 1970s and 1980s. Almost full employment appeared in 1973 and 1979, before the first and second energy crises.

[1]Christopher L. Salter, 1963. "Taiwan's Economic Need for a Population Policy." *Industry of Free China*, Taipei, ROC, May 1963.

THE EMERGENCE OF A POLICY

The term *population policy* refers to government regulations and programs designed to change the growth rate, distribution, or quality of the population. In this chapter I deal primarily with population pressure, that is, growth. Family planning, as the major policy instrument, is used interchangeably with population policy. Family planning operates in two areas. The first is making information on techniques or contraceptive devices available to those who are already convinced of their need for them. The second, more difficult, task is to educate people to the advantage of smaller families. Taiwan had programs of the first type from the early 1950s, and many people, including government officials, spoke in favor of the second, but the creation and implementation of formal policies in both areas came slowly.[2]

In the early 1950s, contemplating the opportunity of recovering mainland China, the central government officially ignored the implications of population growth. Moreover, there was a strong feeling in some circles that the sayings of Sun Yat-sen, the founder of the Republic, emphasized the need for more people to fight imperialism during his revolutionary period. Concerned with the annual rate of population increase of more than thirty per thousand, however, in 1950 the JCRR issued a booklet called *The Happy Family*, which advocated the rhythm method of birth control. The effort was denounced by some as a plot to weaken the country's military strength, but this did not affect the determination of Chiang Mon-lin, JCRR's chairman, and Yin Kuo-ying, the vice-chairman of CUSA, to speak publicly for population control. Nor did opposition prevent their agencies from continuing active involvement in efforts to promote family planning, with a silent and effective program in rural areas to begin with.

---

[2]Many of the quotations in this section are from *Population Policy and Family Planning*, a major compilation in Chinese of material on those subjects. An important English-language source is the papers and proceedings of the *Conference on Population and Economic Development in Taiwan*, held in Taipei in 1976 under the aegis of the Academia Sinica.

Throughout the 1950s, they were the principal senior government officials openly supporting the cause. In July and August 1951, Chiang argued in two articles that, by comparing the amount of arable land and the rate of population growth, it was evident that birth control was essential. Yin also stressed the importance of birth control as an essential measure of solving social problems. American aid officials in Taiwan generally shared this view, although they did not advocate birth control openly for fear of being criticized by the public.

The first officially sanctioned step came in August 1954 with the establishment of the China Family Planning Association whose aim was to introduce wives of military dependents to the idea that family planning had benefits to avoid illegal abortion as well as family burden. The central government's Interior Ministry approved the program, which was financially supported by the JCRR and the provincial government's Health Department. This association was organized in Taipei by a group of people interested in family planning, including legislators and government officials. Its early activities consisted mainly of providing information on infertility and publicizing the benefits of child spacing. During that period, a family planning program was initiated to introduce the rhythm method of contraception to military dependents and the general public. However, implementation of this program was not very successful due to opposition from various quarters. Subsequently, in 1959, the governor of Taiwan Province agreed to set up *Prepregnancy Health* (PPH) services at local public health stations, which then took over the main task of promoting family planning programs.

The large number of births had a highly visible impact on the education system. The number of elementary school students exceeded one million in 1952, and rose by 30% in 1956. Many schools held classes in two or even three shifts. Committed to universal education, the government could barely cope with the numbers.

Yet the absence of food shortages was used to support the claim that the population problem had been exaggerated. Ironically, the success in achieving high yields in agriculture fostered self-righteousness among opponents of family planning. But a drought in

1955 caused many people to seek work outside the agricultural sector, a phenomenon seen by many as a harbinger of a serious imbalance between the number of people looking for work and the economy's capacity to create jobs when the children grew up.

The Chinese have a long history of controlling their numbers at the village level, particularly to maintain a balance with the resources available to support the family. Abortion was common in the period after a drought, but because it was illegal, it was frequently performed under unsanitary conditions. Hospitals were not allowed to dispense information on family planning, and that, too, sent women to quacks.

In August 1956, Yu Soo-young, a member of the Taiwan provincial assembly, suggested population control and legalized abortion. Her views were strongly opposed by a male member, Lee Chien-ho. The provincial governor, C. K. Yen, said the government had no intention of encouraging such activity. He did, however, indicate it was acceptable for civic organizations to promote these ideas, other than abortion. In October, Premier O. K. Yui, of the central government, argued that the way to deal with the high population growth rate was to raise the food supply. Later in August 1957, Li Lien-chun, the director of the Food Bureau, repeatedly expressed confidence in the government's ability to maintain an adequate food supply (meaning enough rice) for the rising population.

As a general statement of the situation in the 1950s, a rapidly growing population was viewed by many, particularly economic planners, primarily as a threat to economic growth—a burden on society as a whole. At the upper reaches of government, this awareness and concern with macroeconomic consequences was not translated into official policy or overt action because opposition to family planning was still too wide spread. Within the government, part of this opposition was based on the military strength argument, but much of it was a reluctance to set the government up as opposing traditional attitudes toward family size and the status of women. Those of us favoring a stronger official policy had to accept that the time was not yet right, and that an open confrontation might well jeopardize the progress that had been made.

Thus, in the mid-1950s the official attitude was neutral. The government would not openly advocate family planning or adopt a population control policy, but it would not interfere with those who practiced birth control, and it cooperated with certain programs such as that of the JCRR. Compared to the need, these were modest programs. The ones that worked best provided women with information on safe and effective means.

In spite of the absence of an official policy to limit population growth, and only limited availability of contraceptive devices, the total fertility rate declined by over 18% in the period 1951–63. There was little decline for women in their twenties, but (reflecting later marriage) the rate for teenagers dropped by over 20%. For women aged thirty and older, the rates declined even more, suggesting that recognition of the fact that it was no longer necessary to have five or more children in order to have three survive was spreading. However, the average desired family size remained over three children into the 1970s. Declines in the fertility rate are an expected part of the modernization process, but it took over a century for a comparable percentage decrease to occur in Western Europe.[3]

TRANSITION, 1957–1963

The annual population increase first exceeded 300,000 in 1954, and the number of births first passed 400,000 in 1956. Looking at this, and being concerned with the ability of agricultural production to keep pace, Pang Sung-chou, in March 1957, added his voice as a senior official in the Executive Yuan to those suggesting birth control. He also advocated encouraging emigration and restrictions on immigration. However, Premier Yui's hands-off policy statement of the year before meant that Pang received little support from his colleagues.

---

[3]The best measure of the underlying dynamics of population growth is the fertility rate. With certain technical assumptions, this is the number of children born during a woman's reproductive years, generally given as children per thousand women. The total fertility rate considers all women of childbearing age; age-specific rates disaggregate this.

In August 1957, two women in the Provincial Assembly, Chang Tsai-feng and Chen Lin Hsueh-hsia, and a male assemblyman, Soo Chen-huei, urged the provincial government to implement birth control and family planning. They were opposed by Assemblymen Kuo Kuo-chi and Wang An-shun. CUSA began to promote increased savings and increased per capita income. In an accelerated economic growth exhibition held on New Year's day 1961, one poster showed a group of worried-looking pregnant women surrounded by their small children. Another stressed that the increase in rice production made possible by the completion of the Shihmen Dam and irrigation project would feed just two years of population increase. This point was reiterated four years later at the dam's dedication in June 1964, as Vice President Chen Cheng noted that 500,000 people could be fed by the project, but the population was increasing by over 350,000 annually.

In 1959, the JCRR and the provincial health department funded a family planning program in Nantou, an agricultural area in central Taiwan, as a prepregnancy health service (PPH). By 1963 this had expanded, as part of the maternal and child health program, to include one-third of the 361 local health stations, including those in twenty-two urban areas. PPH workers would volunteer information on contraceptive methods to women during visits to their homes. Because it was not technically part of the government, throughout the 1950s and 1960s, the JCRR's Rural Health Division, particularly under Dr. Hsu Shih-chu, played a key role in promoting family planning.

Women were interested in family planning and thus were open to programs addressing their immediate needs and problems. Throughout the 1960s women over thirty or those who already had three living children were the most likely participants in the programs. Reduced fertility and the acceptance of birth control to achieve it reflected the need by families to bear fewer babies to have the desired number of children survive. Nevertheless, in the absence of an official policy that included educational efforts and incentives to reduce the desired number of children, population pressure would remain significant.

At the Chinese Medical Association's annual meeting in 1960, a resolution was passed urging the practice of planned parenthood, and a committee was set up to oversee implementation. Farmers' associations and public enterprises also became involved in spreading information on the benefits of small family size. In 1962, with financial support from the Population Council of New York and technical assistance from the University of Michigan, the Taiwan Population Studies Center was established in the provincial Health Department. As the name implies, it was intended as a research organization, although this was understood to include promotion and evaluation of family planning activities. One of the center's first surveys was on attitudes toward family size. It found that 92% of married women aged twenty to thirty-nine approved of doing something to space or limit their children. At this point, in 1962–63, opponents of family planning felt that the government had gone too far in what it allowed and cooperated with, and the various programs were attacked vociferously. At the same time, American aid, which funded many of the programs, was being phased out. However, the Council for International Economic Cooperation and Development (CIECD) and JCRR championed the programs, and opponents backed off.[4]

In 1963, cholera broke out in southern Taiwan. The hardest hit areas were fishing villages, mining towns, and salt fields. Health personnel from JCRR took the opportunity to promote family planning while caring for the cholera victims. The practice of combining disaster assistance with dissemination of family planning information became quite common in the 1960s.

A POLICY EMERGES, 1964–1969

At the dedication of the Shihmen Dam in June 1964, as I have already noted, the ROC's vice president, Chen Cheng, spoke of the importance to economic development of slower population growth. For a senior government official to make such statements at a widely publicized event was significant.

---

[4]The reason for CIECD's support was that the CIECD was the administrator of local funds generated through U.S. aid, which were outside the national budget and therefore could be used without going through the budgetary process.

But there was still opposition to family planning. Liao Wei-fan, a member of the Legislative Yuan, was one of the most persistent opponents. He issued a condemnation of the Executive Yuan for failing to prohibit the use of loops. He considered birth control a conspiracy by foreign imperialists to eliminate the Chinese race. In October, another legislator, Lu Chun-san, also spoke against family planning. Nonetheless, government attitudes had shifted from officially neutral (but positive at the operational level) to officially neutral but concerned, which allowed more open and extensive support at the operational level. Thus, in 1964 the Provincial Government reached an agreement with CIECD to support and fund a five-year program to carry out an island-wide family planning program emphasizing the use of the Lippes Loop (an IUD). Technical advisers and additional funding were provided by the U.S.-based Population Council.

The primary objective was to enable married couples to space their children and prevent unwanted pregnancies, which was an objective consistent with the desires of many families. The original goal was to reduce the annual growth rate from over 3% to less than 2% by 1975. This was translated into an operational target of 600,000 IUD insertions in the first five years. The assumption was that each loop insertion would prevent one live birth during the five years (1964–69) the program was to run. The insertion target was achieved, and with a three-year continuation of the program, about 860,000 women received initial loops. The latter program was financed by the provincial budget. This meant that in the 1964–72 period over 45% of married women were provided with IUDs, while another 3% unable to use them were given oral contraceptives.

From 1964 through 1968 the program was administered by the Committee on Family Planning (called Family Health before 1966), and research and evaluation was done by the Taiwan Population Studies Center (both under the provincial health department). Contraceptive devices were distributed by the Maternal and Child Health Association (MCHA), a voluntary agency set up in 1964 specifically for that purpose, thereby preserving the appearance of official noninvolvement.

The Fourth Economic Development Plan (1965–68) included family planning as part of its public health and the medical care program as a part of its manpower plan. The plan notes, "Rapid growth in population poses a great threat to keeping the benefits of economic development. To raise the people's living standard, joint efforts by all sectors should be made to promote family planning and to lower the rate of population growth." Still, in the absence of an official policy promoting family planning, "the measures to be taken" remained necessarily discreet in the early years of the five-year program, that is, until 1967–68. Through AID channels, however, AID officials from several other countries came to Taiwan to learn how to implement family planning in the absence of open government support.

During the mid-1960s, programs spread to a number of other government agencies, and those in place were expanded. The loop-insertion campaign received a major boost in 1966 when the Government Functionaries Insurance Administration, responsible for health and other insurance for government employees, agreed to let its contracting hospitals and clinics perform loop insertions without charge, although it received a nominal subsidy from the Maternal and Child Health Association (MCHA, which was funded in part by the CIECD/JCRR). The Labor Insurance Administration, which at the time underwrote health care for over 600 000 laborers, expressed interest in a similar arrangement. The China Family Planning Association operated a mobile IUD team for poor people in Taipei, and the Chinese Red Cross provided field nurses. In short, in the mid-1960s, there was a major drive under way, with open government support, to provide Taiwan's women with the means for family planning. But there was still no official policy.

In view of the increasing importance of manpower utilization, the CIECD held its first national seminar on manpower in July 1966. Population policy was on the agenda, and Dr. Sun Fo, President of the Examination Yuan and Dr. Sun Yat-sen's son, was the keynote speaker. Sun, aged 76 and an elder statesman and economist, used the occasion to interpret his father's 1924 lecture on population. Those opposed to population control often cited the following passages from it.

What is the standing of our nation in the world? In comparison with other nations we have the greatest population and the oldest culture, of four thousand years' duration. We ought to be advancing in line with the nations of Europe and America. But the Chinese people have only family and clan groups; there is no national spirit. Consequently, in spite of four hundred million people gathered together in one China, we are in fact but a sheet of loose sand. We are the poorest and weakest state in the world, occupying the lowest position in international affairs; the rest of mankind is the carving knife and the serving dish, while we are the fish and the meat.

Now compare the rate of increase of the world's populations during the last century: the United States, 1,000%; England, 300%; Japan, also 300%; Russia, 400%; Germany, 250%; France, 25%. The large gain has been due to the advance of science, the progress of medicine, and yearly improvement of hygienic conditions, all of which tend to reduce the death rate and augment the birth rate. What is the significance for China of this rapid growth of other populations? When I compare their increase with China's, I tremble.

China has the mildest climate and the most abundant natural products of any country in the world. The reason why other nations cannot for the present seize China right away is simply their population is as yet smaller than China's. A hundred years hence, if their population increases and ours does not, the more will subjugate the less and China will inevitably be swallowed up. Then China will not only lose her sovereignty, but she will perish, the Chinese people will be assimilated, and the race will disappear.

(Speech given in Canton, 27 January 1924, printed in Sun 1927, p. 5).[5]

Dr. Sun Fo also noted Dr. Sun Yat-sen's call in 1924 for more people to fight the type of Western imperialism experienced during the late Manchu dynasty, which brought about the Opium War and other conflicts and ultimately forced the Manchu government to sign the unequal treaties. Today, he said, the situation has changed completely, because Soviet Russia has imposed the Communist system in China and elsewhere. This new form of imperialism, Red Imperialism, is a particular threat to LDCs, whose populations contain a large proportion

[5]Sun Yat-sen, *The Three Principles of the People*, 1927. Most contemporary editions published in Taiwan include supplementary chapters by Chiang Kai-shek.

of poor people susceptible to the message of Communism. This background comparison was very effective in persuading the followers of Dr. Sun Yat-sen to accept population control. Sun Fo then pointed out that with changing international and economic conditions, what determines a country's wealth and strength is not the size, but the quality of its population. He warned against following a rigid interpretation of his father's writings, arguing that promoting family planning was compatible with his father's fundamental view.

One of the most important recommendations made by participants of the seminar was for the central government to formulate a population policy and promote family planning, and to include these in a manpower development plan. Editorials and articles in leading newspapers indicated widespread support for this. The Executive Yuan approved the first Manpower Development Plan in October 1966. For the first time, the central government officially favored lower population growth.

With the appointment of Hsu Ching-chung as Interior Minister in June 1966, the wheels for creating a comprehensive official policy were set in motion. The Population Policy Committee spent ten months preparing proposals, and in July 1967 they were submitted to the Executive Yuan (the Cabinet).

At the plenary session of the Ninth Central Committee of the Kuomintang, in November 1967, in my report as Minister of Economic Affairs I argued the seriousness of population pressure from the standpoint of employment: "According to CIECD's estimates, the number of additional job seekers will reach 140 to 150 thousand each year in the next five years. If employment is not provided, this will be not only a waste of massive manpower but also a cause of social unrest. This is a serious problem, which cannot be ignored."

The session included heated debate on a resolution introduced by General Ho Yin-chin and Dr. Sun Fo, both elder statesmen, calling for a population policy. In the closing session, President Chiang Kai-shek finally announced that a population policy was needed, thereby giving it sanction at the highest possible level. The committee subsequently passed the resolution, "Formulate a population policy, adjust the size of the population, and reduce population pressure."

By having specifically included family planning in the previous economic development plan, as well as in the current manpower plan, the government had a de facto policy since 1964. Now there would be a formal policy and family planning program. A conference on Population Programs in East Asia was held in Taipei in May 1968, and the organizers of the conference, including CIECD and JCRR, suggested to the Executive Yuan that the occasion be used to announce its population policy in Premier C. K. Yen's opening address. This policy was based on a set of recommendations that had been presented to the cabinet in July 1967.

At that conference, Hsu and I presented a paper which we concluded as follows:

> The most important thing that has happened on Taiwan in the last several years in connection with the population problem is the conceptual breakthrough—a change in the attitude of the leaders of the Government—that a large and rapidly growing population can be a real deterrent to socio-economic progress, and that the centuries-old Chinese tradition in favor of large families is no longer compatible with the process of transformation from a backward agricultural economy to a modern industrial society. It is heartening to note that a statement on population policy, clearly recognizing the need for family planning and birth control, and specific measures for the implementation of that policy have been formulated by the Cabinet and are in the process of finalization.[6]

Subsequently, in May 1968, the Executive Yuan promulgated the Regulations Governing the Implementation of Family Planning in Taiwan, officially adopting what had been an unofficial program. There were five major points:

(1) The objectives of family planning were to improve health, raise the level of family life, and achieve a reasonable population growth rate.

---

[6]K. T. Li, *The Experience of Dynamic Growth on Taiwan* (Taipei: Mei Ya Publications, 1976).

(2) Public health agencies would provide married women with free or low cost prenatal examinations, maternal and child health guidance, information on contraceptives, and pregnancy guidance.
(3) A married woman with three or more children could ask a public health agency for contraceptive services. For needy families, the costs could be reduced or waived.
(4) To implement family planning, health organizations could employ additional personnel, including a full-time doctor or midwife and home visitor at each health station.
(5) Motivational and educational activities and short-term training courses and seminars were planned.

This statement, however, contained only part of the recommen-dations; action on the others was deferred.

A year later, in May 1969, the Executive Yuan announced an Outline of Population Policy of the Republic of China. This included implementing eugenic and health measures, promoting physical and mental health, and upholding the family system in order to improve the quality of the population and enhance the happiness of family life. Secondary goals were to encourage proper spacing, a "suitable number" of births, and to reduce death from disease and disasters, so that population growth overall would be "reasonable".

T. M. Hsieh, former Governor of Taiwan Province and former Vice President of the Republic of China, was very much concerned with the implementation of family planning. After he took over the governorship in June 1972, he declared that the work of persuading poor families to reduce childbirths would be included in his Anti-Poverty Plan. In his administrative report, he also pledged that the implementation of family planning would be one of the tasks to be carried out in the movement to increase wealth. After the establishment of the Department of Health under the Executive Yuan in March 1971, expenditures for family planning were for the first time provided for in the national budget.

There was to be a policy on population density, including both internal migration and emigration. Sterilization and induced abortion were allowed. Later marriages— at age twenty for men and at eighteen for women—were to be promoted. Vocational training was to be expanded. Customs duties were eliminated on contraceptives and on supplies for local manufacturers of birth control devices. The child allowance given to government employees was discontinued after the birth of a second child.

Following the 1969 policy announcement the Provincial Institute of Family Planning, formed by merging the Committee on Family Planning and the Population Studies Center, administered the program under the provincial health department, although it was not given official agency status until June 1975. The voluntary MCHA became the Planned Parenthood Association of China.

RESULTS

The 1964 goal of each five IUD insertions reducing the number of births by one per year, according to analysis of the data, was not achieved, but the goal of dropping the population growth rate below 2% was reached in 1973, two years earlier than expected. It has been below that level since, except in 1976 when it was 2.2%; the 1984 rate was 1.5%.

In comparison to other Asian nations, Hong Kong, Singapore, and Korea have had substantially smaller declines in fertility at older ages but larger declines at younger ages. Taiwan appears to be influenced more strongly by traditional familial values, with strong emphasis on having three or four children and one or two sons. This has been changing since the early 1970s, but much remains to be done.

Although Taiwan did not have an official population policy until the end of the 1960s, many of the government's other policies in fact directly affected population. Students of population trends support the theory that fertility declines are associated with rising levels of health and sanitation services, education, and income, among other aspects of modernization. Because the government was actively supporting economic development and improved living standards, it was able to contribute to an environment favoring lower fertility.

Better living conditions directly affect infant mortality rates, and as they fell, so did fertility. Acceptance of programs in the 1950s and 1960s reflected attempts by families to match their desired number of living children with the number they actually had. Absence of a policy supporting this desire meant that more children were born than would have been if the government had been able to do more sooner. Still, a good deal was done through the JCRR and voluntary programs prior to significant direct government involvement. In Table 4.1 the attitudes and practices of women are summarized, and in Table 4.2 the reasons for changes in the birth rate are shown.

Taiwan has gone through the first stage of family planning, in which providing the means to the ready-to-accept group is the main task, and it is now in the second stage, in which further declines in fertility depend on reducing the number of children desired. This has proven to be a massive educational task, and it is being undertaken on a broad front, including in the schools and in programs for military recruits. It is hoped that government policy will encourage and hasten the transition to smaller families.

Besides annual budgetary allocations for family planning, the promulgation of the Regulation Governing the Implementation of Family Planning in Taiwan in 1968 and the Guidelines for Population Policy of the Republic of China in 1969 clearly testified to the government's intention to reduce the growth and upgrade the quality of population and to facilitate an even distribution of population. Subsequently, in 1980 a government policy statement announced that the natural rate of population increase would be reduced to 1.25% in 1989 and that the Eugenic Protection Law would be drafted. In the meantime, the Guidelines for Population Policy were revised and a Program on Population Policy was formulated in 1983. To ensure the successful implementation of these policies, local offices have been set up under various levels of government. Agencies concerned with social and cultural affairs also joined with the health agencies in the promotion of family planning. The Eugenic Protection Law was enacted in 1985. Coordinated measures were taken by the agencies concerned to discourage more than two births per couple.

Table 4.1. Changes in Knowledge and Attitude Toward Family Planning (KAP) and Actual Fertility Behavior for Married Woman Age 22–39 in Taiwan.

Year of Survey (KAP and Fertility)	1965	1967	1970	1973	1980
Knowledge					
Know about loop (%)	48	62	81	89	95
Know about pills (%)	32	47	70	85	93
Know about condom (%)	30	31	38	54	85
Know at least one method (%)	80	80	93	96	98
Attitude					
Approve family planning (%)	77	79	94	95	96
Preferred family size	4.0	3.8	3.8	3.2	2.8
Preferred number of sons	2.2	2.1	2.1	1.9	1.7
Preferred number of daughters	1.8	1.7	1.7	1.3	1.1
Actual Fertility Behavior					
Currently practicing contraception (%)	24	33	44	57	70
Ever practiced contraception (%)	30	43	57	71	82
Ever experienced induced abortion (%)	9	11	12	20	23
Average number of live births	3.8	3.5	3.5	3.3	2.7

Source: Five island-wide KAP surveys conducted by the Taiwan Population Studies Center and its successor, the Taiwan Provincial Committee on Family Planning, in 1965, 1967, 1970, 1973, and 1980.

Table 4.2. Changes in Crude Birth Rates in the Taiwan Area (Selected Time Periods, 1961–1979).

Item	1961–1965	1965–1970	1970–1975	1975–1979
Crude Birth Rate, beginning of period (‰)	37.7	32.1	27.2	23.0
Crude Birth Rate, end of period (‰)	32.1	27.2	23.0	24.4
Change in Crude Birth Rate due to:				
Age structure (%)	−1.2	−0.2	+3.8	+2.7
% married (%)	−0.8	−1.5	−2.5	−0.3
Maritial fertility (%)	−3.4	−3.2	−5.0	−1.7
Interaction (%)	−0.2	0	−0.5	+0.7
All factors (%)	−5.6	−4.9	−4.2	+1.4

Source: See table 4.1.

As a result of these efforts, the crude birth rate was reduced from 3.45% in 1964 to 1.96% in 1984. The natural increase rate of population was down to 1.48% that year. The 1989 target rate of 1.25% was reached ahead of schedule, between 1985 and 1986. Actually the crude birth rate declined to 1.59%, and the natural increase rate was down to 1.1% in 1986.

An aside that might interest in readers is that as society becomes more affluent, more and more people are begetting children in the Year of the Dragon, a creature associated with prosperity and good fortune in Chinese mythology. The last time the dragon ruled the zodiac was in 1988, when around 27,000 more children were born than 1987 and 1989.

5

MANPOWER POLICY

Labor has been Taiwan's most important resource, and its utilization has accelerated Taiwan's development. In this chapter I first outline major problems, then discuss manpower planning. Special attention is given to utilization.

During the late 1950s and early 1960s, Taiwan, as was true of most developing countries, experienced several major manpower problems. These included inadequate absorption of the rapidly growing population into productive economic activity, a shortage of qualified people with adequate training and specialized types of knowledge, outmoded laws and institutions for mobilizing human effort, and a lack of incentives for technocrats and others to undertake the activities essential to national development.

MANPOWER PLANNING AND UTILIZATION

Facing this worrisome demographic and economic situation, the government decided to develop manpower planning. But such planning is an inexact science, and manpower utilization involves a host of economic and noneconomic considerations. For instance, how do the authorities convince students and parents that vocational training is more practical than conventional schooling? How do they persuade the general public that educational spending should be considered as an investment, not just an expenditure desirable for its own sake without regard for society's demand for the right kind of skill and training? With imperfect data and a rapidly changing economic structure, how can the planners forecast future requirements? And once the plan has been drawn up, what if other government agencies are not interested in its implementation, due either to lack of understanding or lack of financial and professional support?

Manpower planning, like family planning, has had a short and sometimes frustrating history in Taiwan. Although problems were identified and given public attention in the early 1960s, the first manpower development plan was not formulated by the government until 1966. It is, however, fair to say that by the late 1970s the concept of such planning, as well as the importance of human resources and how they are utilized, had been gradually accepted by both the government and the public. Still, how to utilize human resources more efficiently and how to implement programs remains a challenge.

In order to raise labor participation and productivity, the following areas for manpower development have been given top priority: family planning, education at all levels, vocational training, employment services, and labor conditions.

In formulating policy and coordinating programs, two things are essential: labor force statistics and employment services. Data are needed to assess changes in the labor force, estimate the demand for manpower, and draw up plans for utilization. The function of employment services is to match supply and demand.

Statistics of one kind or another generally have been available since the early 1950s, but the definition of terms has not been consistent, and standard occupational and industrial classifications were not used until 1967. Data have been collected mainly to meet the requirements of the organizations preparing them, and few of them were concerned with the labor force as such.

The government established employment centers in the larger cities as early as 1947, but without much effect on joblessness. In 1956, an Employment Service Center was set up on a trial basis in Taipei. In 1963 the government added centers in Taichung and Kaohsiung, and later in Tainan and Keelung. The service had no legal foundation other than regulations issued by the provincial government. This made it difficult for the agency to perform as a governmental administrative unit and to coordinate its work with that of other agencies. Low salary levels made it difficult to recruit professional staff; most were general administrative workers with little training in the specialized field.

The centers were not hiring halls or employment agencies. Rather, the service they offered was testing and advising those looking for jobs as to what they might do and where to look. The General Aptitude Test battery, developed in the United States, was used by the service. Because it was not adapted to Chinese conditions, it was not a satisfactory basis for providing vocational counseling. Many employers lacked an understanding of the agency's functions, and so they recruited through private channels. Firms also often refused to furnish the centers with information about openings. Thus, in the early 1960s, the situation in Taiwan was one of spotty data on employment, particularly regarding the number of job seekers and openings. Though concerned about unemployment and manpower resource allocation, the government did not have hard numbers on the specifics of the problem, let alone an agency directly involved in seeking solutions.

Taiwan's population is quite young. In the mid-1960s, 45% of the population was under 15, a proportion even higher than in Puerto Rico, Hong Kong, or India. This also meant a significant demand for education and future employment opportunities. From the mid-1950s to the mid-1960s, the student population roughly doubled, with 3.1 million students making up one-quarter of the population in 1965.

During the decade 1956–65, some 2,263,000 persons aged 12 and above joined the labor force. The percentage employed, however, declined from 53% in 1955 to 47% in 1965. The 1965 labor force survey indicated 65% of the unemployed were under 20 years old. Among them, 75% had no more than nine years of education, and 80% were seeking employment for the first time. Lack of education and unemployment among youths was becoming serious. There was a structural shift toward more skilled jobs, although the ratio of technical workers remained low.

Against this background, Harry Weiss, of the U.S. Department of Labor, visited Taiwan in October 1963. He immediately identified the growing population, serious unemployment and underemployment, lack of planning and coordinated organization, an unbalanced education program, and absence of an apprenticeship program to train skilled workers, as problems. Echoing points made by Chinese government planners, legislators, and labor experts, Weiss made some specific recommendations.

> The most important conclusion I have reached is that the Government of the Republic of China (GRC) urgently needs a manpower plan, and in order to achieve such a plan, it needs a manpower planning organization. At the present time in the field of manpower, the GRC is "flying blind" because it does not know in detail what its manpower resources are and, much more serious, it does not know what its manpower requirements are going to be for the next five to ten years.
>
> In order to achieve a sound manpower plan, it is necessary that a small planning unit be established at a central point in the government where the manpower activities of the various ministries can be coordinated. It would seem to me that the best place for such a unit is the newly established Council for International Economic Cooperation and Development (CIECD).[1]

In January 1964, the CIECD, under Premier and concurrently chairman C. K. Yen, established a Manpower Resources Committee (later renamed the Manpower Development Committee [MDC]) to coordinate and examine plans for the development of human resources. Other members included officials at the vice ministerial level in the central government and directors and commissioners of the relevant departments of the provincial government. (As Vice Chairman of CIECD, I served as convener of the committee, but stepped down on becoming Minister of Economic Affairs in January 1965.)

The MDC, with a staff of seven professionals and two secretaries and a manpower expert from USAID as an advisor, was charged with a number of functions:

1. Formulating policies and plans for manpower development.
2. Coordinating several aspects of the plan such as education, training, recruitment, distribution, and utilization.

1. *Industry of Free China*, Taipei, ROC, March 1964, p. 9.

3. Keeping the overall plan and the operating programs for development under constant review and adjusting them periodically to meet changing conditions and circumstances.
4. Establishing an administration and promoting the public employment service.
5. Promoting programs and facilities for vocational training and adjusting the supply of and demand for labor.
6. Coordinating the manpower plan with the overall economic development plan.
7. Studying special labor problems.
8. Collecting, analyzing, and assessing all available statistics.
9. Studying manpower problems referred by the CIECD.

In 1966, the first national manpower development plan was presented to the National Manpower Conference for consideration, and was subsequently approved by the Executive Yuan. CIECD was then made responsible for overall coordination of policy implementation and review, working through the MDC. In the same manner, subsequent plans were formulated in 1968 and 1970. By the time of the fifth economic development plan during 1969–72, the Manpower Development Plan had become an integral part of the plan to attain the objective.

In spite of the broad charge given the MDC, prior to its merging into the Overall Planning Department of the Economic Planning Council in 1973, it was more involved in research than implementation. In other words, it concentrated largely on the collection of data related to the labor force and on making projections. Although research findings were sometimes used for policy implementation, at other times they were not given proper attention.

One of the persistent administrative problems has been the overlapping of authority and responsibilities assigned to government agencies. Among the agencies dealing with labor administration are a Labor Department in the central government's Ministry of the Interior, and, in provincial government, the first section in charge of labor affairs in the Social Affairs Department, the Industrial and Mining

Inspection Commission, the Labor Insurance Bureau, and several Employment Service Centers in urban locations. In addition, the provincial Department of Reconstruction has been in charge of wage and labor statistics, the provincial Department of Public Health handles industrial hygiene matters, and the Executive Yuan oversees the wages and welfare of workers in government-operated enterprises. Furthermore, there are other government agencies related to manpower matters, such as the Ministry of Economic Affairs, the Ministry of Education, and relevant departments at the provincial level. In the midst of this, besides its research, the MDC served as a catalyst, promoter, advocate and alarmist.

The Manpower Development Committee was renamed Manpower Planning Committee in 1980, and reorganized into the Manpower Planning Department (MPD) of the Council for Economic Planning and Development in 1985. The MPD is responsible for formulating manpower policies and plans, forecasting and analyzing manpower demand and supply, and studying the utilization of manpower resources.

VOCATIONAL TRAINING

Vocational education has usually been a student's second or third choice among educational possibilities. Vocational training in Taiwan has been conducted by both government organizations and private enterprise. However, due to the lack of a central organization to handle overall projects, the effect of training until the mid-1960s was fragmentary. Projects did not meet the requirements of the nation, and their effects were rather limited. In spite of the growing shortage of skilled workers, the Ministry of Education contracted Stanford Research Institute to make a study on Education and Development in 1962. The report stated:

> Only one in seven youths chose vocational education to seek training leading to a career. Fewer than one-seventh had volunteered for apprenticeships, and most of these did so because of limited financial

means. Industry and commerce had given little encouragement to workers to improve their qualifications or further their occupational abilities. As a result, graduates from commercial-vocational schools working in offices received preferential treatment over graduates from industrial-vocational schools working in factories.[2]

According to estimates of the first manpower development plan and the forecasts made by Alice W. Shurcliff of the International Labor Office, an average of more than 77,000 people would have needed training each year from 1965 to 1970, and available facilities could not have accommodated that number.

In the process of formulating the manpower development plan in 1966, it was found that while the number of primary school graduates had increased rapidly, only about half of these could be accepted into the existing junior high schools. As a result, every year some 140,000 primary school graduates did not have the opportunity to further their education. Because those denied places were too young to work, the resulting situation created difficulties for parents and society. A survey of various levels of schools and the demand for labor revealed that almost all schools had focused their attention on preparing students to enter the next level of education.

Traditionally, Chinese have believed in the scholar-official sequence, or "learning tops all trades". Those engaged in trade and commerce have generally been looked down on. Although more people are rejecting these concepts, few have accepted the idea of learning by doing. Graduates have been disinclined to do technical or manual work, and they yearn to be white-collar workers, such as government employees and teachers.

The target ratio of 4 to 6 was attained between senior high school and senior vocational school enrollments in 1970. A later target at 3 to 7 was set for 1981, which turned out to be 2.8 to 7.2. It further dropped to 2.7 to 7.3 in 1986. The government extended primary education from six years to nine years in 1968. Since there were not so many schools for junior high graduates, the Ministry of Education initiated a program

[2]*Education and Development*, Stanford Research Institute, November 1962.

under which five-year junior colleges accepted students completing nine years of compulsory schooling. All of the junior college are vocational in nature. Because the five-year junior college students were included in senior vocational schools, the ratio between senior high school and senior vocational school changed rapidly after the 1970s.

On the other hand, skilled blue-collar applicants found it easy to find a job and were better paid than white-collar employees. As a result, the turnover rate of skilled workers was high, and changing jobs for higher wages became common. Students, their parents, and school authorities began to realize that education had to be fashioned to equip students with both knowledge and skills to earn a living.

Until the mid-1960s, there was no comprehensive statutory basis for vocational training programs. Existing laws dealt largely with apprenticeships and handicraft training and were thus too simple and restricted. They could not be applied effectively to promote nationwide vocational training. Standards had not been established; a system for screening and licensing schools had not been created; and there were no training budgets or any coordination between societal needs and training programs.

As Minister of Economic Affairs, I asked two government enterprises, Taiwan Shipbuilding Corporation in Keelung and Taiwan Machinery Manufacturing Corporation in Kaohsiung, to set up one vocational training center in each city, concentrating on the training of qualified welders, machinists, and other skilled tradesmen in great demand by industry. The shortage of welders and machinists was eased within less than two years. In subsequent years, the government set up institutions to train seamen, drivers, and fishermen.

At the same time, I requested the United National Development Program to support the funding of an institute to train more instructors and supervisors for various local Vocational Training Centers. This project was cosponsored by the Ministry of the Interior.

Later, in 1970–71, Japan's Labor Ministry supported a project for providing technical personnel and necessary equipment to the modern Vocational Training Center located in Taichung, where many small- and medium-sized machinery works were located.

Both the education and the vocational training systems began to devote greater attention to the training of skilled workers. An *ad hoc* committee was organized in 1976 with a Minister without Portfolio in charge of coordination. A five-year program for the continuous financing of such training programs was implemented. In 1982–83, a Vocational Training Bureau was set up under the Ministry of the Interior.

To drum up public support for apprentice training, I sent some experts in 1968 to study the activities of the International Apprentice Contest. We then started up an annual National Apprentice Contest of our own, the winners of which were sent to attend the International Apprentice Contest.

The apprentice-training provisions of the Factory Law were superseded by those of the 1983 Vocational Training Act and the 1984 Labor Standards Law. Both laws require the employer, when hiring an apprentice, to sign a written training agreement specifying his training program, with details on training courses, duration of training, instructors, living accommodations and allowances.

As the economy moved through the 1960s and into the 1970s, industries gradually became more capital- and skill-intensive through the process of backward integration to produce intermediate goods. This was especially true of the textile and plastics fabrication industries. With the two energy crises in 1973–74 and 1979–80, the government placed emphasis on encouraging high-technology industries as well as higher-value-added products for traditional industries to meet the competition with low-labor-cost developing countries.

The program for manpower development also underwent continuous change. The Science and Technology Development Program approved by the Cabinet in May 1979 focused on education and training at higher levels. Hence, university education and post-graduate education were heavily emphasized, along with key technologies which would be needed by industry. The ratio of students majoring in science and engineering to students majoring in social science and liberal arts showed a remarkable change, rising from 4:6 in 1971 to 5.4:4.6 in 1991.

The quality of college and post-graduate students, both masters and doctors, was greatly enhanced. The university provided the upstream high-level manpower, while the applied research institutes, such as the Industrial Technology Research Institute and the Chung Shan Institute of Science and Technology (for defense research) provided the intermediate high-level manpower. It was therefore much easier for the downstream industries engaged in the manufacture of high-technology products to find trained technical personnel to start up their plants.

A special training program can be cited here as an example. The information and computer industry is our future leading sector, but the number of college graduates in electrical engineering and computer science cannot always meet the demand. A five-year program sponsored by the Ministry of Education provides:

(1) six months of intensive training for noncomputer major graduates who, after passing a competitive exam, are qualified for employment in the computer field;

(2) computer training for teachers in junior colleges, vocational high schools, senior high schools, and junior high school;

(3) training of civil servants to manage computerization programs in government agencies.

6

EXPORT PROCESSING ZONES

It was easy for foreign companies in the 1950s and 1960s to think of reasons not to establish factories in Taiwan, and many of them can be summarized simply by "red tape". Although it can be, and was, argued that the regulations and procedures that investors found discouraging were felt by the authorities to be justifiable or necessary aspects of the government's responsibilities, the fact remained that many of the rules were considered unduly burdensome even by Chinese investors who understood their cultural and historical context. There was also Hong Kong. The colony's investment climate was considered very favorable, particularly compared to Taiwan's. The ROC government recognized that something needed to be done in the direction of liberalization. The idea of a free trade zone was discussed, and out of these discussions emerged the concept of an export processing zone (EPZ). In this chapter I look at the creation of EPZs.

EPZs were created to reconcile the conflict between the government's goal to create employment opportunities (economic development in general) and several other goals. With hindsight, the simplicity of the solution makes it seem obvious, but many policymakers were not easily convinced. Taiwan's experience demonstrates that in the process of development, even when an innovation is consistent with the development strategy, its gestation period can still be quite long. Thus, an entire decade elapsed between conception of the idea in 1956 and the opening of the first EPZ.

THE NATURE OF AN EXPORT PROCESSING ZONE

In the early 1950s, concern over Taiwan's security under the threat of Communist attack deterred private investment, but this had largely receded by the early 1960s. By then, increasing social and in Taiwan and the strong American commitment made Taiwan a potential plant site not just for overseas Chinese but also for non-Chinese. Even when an investor was eager to move ahead with a project, however, procedures were considered cumbersome; it was easy to become frustrated and conclude that red tape was excessive.

Foreign trade zones (free ports), where trade restrictions are relaxed and items that will be reshipped can be brought in duty free, date back to the Middle Ages, when such German ports as Lübeck and Hamburg were centers of entrepôt trade. Through the centuries, the foreign trade zone had been extended beyond being a mere transshipment point to include processing imports for export (generally referred to as re-export). Originally this meant, for example, turning grain into flour or logs into lumber. In post-World War II Asia, Hong Kong and Singapore enhanced the value of their geographical locations by establishing themselves as free ports.

But government regulation extends beyond trade and tariff laws. Although there were proposals for establishing free trade zones in Taiwan, the concept was not comprehensive enough to deal with the full range of problems investors encountered. In competing for foreign and overseas Chinese trade, it was also necessary to address the issues of administrative complexity and delay.

The EPZ is an expansion of the free trade zone concept. It is innovative in two ways: it has an integrated, simplified administration, and it puts primary stress on production for export (rather than any processing being merely an extension of an essentially transshipping activity). Dealing with complaints over red tape was the principal concern at the time the first EPZ was created, with the immediate goal being to encourage foreign investment. In this sense, establishment of an EPZ was a definite liberalization, albeit a partial one. The larger goals were promoting employment and earning foreign exchange, and in addressing them, the EPZs became an important element in Taiwan's export-oriented growth phase. In fact, investors who located in the EPZs were urged to bring a ready market and ample competitive know-how with them. What they wanted to do was start up their operations as soon as possible.

EPZs represented a liberalization, but only of a slice of the export part of the market. By foregoing access to the domestic Taiwanese market (probably not considered much of a sacrifice initially), firms were able to utilize the island's abundant low-cost labor and duty-free imports of machinery, parts, and raw material. These two—labor and imports—were combined into products exported at world market prices. The zones were open to investment by both foreign and domestic firms, which meant that the Chinese could gain experience in competitive markets.

The first EPZ was developed on reclaimed land at Kaohsiung Harbor, and another two were later added in order to meet demand for more space. In the year immediately after the opening of the first EPZ in 1966, many foreign government officials, businessmen, development economists, and reporters visited it. More than a dozen developing countries sent study teams to Taiwan, and Chinese consultants visited countries interested in the concept. The United Nations Industrial Development Organization (UNIDO) had scheduled a workshop on the EPZ to be held in Taiwan in November 1971. After the withdrawal of the ROC from the United Nations in October 1971, the workshop was canceled, but in October 1975, thirty-eight countries attended a week-long symposium on the EPZ in Seoul sponsored by the Asian Productivity Organization of Japan. A second symposium was held five years later in Colombo, Sri Lanka.

By 1978, EPZs had been established in twenty-two countries, including South Korea and the Philippines, as well as in Singapore and Malaysia (where they are part of larger free trade zones). In Taiwan, progressive liberalization has reduced the advantages of being in an EPZ, and their usefulness as originally formulated has probably run its course. In the latter part of the 1970s, however, the National Science Council proposed to build a science-based industrial park after the pattern of an EPZ in an area near Taipei where a number of academic and industrial research institutions are located, with a view to attracting companies which could stimulate the development of high technology in Taiwan. Although the general reduction in government involvement in the market has reduced the perceived need to be in an EPZ in Taiwan, the concept remains a useful model for other countries actively seeking to expand their exports and employment.

ISSUES IN THE DEBATE ON THE EPZ

The idea of an EPZ emerged in 1956. Two major psychological barriers and a number of minor problems had to be overcome before the idea evolved into an actual program and then a reality. These same concerns also influenced debate over the more traditional free trade zone.

Chinese resentment of the extraterritoriality (freedom from local jurisdiction) enjoyed by foreigners in prewar China created opposition to both free trade zones and EPZs. There was a sincerely held concern that Taiwan was yielding sovereignty in the zones to foreign investors in the name of trade and investment. Although it is true that the zones allowed investors to operate under a different set of rules than those outside—which was the whole point—they were nonetheless Chinese rules. As this came to be recognized and accepted, sovereignty ceased to be an issue.

Exploitation—the sale of relatively cheap Taiwanese labor for the enrichment of foreign investors—was another concern. This is a matter of perception. Supporters of the EPZ argued it was better to provide a job to someone who would otherwise be unemployed than to be concerned with the profits of the employer. It was largely an investor's market in the 1960s and 1970s, whether one liked that fact or not.

Would firms in the zone affect sales of exporting firms operating outside the zone? This was a serious matter, as any negative impact on existing businesses would reduce one of the justifications for establishing an EPZ. Actually, firms in the zone are those that have established their export market outlets before their investment in the zone. So they should pose little or no threat to the exporting firms operating outside the zone. Indeed, during the early years they helped promote Taiwan as a supplier of light consumer goods and not merely as a source of agricultural products. In fact, after visiting factories located in the EPZs, foreign buyers would necessarily come to Taipei to examine products produced by firms outside the EPZs. In this way, many new business connections were established. Consequently, I have always regarded the EPZs as showcases for our industries. To reduce the likelihood of competition between EPZs and domestic firms, the Ministry of Economic Affairs decided to limit the kinds of industries allowed, excluding ones (such as cotton textiles) that already had many exporting firms. Seventeen kinds of industry were allowed. It was also made clear in the regulations that, regardless of world market conditions, products manufactured in the zone could not be sold in the domestic market. Such regulations have since been liberalized to permit limited sales in the domestic market upon approval and payment of customs duty.

The concern over competition was also allayed by pointing out that most of the foreign firms being sought as investors already had the intention of building somewhere, and that their output would compete with Chinese firms regardless of where they built. Moreover, unlike those of Korea, EPZs in Taiwan were open to domestic investors. If a Chinese firm felt it would be more profitable to operate in the zone, it was not discriminated against. A number of firms, foreign and domestic, operated plants both inside and outside the zones.

Among the minor issues was the possibility of smuggling duty-free imports out of the zone into the domestic market. This was dealt with by surrounding each EPZ with a wall with watch towers and police patrols. The government wanted to be sure that the output of factories in the EPZ could only be exported and purchased by foreign consumers while domestic consumers would have to pay higher prices for products of the same quality in the highly protected domestic market. The EPZ is thus a device to foster labor-intensive manufactured exports by exempting foreign consumers from paying the exorbitant import duties imposed on domestic consumers.

FROM IDEA TO IMPLEMENTATION

In 1960, a trade zone that could compete with Hong Kong became the topic of formal studies by the Industrial Planning and Coordination Group of the Ministry of Economic Affairs and by CUSA's Industrial Development and Investment Center. Special emphasis was given to management, tax exemption, customs duties, foreign exchange controls, capital requirements for firms in the zone, and location. These studies helped form the basis for the subsequent implementation of the broader EPZ concept.

By May 1963, the EPZ approach was sufficiently accepted by economic and financial leaders in the government and, in reviewing the statute for the encouragement of investment in light of the phasing out of American aid, it was proposed that export processing zones be added. This led to a decision by the Executive Yuan to proceed with the establishment of an EPZ, under a special law separate from the investment statute. Kaohsiung was selected as the tentative location, partly because a harbor extension project meant that a landfill site would be available, plus deep water wharves and warehouses surrounding the zone.

The following summer, a proposed text of the statute for establishment and management of export processing zones was sent by the Executive Yuan to the Legislative Yuan. After a final airing of the concerns already discussed, a modified version gained approval in January 1963. The legislature went further than the Executive Yuan did in centralizing the administrative responsibility and authority in the zone's administrative body. Specifically, several government agencies closely related to the operation and management of the zone had some of their functions and authority delegated to the zone administration. The Ministry of Economic Affairs of the central government was given jurisdiction through an agency specifically created for the purpose. Actual construction began on July 1, 1965. Formal inauguration came on December 3, 1966.

DEVELOPMENT OF EPZS

When the Kaohsiung EPZ (KEPZ), with an area of 67 hectares, opened in 1966, a target of 120 firms had been set. Perhaps appropriately, the first application was from a Hong Kong garment maker. Within two years, 128 firms were approved, and plans were underway for a second and then a third zone, one located in Nantze near Kaohsiung (88 hectares) and one in Taichung (23 hectares), both of which opened in April 1971. The slowdown of world economic growth in the 1970s meant that these two did not meet their original goals for number of firms, but the actual amount of investment was substantially greater nonetheless. In 1991, 241 firms were operating in three zones. There have been a number of mergers and few newcomers as investment opportunities outside the zones have expanded, so this number was down from 272 firms in 1979. By 1991 cumulative investment had reached US$886 million, more than thirty-eight times the initial expectation in 1966, and almost 6% of private foreign and overseas Chinese Investment in Taiwan for the period 1966–1991.

In spite of the importation of most of the machinery and raw materials, except for the first three years when there was heavy initial investment, the zones have exported far more than they imported. In 1991, exports reached US$3,990 million and imports US$1916 million, turning in the best performance ever.

Employment peaked in 1973 at over 75,000, but then declined in the wake of the energy crisis. Afterwards, the number reached 90,876 in 1987 (the newest peak), and then in 1991 there were 65,733 workers, over half of them in electronics. Women accounted for 80% of the labor force, and some 60% of them (almost half the zones' total labor force) were between sixteen and twenty-nine years of age.

EVOLUTION OF THE EPZ

Significant improvement in the overall investment climate in Taiwan since the early 1960s, along with relaxation of many government regulations, has reduced the advantages initially offered by the zones.

Moreover, several neighboring countries—mainland China, the Philippines, Thailand — are equally or even more attractive with regard to low-wage labor. This is crucial, as an abundant labor supply at low wage rates is a prerequisite for successful operation of an export processing zone. Of course, low-cost labor is not everything, as labor productivity needs to be taken into consideration also.

Prior to the worldwide recession of 1974–1975, there was a serious shortage of workers in the zones. Firms resorted to a variety of ploys, such as paying bonuses to employees who recruited additional workers. At the same time, firms were forced to lower such requirements as educational levels, skills, and age. As a consequence, the wage bill rose, costs of operations increased, and profit margins narrowed. In the midst of expanding production, and plagued by increasing costs, firms were badly hit by the 1974–75 recession. In the KEPZ alone, 13,000 workers were laid off. Workers' feelings were hurt on being dismissed, many moved to other cities or took other employment, others returned to the farms or rural areas they had come from, and a number of the women married and left the labor force.

At the same time, foreign investors began to regard government regulations in the zone as limiting and burdensome. Many of these complaints were patently self-serving, such as objections to selling a plant only to investors qualified to locate in the zone, or to the prohibition against selling imported production machinery in the domestic market without legally winding up plant operation, or complaints about not being able to own land in the zone (the land had increased substantially in value, and the investors felt they should have had the profits). The original rule of no sales into the local market had been relaxed to allow sales with specific approval, but even the relaxed limitation was resented.

In short, what made zone investors dissatisfied in the mid-1970s was that investors outside the zones had some advantages and concessions that they did not, even though the reverse was also true. It was claimed the administrative and public service assessments (0.3% of sales) offset to a certain extent the duty-free benefits. By 1978 firms in the zone argued that there were only two major benefits left: the simplified government procedures and duty-free imports of machinery, equipment, raw materials, and semifinished goods. Even the duty-free benefit was no longer unique.

If firms in the EPZs were no longer enthusiastic, and potential investors were reluctant, then an important policy decision had to be made: should the zones be phased out or should the government make changes to make the zones more attractive? Has the EPZ been useful? To answer this question, two periods must be kept in mind. The first is 1966–72, and the second since 1973. There is little question that both the investors and the Chinese government were satisfied and proud of the economic performance in the first period. In the second period, as the impact of the first oil crisis began to be felt, the performance of the zones suffered, as did that of the rest of the domestic economy. As the domestic economy moved toward recovery in 1984, however, the performance of the zones began to experience a strong comeback. The situation was even better in the latter half of the 1980s, and in 1991, total exports of the three zones amounted to nearly US$4 billion.

Have in EPZs outlived their usefulness? There has been no serious discussion of maintaining the status quo or of phasing the zones out. Nantze and Taichung have reached maximum expansion; in fact, the three zones are all saturated. Some agencies have recommended that the opening of additional zones should be liberalized to the greatest extent possible. The authorities have concentrated more on the general liberalization and internationalization of the economy. Personally, I think the EPZs will continue to adopt modern technology, rising to the status of science parks.

SIGNIFICANCE OF THE EPZ

According to a survey conducted by the Zone Administration, more than 50% of the factories in the zones have adopted automation and are producing higher value-added products. Philips of Holland built a very large IC package plant in 1986. These facts show that private enterprises have a way of surviving and winning, and that the life of the EPZ can be prolonged.

With the government emphasizing the liberalization and internationalization of the economy at a faster pace in the latter half of the 1980s in order to reduce the export surplus and encourage more imports, tariff reduction and import liberalization have gained greater momentum. A value-added tax was adopted in 1986 to replace the local sales tax. All these measures will move the economy in the direction of Hong Kong and Singapore and make the EPZ more like a free-trade zone.

7

DEVELOPMENT OF SCIENCE AND TECHNOLOGY

EARLY POLICY OF SCIENCE & TECHNOLOGY (S&T) DEVELOPMENT—EMPHASIZING SCIENCE EDUCATION AND RESEARCH

In January 1959, the ROC government promulgated the Guidelines for National Long-term Science Development. While aimed at providing guidelines for the development of science, it marked the advent of formulating a science policy at government level. At that time, the economy of ROC was mainly based on labor-intensive industry and the domestic research climate was not as well-established. Furthermore, there were problems, such as brain-drain, shortage of R&D expenditure, research facilities, etc. Under these circumstances, emphases were put on providing academic research funding and recruiting and cultivating S&T manpower. To implement the guidelines, the government also established a special fund to set aside a proper percentage of the national budget each year to be used for science development. This fund was allocated to U.S. aid-sponsored universities and R&D institutes for activities such as upgrading research facilities, purchasing periodicals, setting up visiting lectureships and professorships, building dormitories and offering research grants.

To effectively utilize this special fund, a task force was established bearing the name "National Long-term S&T Development Committee", in which representatives of Academia Sinica and the Ministry of Education were included. The objectives of the Committee were:

1) Planning and promoting long-term scientific research
2) Reviewing R&D budget allocation
3) Recruiting and inviting visiting professors as well as sponsoring S&T personnel to go abroad for advanced studies.

Generally speaking this Committee, being the first administrative institute for S&T development, focused its efforts on promoting basic scientific research.

In the 1960s, additional attention was paid to industrialization. Concurrent steps undertaken at the time included the promotion of science education and research. Among these steps was the establishment of five science centers, the mathematics and chemistry centers at the National Taiwan University, the physics center at the National Tsing Hwa University, the biology center at the Institute of Botany in the Academia Sinica, and the engineering science center at the National Cheng Kung University, with the support of the Council for International Economic Cooperation and Development. In addition, universities were encouraged to set up research institutes that would offer Masters degrees in the initial stage. This contributed greatly to the growth of S&T manpower and the upgrading of R&D capability.

In 1969, the government instructed the National Science Council to formulate a "National Science Development Plan (1969–80)". The program was implemented in three phases, taking the following as national goals for S&T development:

1. Strengthening basic science education by upgrading curricula, faculty and facilities at elementary schools, and junior and senior high schools.
2. Improving the research environment at universities and research institutes to produce hi-tech manpower.
3. Enhancing R&D in the fields of industry, agriculture, transportation, medicine, and public health.

The purpose of this plan was to coordinate S&T and economic development as well as to stress applied technology research. However, because the division of responsibilities was not well-coordinated among the various ministries and agencies concerned, the accomplishments of the plan were somewhat limited in academic research, and the result of R&D was not efficiently and effectively transferred to private industry.

In 1967, the National Long-term S&T Development Committee was reorganized into the National Science Council (NSC), whose mission remains to promote basic scientific research and manpower training, invite visiting research lecturers and professors, and carry out measures to sponsor and encourage S&T research.

CURRENT S&T POLICIES — A COMBINATION OF PROMOTING S&T WITH PRIVATE INDUSTRIAL DEVELOPMENT

First National Science and Technology Conference — the First Attempt to Identify Strategic Areas of S&T Development

In the 1970, the first energy crisis in late 1973 dramatically affected the world economy and gave rise to many difficult economic challenges. To successfully respond to those challenges, Taiwan had to upgrade its economic structure and quickly move from labor-intensive industry to capital- and technology-intensive industry. There was much more earnest recognition of the importance of promoting applied research. At the end of 1976, the Executive Yuan (Cabinet) designated an *ad hoc* committee named the "Committee for Research and Development on Applied Technology", consisting of the Ministers from the Ministries of Economic Affairs, Communications, Education, National Defense, the Chairman of the Joint Commission on Rural Reconstruction (JCRR, later known as Council of Agriculture) and National Science Council, and the Head of the Taiwan Provincial Government. The Committee's mission was to coordinate applied science and technology related policies and promote industrial development in key areas. This author, then holding the position of Minister Without Portfolio, was appointed convenor of that committee.

As a major step, in January 1978, the First National Conference on S&T Development was held with participation from academia, industry and government to discuss nation-wide S&T policy and carefully review the status of industrial development. Based on the conclusions and recommendations of the conference, an S&T Development Program was approved by the Cabinet in 1979. This program outlined the Objectives, Strategies and Tactics (OST) Management that set forth the overall approach to S&T development undertaken by various government agencies. The major goals were:

1) Supporting economic development,
2) Improving the well-being of the populace,
3) Strengthening national defense industry.

In the program, the government identified four major areas of science and technology for development through national effort, namely energy, materials, information, and automation. Establishment of the Hsin Chu Science-Based Industrial Park was part of the program to accommodate the initiation of hi-tech industries. This was the first time that the S&T policy was made in coordination with industrial development. The process of S&T policy formation through nationwide forums was accepted as an important model.

In 1979, while the ROC government launched nationwide efforts to carry out the Science and Technology Development Program, the Board of S&T Advisors was formed in the office of the Premier. The Board consists of a number of eminent leaders from abroad in various fields of science and technology. They are invited to advise the Premier and relevant members of the cabinet on various fields, including basic science, manpower education, health and medicine, materials, energy, agriculture, telecommunication, electronics and information, ocean S&T, manufacturing technology, etc. The Board members meet at least once a year for the annual board meeting, and visit the ROC with the invitation from ministries concerned at mutually convenient times to follow up the implementation of recommendations and advise on specific issues.

At that time, the Committee on R&D for Applied Technology was responsible for the coordination of the development of science and technology. To ensure the effective operation of the above-mentioned

Board of S&T Advisors, the Convenor of the Committee for R&D on Applied Technology, Minister K.T. Li, was also given the responsibility to maintain close liaison with members of the Board. Therefore a task force office called the Science and Technology Advisory Group (STAG) was established in December 1979, under the supervision of Minister Li, to provide logistical support to the Board.

Also acting as a think-tank for the development of Science and Technology in the Cabinet, STAG is entrusted with the responsibility to provide an advisory service at the inter-ministerial level to mobilize and manage the country's resources for S&T to the full. Within its mandate, STAG provides recommendations aimed at reducing unnecessary duplication of S&T investment and enhancing the across-the-board effect of national endeavor.

In the meantime, as a result of the enactment of the Science and Technology Development Program and the growing need to strengthen inter-ministerial cooperation in S&T projects, new ministerial S&T advisors' offices—consisting primarily of domestic talent—were established in individual government departments, including the Ministries of Education, Economic Affairs, Communications, National Defense, and the Department of Health. They work closely with the S&T advisors in their respective areas of interest. NSC has also set up a coordinating system for overall evaluation. These modifications of the governmental administrative structure represented a significant step in the process of making certain that the nation would be well prepared for the advent of S&T development of the 1980s.

The Second National S&T Conference — Expanding Strategic S&T Areas

In January 1982, after the second energy crisis, the Second National S&T Conference was held to address the challenges following international economic changes and the transformation brought about by domestic industrial restructuring. The implementation of the S&T development program was reviewed and revisions were made to cope with economic changes as follows:

1) Increasing the percentage of national research expenditure in GNP from 0.6% to 1.2% by 1985,
2) Emphasizing basic research,
3) Adding four strategic areas, i.e., biotechnology, optoelectronics, food processing technology, and hepatitis control to the four original technologies, making eight major areas of thrust in the development of Science and Technology in Taiwan.

In addition, the Technical Manpower Cultivation and Recruiting Program was approved in 1983 as a plan of action for the S&T development program. It also served to upgrade S&T manpower at universities and research institutes.

The contents of the plan were as follow:

1) Setting up research centers of excellence to provide favorable research environments in the four major universities
2) Providing professors with research grants in accordance with their performance; getting rid of equalitarian grants
3) Providing universities with flexibility to utilize S&T project funds
4) Reducing the limitation on the number of faculties in national universities providing MScs and PhDs in order to meet the increasing number of postgraduates in key areas of technology.

With the implementation of this program, most limitations in the systems of personnel, accounting and budget were removed and more distinguished researchers were produced.

After the second National S&T Conference, NSC has taken up the responsibilities of reviewing and evaluating the S&T projects undertaken by the related ministries and agencies. It was also required that each ministry set up its review system to facilitate the development of S&T, and meet the requirements of economic and social development in a more efficient way.

The Third National S&T Conference — Enacting the Long-term and Mid-term S&T Development Programs

The Third National S&T Conference in January 1986, passed the

National Ten-year Science and Technology Development Plan (1986–1995), which identified the following six major strategies for S&T development in the ROC:

1) Broadening R&D base, raising the quality and quantity of researchers, increasing overall R&D expenditure to around 2% of GNP.
2) Enhancing R&D efficiency, strengthening research project evaluation systems, carefully selecting R&D subjects to meet the requirements of basic research, economic development, social welfare, and national defense.
3) Encouraging private industries to invest in R&D through tax incentives and other financial measures to boost the R&D investments of private industries.
4) Expanding further the Hsinchu Science-Based Industrial Park; introducing more hi-tech industries into the ROC; supporting industrial Technology Research Institutes develop hi-tech products and technical know-how.
5) Promoting international S&T cooperation and strengthening technology transfer.
6) Broadening public awareness in science and technology.

To implement the long-term plan, which added four more areas, i.e., disaster prevention, synchrotron radiation, ocean S&T, and environmental protection, the Encouragement of Private Industries to invest in Research and Development and the Mid-term plan for the Development of Twelve Strategic S&T, were formulated. The ministries concerned followed the guidelines to plan for implementation year by year and set up the review and evaluation system of the long-term, mid-term, and annual projects.

The Fourth National S&T Conference — Revising the Long-term and Mid-term Development Plans to Cope with National Development

In January 1991, the Fourth National S&T Conference was held to discuss S&T development in order to meet the requirements of the 21st century and to plan for future national development.

Based on the consensus achieved, the National Ten-year S&T Development Plan (1986–1995) was revised as the Twelve-year Long-term Development Plan of Science and Technology (1991–2002).

In accordance with the Six-year National Development Plan (1991–1996), the Mid-term Six-year Development Plan of Science and Technology was drafted to fully utilize the ROC's limited S&T resources, develop industrial technology, and strengthen academic research so that the ROC could catch up with the advanced countries in some areas of basic research and industrial technology development.

IMPORTANT MEASURES IN SCIENCE & TECHNOLOGY DEVELOPMENT

Academia Sinica — Expansion of Research Institutes and Implementation of the Five-year Development Plan

As the highest academic institution in the Republic of China, the Academia Sinica was founded in Nanking in 1928. When the ROC government retreated to Taiwan in 1949, only two institutes were moved to the island. Despite the adverse conditions in the early 1950s the Academia Sinica has gradually built up its strength at the present site in Nankan, Taipei.

But due to limited budgets and S&T manpower, the effective promotion of basic research was constrained. Since 1981, the Five-Year Development Plan was formulated for the long-term academic development of science and technology. Research talent, equipment and expenditure were adequately strengthened. The performance of the institutes and the expansion or research fields were significant.

In the 1990s two phases of the Development Plan were implemented. The scale of the Academia Sinica was greatly expanded, and total annual expenditure increased from NT$310 million in 1981 to NT$4 billion. At present it is made up of nineteen research institutes. There are about five hundred senior research fellows and three hundred junior research fellows and assistants. In order to keep up the effort, phase three of the Five-Year Development Plan was started in 1991. It is expected that 530 researchers are to be added. Total expenditures will be NT$22.4 billion (on average NT$4.5 billion per year).

National Laboratories

To respond to the characteristics of large-scale research projects, the National Science Council has since the mid-1980s coordinated with agencies and research institutes concerned to conduct planning for the setting up of national laboratories. NSC provided large-scale research facilities at domestic universities, research institutes, and the Science Park, open to researchers and scholars to facilitate the localization of S&T research and upgrade the capability of S&T manpower.

There are five national-level research laboratories under construction. The following is a brief description of their mission and efforts for promotion.

1) *Synchrotron Radiation Research Center* (*SRRC*)

The engineering and construction of the SRRC was started in August, 1986 and completed in January 1992. It includes light source buildings, a research building, an administration building, and a guest house. The main facility is a 1.3 GeV electron storage ring with a fuel-energy injection booster ring, connected by a transport line. Three beelines and corresponding stations have been installed around the ring.

The design and fabrication of most components have been undertaken by Chinese scientists. The installation of an injection system was completed in November 1992. The installation of the storage ring was completed at the end of December 1992. After the first success of commissioning in April 1993, the beam current of the storage ring reached the design value of 200 mA. in August 1993. It will put Taiwan at the cutting edge of advanced physics research.

The shift from construction of the SRRC to an operating facility will take place in October 1993.

2) *Laboratory Animal Breeding and Research Center*
The goal of this center is to provide high-quality, healthy, and genetically pure of animals for use in medical research and in modern hi-tech life sciences research to ensure the accuracy and reliability of research results. The construction of the center is scheduled to be completed by the end of 1993. The center will produce four species of laboratory animals: mice, rats, hamsters, and guinea pigs.

3) *Nanodevice Laboratory*
The Laboratory is designed to meet the manpower and technological needs of the rapid growth in the semiconductor and IC industry. It will train high-calibre research and engineering personnel and will conduct research toward the development of key technologies. Cooperation with industry and research institutes is highly emphasized. Construction of the laboratory, located at the National Chiao Tung University, was completed at the end of 1992. The goal of the laboratory is 0.35 micrometer technology, accelerating the development of the IC industry.

4) *Seismic Engineering Research Center*
Since Taiwan is located on the Pacific earthquake zone, and earthquakes occur frequently, the importance of research concerning seismic engineering has been emphasized. The Center will raise the level of academic seismic research and improve the standards of quake-proof designs to lessen damage caused by seismic disturbances. The site of the Center is at the campus of the National Taiwan University. The construction of the center was started in August 1993, and will be completed in 1995.

5) *Center for High-performance Computing*
The National Center for High-performance Computing oversees the use of high-speed computation for research to raise the level of academic work and to promote professional computing applications. The Center was founded in January 1991, to be located in the Hsinchu Science-based Industrial Park, and externally linked by high-speed computer networks with major research institutes. The services of the center

were already open to the public in February 1993. The initial facility in the center includes a high-performance computing engine, a front-end system and a large number of workstations for visualization computing and software development.

Besides the above five national labs under operation or construction, other labs designed to facilitate future S&T development are being planned, for instance the National Space Laboratory, High-temperature Superconductor Laboratory, etc. The establishment of national labs will contribute greatly to Taiwan's advancement in academic research, hi-tech industrial development and manpower development.

Industrial Technology Research Institute (ITRI)

The promotion of S&T should be based not only on a well-defined goal and a concrete implementation plan but also the advice of qualified research institutes of high calibre. This paved the way for the setting up of ITRI, which has now become the most important research institute in promoting Taiwan's industrial technology. In 1973, the Ministry of Economic Affairs (MOEA) reorganized three research institutes, namely, Union Industry, Union Mining Industry and Metal Industry, into ITRI. The missions of ITRI are accepting the government's contracts to conduct key technology research programs, disseminating research accomplishments to the private sector and assisting small- and medium-sized enterprises to improve production processes or to upgrade technology.

In line with technology policy formulation and industrial development, ITRI kept adjusting and expanding its organization. It initially consisted of 3 laboratories initially and it now owns 7 laboratories and 3 research centers. The fields of research have expanded to cover electronics, materials, optoelectronics, computers and communication, measurement technology, chemical engineering, energy and resources, mechanical engineering, pollution abatement, industrial safety, aerospace, and so on. ITRI has played a leading role in both industrial technology development and manpower development.

In the beginning, the budget of ITRI was so limited that it could only focus on offering technical services to private sectors. However, its budget greatly increased since the promotion of the S&T Development Program in 1979. Thanks to the growth of government-sponsored S&T projects, ITRI's budget was rapidly increased from NT$1,100 million in 1980 to NT$13,100 million in 1993. The budget of government-sponsored projects in 1993 was NT$8,800 million, accounting for two-thirds of its total budget in 1993. The results of government-sponsored research projects were spread to the private sector by way of technology transfer, symposia and publication of papers. For example, in 1993, ITRI transferred 209 cases of technology to 297 companies, and conducted 707 seminars to train 38,341 man-hours.

In addition to the establishment of ITRI, the ROC government has also set up some nonprofit R&D organizations such as the Institute for Information Industry (III), the Development Center for Biotechnology (DCB), and the Food Industry Research & Development Institute (FIRI). Each institute is responsible for key technology R&D and technology transfer. R&D and technology transfer in strategic areas are undertaken by these research institutes to get S&T development policies implemented.

Hsinchu Science-Based Industrial Park (HSIP)

Besides setting up nonprofit R&D organizations, the ROC government also followed the development model of hi-tech industry at Silicon Valley in the U.S. to set up the Hsinchu Science-based Industrial Park, which is located near the National Tsing Hua University, the National Chiao Tung University, and ITRI. With the incentives of a convenient transportation network and simplified administrative procedures, the Park had attracted several enterprises to invest and operate in the Park. The administration of the Park has strict selection processes in introducing suitable hi-tech industries.

It also made efforts to offer excellent job opportunities and a favorable living environment to attract talented hi-tech S&T personnel overseas to return and work in the home country. The Park is now regarded as the window of Taiwan's hi-tech industries.

The growth of the HSIP has been very rapid since 1987. By the end of 1992, the number of the companies operating in the Park was 140 and total annual turnover was US$3.5 billion. So far, computer and computer peripherals companies take the lion's share. This indicates the phenomenal development of the information technology industry in Taiwan. Besides, most IC manufacturers in Taiwan are located in the Park now. In order to expand the field of R&D, the Park administration has accelerated the introduction of biotechnology, environmental protection technology, etc., to stimulate the development of related industries.

Generally speaking, the creation of HSIP has had the following impact on hi-tech industries in Taiwan:

1) *Encouraging venture capitals into hi-tech industry*
   High risk and high returns are two characteristics of hi-tech industries. The government must provide the incentives of a favorable climate and promotion programs to encourage traditional enterprises to invest in venture capital companies and introduce high technology from abroad to serve as the important medium for technology transfer.

2) *Disseminating technology to accelerate the upgrading of industries*
   Many components needed for production in the Park were supplied by small- and medium-sized enterprises outside the Park. To ensure the quality of the components, the hi-tech companies in the Park have to assist their suppliers in technical education and personnel training. This has also helped upgrade the technology of many satellite companies.

3) *Attracting overseas Chinese S&T manpower to start up business in Taiwan*

Due to the attractions of the favorable working and living environment in the Park, many overseas Chinese S&T talents returned home to invest in the Park. At present, more than half of the companies in the Park were founded by overseas Chinese scholars and engineers who brought back a lot of specialized and unique production technology.

Following the success of HSIP, the government has planned to conduct an extension program in the Six-year National Development Plan, namely, to set up a Hsinchu Science City to magnify the functions of the HSIP. In the meantime, the government would set up a new S&T industrial park at Tainan to upgrade technology in coordination with the development of local industry.

Human Resource Planning and Development

The effective education system and application of human resources have been one of the major factors leading to successful development in Taiwan. From the 1960s, we have cultivated technical manpower at every level to meet the needs of economic and scientific development. Different measures were taken at different stages:

1) It is clear that technicians and skilled workers are needed in industrialization. In the 1960s, vocational education was first promoted, but at that time the ratio of the number of high schoolers to that of vocational students was 6:4. Today, it is 3:7. Nowadays, all sorts of technical manpower and training systems are well designed.

2) Throughout the 1970s and the 1980s, we also increased the number of colleges and universities and departments for the development of S&T manpower. The ratio of university graduates in science and engineering to that of all disciplines is now about 1:1. The number of masters and doctoral programs has been greatly increased in both public and private universities. Great strides have been made both in quantity and quality. These are favorable conditions for the promotion of the hi-tech industry in Taiwan.

3) On the manpower resources for applied research, the government has in the past asked such research organizations as ITRI through the so-called consigned S&T research programs to establish common industrial technologies and train talent. Through the proliferation of technology and manpower in the private industry, the development system of emerging industries has gradually formed.

At the level of advanced S&T manpower, a big manpower bank has been accumulated abroad in the past years. Chinese scientists and engineers have increasingly returned home for work, and have been and will be a driving force in the overall development of this country.

CONCLUSION

The government has taken the initiative in the promotion of S&T research for over thirty years since the promulgation of the Guidelines for National Long-term Science Development in 1959. In retrospect, over this long period of S&T development, the policies at earlier stages emphasized the importance of basic science research and the cultivation of manpower. Following the promulgation of the Science and Technology Development Program, which identified strategic technologies for development, the policies of S&T development were more closely connected with those of industrial development.

In the last ten years, hi-tech industries grew rapidly with joint efforts between government agencies and the private sector. For example, the information industry, whose total turnover rose from US$10 million in 1981 to US$9 billion in 1992, was ranked 7th in the world. The ROC IC industry, whose total turnover was 1% of the world market, was ranked 7th in the world since the setup of the Taiwan Semiconductor Manufacturing Company in 1987. Besides, the total turnover of communication products has reached US$1,800 million and was ranked 10th in the world. The export value of mechanical and electronic products has been rising yearly, surpassing traditional industries like textile and food processing. The mechanical and electronics industry has become the biggest export-oriented industry.

For years, the government not only provided funds for S&T projects but also initiated several tax incentives such as the Articles of Encouragement to New Product Development by the Private Sector and the Statute of Encouragement to Investment (later replaced by the Statute of Enhancing Industrial Development in 1991) to encourage research and development in the private sector. The nation's R&D development expenditure was US$420 million (0.93% of GNP) in 1981 and had increased to US$3,175 million (1.7% of GNP) in 1991, with an annual growth rate of 22.7%. In recent years, the percentage of increase in growth in the private sector has surpassed that of the government. This tendency matched the development trend of the advanced countries where research activities were concentrated in the private sector.

With respect to the S&T manpower, the number of researchers was 19,604 in 1981, which had grown to 46,173 (1.35 times that in 1981) in 1991. There were 23 researchers per 10,000 people, close to the level in industrialized countries. The growth of high-level manpower was rapid. The percentage of PhD holders rose from 8% in 1981 to 12.9% in 1990 and the researchers with a Masters degree rose from 16.3% to 21.3% while Bachelor researchers fell from 47.3% to 35.1%. Therefore, the quality of researchers has improved greatly.

Although research expenditure and manpower has increased every year, there is still a gap that must be closed for the ROC to catch up with advanced countries. In order to upgrade technology and improve industrial structure to enhance the competitiveness, the government is going to invest more in S&T development, especially in hi-tech industry. Therefore, the government has selected tele-communications, information, semiconductors, consumer electronics, precision machinery automation, aerospace, advanced materials, specialty chemical, pharmaceuticals, healthcare, and pollution prevention as the top ten newly emerging industries. In addition, eight core technologies, namely, optoelectronics, software, industrial automation, materials application, advanced sensors, biotechnology, resource development and energy conservation have been identified for development to reach the goal of making the ROC as an S&T-based country. As estimates show, the R&D expenditure would be 2.2% of GNP and the percentage of the R&D expenditure by private enterprises out of total R&D expenditure would be over 60% in 1996.

To complete its transition to a fully developed economy by the year 2000, economic development in Taiwan should make further leaps. The 1990s will mark a new era of science and technology development in the Republic of China.

8

CROSS-STRAIT POLICY

For more than thirty years after the Nationalist government relocated to Taiwan in 1949, there was little economic and trade contact across the Taiwan Strait. Not only did the two sides institute radically different political and economic systems, but they were also locked in a tense military confrontation. In 1979, however, mainland China, discredited by 30 years of economic stagnation and inspired by Taiwan's successful achievements, adopted a policy of "internal reform and external openness" and dramatically changed its attitude toward trade and economic links with Taiwan. As a result, tensions between the two sides began to abate.

Nevertheless, despite the introduction of economic reforms, the mainland continued to be guided politically by communist doctrine. For this reason, contact across the Taiwan Strait before 1987 consisted of a limited amount of indirect trade. It was not until October 1987, when the Kuomingtang (KMT) government lifted a ban on visits by Taiwan residents to the mainland that economic interchange between the two sides began to grow rapidly. This process has been promoted by changing political and economic conditions on both sides of the strait and throughout the world.

Since the 1980s, when Taiwan adopted economic liberalization and internationalization as the guiding principles of economic development, trade and economic ties with the mainland have taken on added importance. Indeed, cross-strait relations have become a critical concern in Taiwan's overall economic strategy. Nevertheless, given the political and economic differences that continue to exist between the two sides, as well as their history of mutual hostility and suspicion, Taiwan must proceed cautiously in the development of trade and economic relations with the mainland.

AN OVERVIEW OF TRADE AND ECONOMIC RELATIONS ACROSS THE STRAIT

Only the narrow Taiwan Strait lies between the mainland and Taiwan, but the two sides are separated by much more than this geographical barrier. Mainland China isolated itself behind a bamboo curtain from 1949 to 1987, and repeatedly threatened to "liberate" Taiwan by force. Several military conflicts broke out between the two sides during this period, and there were no economic or cultural contacts. Not until 1979, when the mainland began to emphasize "internal reforms" and "external openness", and radically changed its Taiwan policy did cross-strait links begin to develop.

Evolution of Cross-Strait Relations

The evolution of cross-strait contacts since 1979 can be divided into three stages:

(1) a period of no contact;
(2) a period of tacit contact; and
(3) a period of expanded contact.

(1) *Period of no contact (January 1979—June 1985)*

Mainland China undertook economic reforms and introduced dramatic changes in its Taiwan policy in 1979. It toned down previous calls for the "liberation of Taiwan", expressing a desire for "peaceful reunification of the motherland" instead. Among its open-door economic policies, the mainland advocated direct trade, and postal and transportation links with Taiwan, both to develop the mainland's foreign trade and to attract investment from Taiwan and the rest of the world. But Taiwan responded by declaring a Three-No's policy— that is, no contact, no compromise, and no negotiation with the mainland until Mainland China implemented democracy and a free economic system, and renounced her threat of using force against Taiwan. Military confrontation had shifted to a peace offensive, but there was no noticeable improvement in cross-strait relations and only a trickle of indirect trade flowed through Hong Kong.

(2) *Period of tacit contact (July 1985—October 1987)*

During this period Taiwan's businessmen, attracted by the low cost of labor and land on the mainland, and encouraged by the mainland's deliberate efforts to promote trade and economic ties with Taiwan, began to pressure the Taiwan government to loosen restrictions. The KMT government, taking a more pragmatic stance, began to modify its mainland policy. In early 1985, it announced that it would neither encourage nor interfere with indirect exports to the mainland, meaning that it would turn a blind eye to Taiwan's exports to the mainland through a third country. However, indirect imports from the mainland to Taiwan were not yet allowed. Consequently, exports to the mainland grew much more rapidly than imports from the mainland. There was almost no growth in indirect bilateral trade through other countries.

(3) *Period of expanded contact (November 1987 to the present)*

In November 1987, the KMT government opened up a new channel of communication with the Mainland by allowing Taiwan residents to visit relatives there. With a major thaw in cross-Strait relations now under way and the economic symbiosis between the two sides growing, trade and economic ties took an unprecedented turn for the better. And in addition to existing indirect trade through Hong Kong, an extensive division of labor began to develop in industrial production.

Factors Promoting Cross-Strait Economic Links

For reasons of politics and history, the development of cross-Strait ties has been motivated mainly by economic concerns, although internal and international political conditions have also played a part.

(1) *Economic reforms in the mainland*
Taiwan's economic success was a catalyst in the mainland's economic reform. In 1950, per capita GNP was around US$50 on both sides of the Strait. But by 1990 the figure for Taiwan had jumped to US$8,000, almost 20 times the mainland's. This success is believed to be rooted in export-oriented planning within a free-market system. To remedy the effects of decade-long stagnation, the mainland authorities are opening up their economy to market forces, allowing the private ownership of property, and promoting foreign trade and international investment on the mainland. Since November 1987, they have made a special effort to reduce tensions and improve ties across the Strait, both to benefit from Taiwan's experience in economic development and to re-energize the mainland economy by attracting more investment capital from Taiwan. In July 1988, the mainland's State Council announced a set of "regulations to encourage investment by Taiwan compatriots", and in March 1989 and then in February 1990, new measures were introduced that opened up more channels to investment from Taiwan and provided preferential tax treatment to Taiwan businesses.

Deng Xiao-ping's recent public speech made during his South China trip (1992) signaled the start of a second wave of reform. Not only will the opening of coastal economic zones, technology development zones and cities be accelerated, but inland towns and cities will be opened up as well, while special tax incentives will be offered to stimulate investment in tertiary industries.

Economic reform has been given highest priority in the mainland since the 1980s, and accompanying programs in accelerating openness and increasing preferential treatment have been a great encouragement to potential Taiwan investors and to cross-Strait economic and trade ties.

(2) *Structural economic changes in Taiwan*
Taiwan's traditional labor-intensive industries have been losing their competitiveness since 1986, when the cost of production began to rise sharply along with wages and land prices, and the domestic currency

began to rapidly appreciate. Increasing labor and environmental disputes, as well as rising crime, are also adding to these industries' difficulties. These problems prompted labor-intensive industries — such as shoes, textiles, and toy manufacturing—to relocate to Southeast Asia, a region that still possessed the advantages that Taiwan used to enjoy. However, given the strong historical, cultural and linguistic ties binding the two sides of the Taiwan Strait, Taiwan industrialists expressed a strong preference for the mainland when the ban on mainland visits was removed in 1987. As a result, investment by Taiwan businesses in mainland industries began to overtake their investments in Southeast Asian countries.

In addition to social and cultural bonds, complementary resource endowments provide a powerful impetus to closer cross-Strait economic ties. This resource complementarity allows each side to specialize in those forms of production in which it enjoys an advantage. The greater division of labor and economies of scale that result from such specialization provides significant benefits for both sides.

SPECIAL ASPECTS OF CROSS-STRAIT TRADE AND ECONOMIC TIES

Mainland China launched its open-door policy in 1979, but it was not until 1987 that trade and investment across the Strait began to develop rapidly. From under US$1 billion in 1986, indirect trade between the two sides jumped to around US$5.8 billion in 1991. According to the Investment Commission of the Ministry of Economic Affairs, there were 2,552 reported cases of Taiwanese investment in the mainland as of the end of 1991, amounting to US$820 million. The actual figure should be larger, since many firms are reluctant to fully disclose their mainland investments. Other special features of cross-Strait trade and economic activity include:

Rapidly Increasing Trade Interdependence

Judging from shares in total trade, indirect trade across the Taiwan

Strait is becoming more important for both sides. Taiwan's indirect exports to the mainland as a percentage of its total exports remained around 2% before 1984, but shot up to 6.2% in 1991. Its indirect imports from the mainland, around 1% of total imports before 1988, rose to 1.8% in 1991. For the mainland, exports to Taiwan, which used to account for less than 1% of total exports, increased to 1.6% in 1991. In the meantime, imports from Taiwan climbed from 3% to 7.4% of the mainland's total imports.

Today, the mainland has become Taiwan's fifth largest trading partner, and Taiwan the mainland's sixth largest partner. Both figure importantly in each other's trade development. However, since Taiwan's geographical size, population, and overall production are much smaller than the mainland's, and Taiwan is far more dependent on foreign trade, it is more vulnerable to sudden changes in cross-Strait indirect trade.

Large Imbalance in Trade

The trade imbalance in Taiwan's favor has been widening considerably since the 1980s. Only US$0.2 billion in 1980, Taiwan's trade surplus with the mainland zoomed to US$3.6 billion in 1991, or 27% of Taiwan's total trade surplus. From the standpoint of the mainland, its deficit with Taiwan accounted for 44% of its total trade deficit of US$8.1 billion.

Two factors are believed to be responsible for the imbalance. One is that the two sides of the Strait are at different stages of economic development. Exports from the mainland to Taiwan consist mostly of low-value-added primary agricultural and industrial products, while exports from Taiwan to the mainland are mostly industrial raw materials, machinery and equipment, and electronic parts, which embody higher value-added goods. The second factor is that Taiwan firms have to ship Taiwan-made machinery, equipment and parts to their mainland plants, because mainland industries are not yet capable of providing such items. And as the pace of industrial integration across the Taiwan Strait quickens, increasing imports of such products contribute to a growing trade deficit for the mainland.

Deepening Trade and Economic Ties

Trade across the Strait has graduated from simple entrepôt trade through a third country to investment-driven trade. And this process promises to deepen and intensify the economic integration that is already under way.

Initially, investment by Taiwan businesses in the mainland was of an exploratory nature. Most investors were small-scale, labor-intensive firms who tended to concentrate their investments along the southeast coast in such locations as Shenzhen, Canton, Hsiamen, and Shanghai. But today, with Taiwan's investment rapidly expanding in the mainland and with more areas of the mainland opening up to foreign investment, the scope, amount, location, number, and nature of investments have changed dramatically. Longer term investments are being made. Investors are turning their attention from coastal to inland areas, and from the south to the north. More investment is flowing to upstream industries that are capital- and technology-intensive. Medium-sized and large enterprises are more frequently selected for investment. And some Taiwan businesses are even renting large industrial estates for multi-purpose development.

CURRENT POLICIES

Because of the unique historical and political factors that have shaped Taiwan-mainland relations, the cross-Strait trade and economic policies of each side are very different from their policies vis-à-vis other countries. In particular, given the critical importance of mainland trade to Taiwan's economic development, there is no margin for error in its cross-Strait policy. Consequently, Taiwan's approach to the development of trade and economic ties with the mainland tends to be cautious and incremental.

The Mainland's Policy on Trade and Economic Ties with Taiwan

Mainland China launched its economic reforms and open-door policy in 1979, the same year that it began to promote accelerated development under the banner "four modernizations". In order to attract overseas investment to the mainland, the mainland toned down its bellicose rhetoric regarding Taiwan, no longer calling for "liberation through military force" but for "peaceful unification". It issued a "declaration to Taiwan compatriots" in January 1979, calling for faster progress in the establishment of communications links ("three communications") and the promotion of exchanges across the Strait ("four interflows") in academic work, science and technology, sports, and cultural activities, and proposing that "both sides should work for the development of trade and economic ties." Later, in speeches by chair leaders such as Yeh Jian-ying (September 1981), Deng Xiao-ping (June 1983) and Hu Yao-bang (May 1985), a policy of "one country, two systems" and "peaceful unification" appeared to emerge. This theme has been implicit in all recent mainland policy pronouncements regarding economic and trade links with Taiwan.

In the 1980s, the mainland offered a great many trade and investment preferences to businessmen from Taiwan, a move consistent with the principle just mentioned and with the "four modernizations" and "peaceful unification".

The mainland's latest policy statement regarding trade and economic links with Taiwan, released in July 1991, calls for "direct, stable, mutually beneficial and multi-faceted" ties between the two sides, and emphasizes the importance of "keeping commitments and promises". The Communists' real intentions were clarified in a speech by Yang Shang-kun at the "National Conference on Taiwan Affairs" in December 1990, in which he:

— Cited the "one country, two systems" concept and the expansion of communications links and exchanges as the guiding principles of cross-Strait ties.
— Urged the use of communications links to promote political contacts.
— Called on Taiwan businessmen to pressure their government toward unification.

— Encouraged the use of incentives and preferences for attracting investment from Taiwan to stimulate the mainland's economic growth.

Taiwan's Policy on Trade and Economic Ties with the Mainland

Business and economic interests are only one concern of Taiwan's overall mainland policy. Increasing dependence on cross-Strait economic and trade activities and memories of political hostility have led Taiwan to be cautious and skeptical in the development of cross-Strait links. Moreover, Taiwan regards economic concerns as secondary to national security, and believes that trade and economic activity, as well as other cross-Strait exchanges, should be subject to regulation. Therefore, to gain a thorough understanding of Taiwan's policy on trade and economic ties with the mainland, one must look at Taiwan's mainland policy as a whole.

(1) *Current policy in general*
Taiwan's mainland policy is meant to bring about the reunification of China through the principles of freedom, democracy, and prosperity for all. Since the disparity in economic and political conditions across the Strait is still great, the unification process can be achieved only gradually, and only if equality and reciprocity are ensured.

In March 1991, the government announced "Guidelines for National Unification" to explain Taiwan's mainland policy. According to the guidelines, unification will proceed in three stages. Goals are set for each stage, and only after those goals have been realized can the succeeding stage begin. The three stages are briefly described as follows:

A. *Short term — expanding exchanges and encouraging reciprocity*
Objectives include recognition of each side as a political entity, the expansion of people-to-people contacts, continued reform on both sides, the peaceful resolution of disparities, an end to hostility, and greater respect for each other in the international community.

B. Medium term — promoting mutual trust and cooperation

Goals to be achieved during this stage include establishing official channels of communication on an equal footing; removing the ban on direct postal, transport, and commercial links; cooperating in international organizations and activities; and promoting exchange visits by high-ranking officials of both sides.

C. Long term — beginning consultations on national unification

This stage will begin only after disparities between the political and economic systems of the two sides and between their living standards are significantly narrowed. A consultative body will be established, which will deliberate the great tasks of national unification and lay the foundation for a constitutional government founded on the principles of freedom, democracy, and prosperity for all.

(2) Trade and economic policy

Until the mainland renounces the use of force against Taiwan and recognizes it as a political entity, trade and economic ties between the two sides will not advance beyond the current stage of short-term exchanges. To preserve economic stability and prevent the hollowing out of domestic industries, Taiwan must avoid becoming overdependent on the mainland market. And its policy toward the mainland must remain forward-looking, pragmatic, pro-active, and incremental.

A. Strategy

— Contacts will be indirect and people-to-people. A Taiwan business that wishes to invest in the mainland will have to do so through a subsidiary it has set up in a third country or region that has concluded an investment protection agreement with the mainland. Trade also will have to be conducted through a third country.

— A trade and investment monitoring system should be set up to alert policymakers in Taiwan to changes in mainland conditions that could lead to the hollowing-out of domestic industries.

— Small and medium-sized firms losing comparative advantage in Taiwan should be allowed to set up operations on the mainland, provided that their relocation does not hinder Taiwan's industrial upgrading.

— The "Taiwan experience" should be shared with the mainland to help accelerate its economic reform and raise its living standard.

The following regulations regarding trade and investment with the mainland have been designed in compliance with the strategy described above.

B. *Key regulations*

Regarding indirect trade, a negative list applies to exports and a positive list to imports. Only high-tech items appear on the negative list for exports; all other products are allowed to be exported to the mainland. The positive list for imports include all products that pose no threat to national security or industrial development, and that can help improve industrial competitiveness. Since August 1988, under the Regulations Governing Mainland Goods and the Regulations Governing Indirect Imports of Mainland Products, 2,282 agricultural and industrial raw materials and eight categories of footwear and hand-made products have been approved for import from the mainland.

According to the Regulations Governing Indirect Investment and Technological Cooperation with the Mainland, announced by the Ministry of Economic Affairs in 1990, Taiwan investment in the mainland is governed by a positive list. The list permits any investment that will not harm national security or economic development, and that meets at least one of the following requirements:

a) The investment is in the development of raw materials which the mainland possesses in abundance and that are needed for Taiwan's industrial development;

b) The investment is in labor-intensive industries;

c) The investment has a low industrial linkage effect; and

d) The investment is in an industry that no longer enjoys a comparative advantage in Taiwan.

At present, investment in as many as 3,679 industrial categories is permitted on the mainland.

THE SPECIAL NATURE OF TAIWAN'S POLICY ON TRADE AND ECONOMIC TIES WITH THE MAINLAND

Because of unusual political and economic factors, the formulation of Taiwan's policy governing trade and economic ties with the mainland must take into account a number of important concerns. Among these are not only economic concerns but also the impact of mainland policy on national sovereignty, welfare, and security. Since the mainland still regards Taiwan as a province and objects to its diplomatic ties and international standing, the KMT government naturally exercises great caution in formulating its mainland policy.

In the 1980s, liberalization and internationalization were adopted as the cornerstone of Taiwan's long-term economic development. These principles have shaped Taiwan's trade and economic relations with every country and territory excluding the mainland. This exclusion has remained a unique feature of cross-Strait trade and economic ties. Other special characteristics of mainland policy are described below.

Flexibility

Given that cross-Strait relations are subject to sudden and unpredictable change, flexibility is a key criterion of Taiwan's mainland policy. In addition, special measures must be taken at each stage of development in the relationship to protect the interests of both business enterprises and the general public. Both of these concerns are addressed by the short-, medium-, and long-term plans developed in accordance with the Guidelines for National Unification, which were adopted in 1991 as the guiding principles of Taiwan's mainland policy.

Government agencies concerned with cross-Strait trade and economic ties are constantly evaluating changing economic and political conditions on the mainland in the light of Taiwan's development needs. And the frequent revision of regulations governing trade with and investment on the mainland are evidence of the government's timely and flexible response to such changes.

Regulatory and Advisory Functions

Under the principles of economic liberalization and internationalization, the government allows free rein to the market mechanism in trade and economic relations with other countries. However, given the significant role played by politics in cross-Strait ties, the interests of both national security and economic development demand that the government exercise certain regulatory and advisory functions with regard to trade and economic activity across the Strait. The establishment of positive lists for imports from and investment in the mainland is a good example of the government's regulatory function. In its advisory capacity, the government has helped set up cross-Strait trade councils under the National Federation of Industries, the General Chamber of Commerce, and the Straits Exchange Foundation. These councils help local businesses collect and analyze information important to cross-strait trade and economic ties. They also provide advice and assistance to mainland-bound business executives.

CONCLUDING REMARKS

We have noted earlier in this chapter that the economic reform adopted by mainland China in 1979 has an *internal* as well as an *external* dimension. The latter dimension, centered on an orientation of "openness", changed the attitude of the mainland toward trade, investment and other economic links with the outside world in general and with Taiwan in particular. The evolution of economic and trade relations across the Taiwan Strait in recent years (for example, from "tacit contact" after 1985 to "expanded contact" after 1987) was the direct consequence of the "external dimension" of economic reform. It is quite inevitable that the economic contact in the past will lead to some forms of political contact in the years ahead that will, in turn, pave the way for a political unification of China in the early part of the 21st Century. The prospect of political and economic unification of

China can only be assessed in reference to the internal dimension which is far more important and complex than the external (or "openness") dimension.

From a long-run, historical perspective, the rise and fall of the socialist experiment in the 20th Century (as guided by Marxist ideology) has been a major epoch-making event in human societies. The sudden collapse of the socialist "Party State" in the ex-socialist countries of Eastern Europe proved conclusively that socialism—formed of the political system of totalitarianism (i.e., one in which the Communist Party monopolizes political power), and the economic system of "centralism of planning and command" — is incompatible with, and not accommodative of, the requirements of modern economic life. What lies behind the economic reforms of mainland China after 1979 has been a Chinese manifestation of her frustration with the socialist experiment (1949–1978) and her quest for modernization toward the end of the 20th Century.

The cardinal principle that guides the "internal dimension" of economic reform after 1979 has been a movement toward liberalization that represents the atrophy of political forces and the rehabilitation of the roles of private societies (including private property, private markets, private family, relations, and privatized education) that, though valued highly in traditional China, have been brutally suppressed by political forces before 1978. This liberalization process has found political and economic expression. The heart of the political liberalization movement was centered on the societal demand for the initiation of a "government-society dialogue" in the Party State, heralded, for example, by the social movement at Tien-An-Men in June 1989, that constituted an essential precondition for constitutional democracy. However, what is directly relevant to this volume is the liberalization in the economic arena.

After fourteen years of economic reform since 1979, the focus of reform at the present time (1993) centers on the quadruplet of reform measures:

i) *Financial market reform*: construction of financial markets that regulated the allocation of investment funds to ensure rapid growth, with structural flexibility.

ii) *Ownership reform*: construct economic decision-making units, with cooperation between government and society, to ensure a system of accountability in the decentralized formation of investment plans.

iii) *Reform for indirect control of the market* via the exercise of monetary and fiscal policies to promote growth and/or to ensure economic stability.

iv) *Legal reform* to protect property rights and to settle contractual disputes—essential for the orderly operation of the "socialist market economy".

While the purpose of this volume is to analyze the formation and evolution of policies (including monetary and fiscal policies) in Taiwan during the post-War period (1950–1990), there is the prospect that this very successful policy experience of Taiwan can be transferred to, and shared by, those who are responsible for the design of growth promotion policies on the mainland.

This brief discussion of the "internal dimension" of reform given above immediately suggests that the *very transferability of the policy experience from the ROC to the PRC is an academically debatable issue*. Notice that the foundation for the effectiveness of policies in Taiwan was due to the fact that Taiwan had always accepted the privatized market economy as well as a political culture (i.e., one that curbs the arbitrariness of totalitarian government power) underlying the exercise of monetary and fiscal policies. For example, taxation policy in the ROC (or any capitalist country) is founded on the assumption of the principle of "taxation with consent" which is a political culture that is quite immature on the mainland at the present time. As long as the Party believes that it can retain "totalitarian power", all efforts at tax reform will be resisted.

The "internal dimension" of economic reform is far more important than the "external dimension" because when and if all these (and other) reform measures are brought to a successful conclusion, the lifestyle on the mainland will be altered fundamentally and irrevocably. In the Guidelines for National Unification (announced by the ROC government in March 1991), the vision of a sequence of "short-term", "medium-term", and "long-term" objectives was entertained. The "political consultation", specified as the "long-term" objective, will begin only after disparities between the political and economic systems of the two sides are significantly narrowed — as has been stated earlier in the text.

The successful conclusion of economic reform will bring about a *convergence of socio-political-economic institutions on both sides of the Taiwan Strait*. It will take a volume of a different nature to outline the process that is expected to happen in the near future. To the extent that this convergence occurs, the policy experience of Taiwan analyzed in this volume, will become relevant and transferable. However, what is even more important is that the convergence of institutions will pave the way for a political unification of China into "one country under one system". This will bring about a full economic integration of both sides of the Taiwan Strait — to an extent that will far exceed the vision painted in this chapter. This will also bring about a full political integration under constitutional democracy to realize a lifestyle of freedom and creativity in a modern China.

Table 8.1. Indirect Trade Across the Taiwan Strait

Unit: US$ million

| Period | Two-way Trade | | Through Hong Kong | | | | Taiwan's trade dependency on the mainland |
| | Value | Change from previous year (%) | Exports to the mainland | | Imports from the mainland | | |
			Value	Change from previous year (%)	Value	Change from previous year (%)	
1979	77.76		21.47		56.29		0.25
1980	311.18	300.18	234.97	994.41	76.21	35.39	0.79
1981	459.33	47.61	384.15	63.49	75.18	-1.35	1.05
1982	278.47	-39.37	194.45	-49.38	84.02	11.76	0.68
1983	247.69	-11.05	157.84	-18.83	89.85	6.94	0.55
1984	553.20	123.34	425.45	169.55	127.75	42.18	1.06
1985	1,102.73	99.34	986.83	131.95	115.90	-9.28	2.17
1986	955.55	-13.35	811.33	-17.78	144.22	24.43	1.49
1987	1,515.47	58.60	1,226.53	51.18	288.94	100.35	1.38
1988	2,720.91	79.54	2,242.22	82.81	478.69	65.67	2.47
1989	3,483.39	28.02	2,896.49	29.18	586.90	22.61	2.94
1990	4,043.62	16.08	3,278.26	13.18	765.36	30.41	3.32
1991	5,793.18	42.27	4,667.15	42.37	1,125.95	47.11	4.16

Source: Board of Foreign Trade, Ministry of Economic Affairs, ROC.

Table 8.2. Trade with Hong Kong and Indirect Trade with the Mainland Through Hong Kong

Unit: US$ million

Period	Exports to Hong Kong			Imports from Hong Kong			Two-way trade with Hong Kong			Balance of indirect trade with the mainland
	Value	Re-exports to the mainland		Value		Imports from the mainland through Hong Kong	Value	Indirect trade with mainland through Hong Kong		
		Value (A)	Total exports to Hong Kong (%)		Value (B)	Total imports from Hong Kong (%)		Value	Total trade with Hong Kong (%)	(A) – (B)
1980	1,551	243.97	15.1	250	76.21	30.5				158.76
1981	1,897	384.15	20.3	309	75.18	24.3				308.97
1982	1,565	194.45	12.4	307	84.02	27.4				110.43
1983	1,644	157.84	9.6	299	89.85	30.1	1,943	247.69	12.75	17.99
1984	2,087	425.45	20.4	370	127.75	34.5	2,458	553.2	22.51	297.70
1985	2,540	986.83	38.9	320	115.9	36.2	2,859	1,102.7	38.57	870.93
1986	2,921	811.33	27.8	379	144.22	38.1	3,300	955.55	28.96	667.11
1987	4,118	1,226.5	29.8	754	288.94	38.3	4,877	1,515.5	31.07	937.11
1988	5,580	2,242.5	40.2	1,922	478.69	24.9	7,509	2,720.9	36.23	1,763.51
1989	7,030	2,896.5	41.2	2,205	586.9	26.6	9,248	3,483.4	37.67	2,309.60
1990	8,556	3,278.3	38.3	1,446	765.36	52.9	10,002	4,043.6	40.42	2,512.94
1991	12,430	4,667.2	37.5	1,944	1,125.95	57.9	14,375	5,793.1	40.30	3,541.20

Source: Same as Table 8.1.

Table 8.3. Dependence of Taiwan and the Mainland on Cross-Strait Trade

Period	Taiwan's total exports to the mainland (%)	Taiwan's total imports from the mainland (%)	Mainland's total exports to Taiwan (%)	Mainland's total imports from Taiwan (%)
1979	0.13	0.38	0.41	0.14
1980	1.19	0.39	0.42	1.2
1981	1.70	0.35	0.34	1.75
1982	0.88	0.44	0.38	1.01
1983	0.63	0.44	0.40	0.74
1984	1.40	0.58	0.49	1.55
1985	3.21	0.58	0.42	2.34
1986	2.04	0.60	0.47	1.89
1987	2.30	0.84	0.73	2.84
1988	3.70	0.96	1.01	4.06
1989	4.38	1.12	1.19	4.9
1990	4.88	1.4	1.23	6.08
1991	6.16	1.8	1.57	7.35

Sources: 1. Hong Kong Customs.
2. Ministry of Finance, Monthly Statistics of Exports and Imports, Taiwan Area, the Republic of China, various issues.
3. Economic and Trade Yearbook of Mainland China.

Table 8.4. Investment by Taiwan Businesses in the Mainland — by Industry (1991)

Industry	Value (US$1,000)	Number of firms	Industry	Value (US$1,000)	Number of firms
Electrical Engineering	102,748	242	Rubber	6,478	31
Transportation Equipment	78,923	202	Foreign Trade	6,393	37
Footwear Manufacturing	58,751	306	Eyeglasses	5,593	14
Services	56,472	62	Toys	5,126	56
Plastic Products	44,582	129	Knitware	4,945	24
Textiles	31,995	74	Glass	4,920	10
Metals	30,400	85	Frozen Seafood	4,557	19
Farm and Livestock	21,378	35	Kitchen and	3,761	22
Sporting Goods	20,348	59	Sanitary		
Garments	17,876	106	Facilities		
Decorative Lamps	17,566	67	Medicine	3,007	11
Handbags, Suitcases, and	16,466	40	Furniture	2,891	15
Bags			Printing	2,793	21
Wood Products	15,688	46	Hand Gloves	2,247	15
Food	13,807	39	Automobiles	2,185	7
Electrical Appliances	13,343	37	Printing and	2,030	5
Sweaters	13,012	62	Dyeing		
Handicrafts	11,062	48	Feed	1,800	1
Clocks and Watches	10,989	12	Paint	1,655	15
Umbrella Manufacturing	10,829	62	Educational	1,518	6
Vegetable and Fruit	10,609	36	Materials		
Processing			Fishing Equipment	1,328	2
Porcelain	10,214	54	Hand Tools	1,318	6
Bamboo and Rattan	10,210	48	Unclassified	989	68
Products			Industries		
Machinery	9,461	30	Gifts	903	14
Medical Instruments	9,251	10	Optics	751	4
Stone and Mineral Products	8,964	28	Jewelery	410	7
Petrochemicals	7,158	37	Synthetic Resin	400	3
Paper Products	6,920	15	Aquaculture	185	2
Leather	6,680	58	Dyestuffs and	185	1
Paper Making	6,680	11	Pigments		
Tissue Paper	6,675	36	Fireworks	0	1
Zippers	6,490	10	Total	753,915	2,503

Source: Compiled by Investment Commission, Ministry of Economic Affairs, from data filed by firms in the classification of trade associations.

Table 8.5. Investment by Taiwan Businesses in the Mainland — by Area (1991)

Area	Number of firms	Value (US$1,000)	Area	Number of firms	Value (US$1,000)
Fukien Province	204	42,415	Szechwan Province	6	2,103
Foochow	119	44,903	Chungking	7	1,622
Amoy	275	92,205	Hunan Province	13	2,173
Shantou	39	12,040	Hupeh Province	15	5,418
Kwangtung Province	411	121,104	Shantung Province	46	18,081
			Sian	1	220
Canton	149	55,996	Honan Province	7	1,479
Shenzhen Economic Zone	379	111,682	Hopeh Province	11	3,547
			Liaoning Province	45	10,092
Tungyuan	188	15,776	Kirin Province	5	2,406
Zhuhai	42	11,301	Sinkiang Province	2	91
Kwangsi Province	15	2,983	Ningshia Province	2	430
Yunnan Province	1	50	Kansu Province	4	1,254
Kweichow	4	400	Heilungkiang Province	1	240
Shanghai	78	87,032			
Nanking	20	2,961	Harbin	2	100
Peking (Bejing)	30	25,029	Hainan Special Economic Zone	49	15,023
Tientsin	13	8,793			
Kiangsi Province	16	7,273	Others	188	7,846
Kiangsu Province	56	24,696	Total	2,503	753,915
Chekiang Province	56	14,851			
Anhwei Province	4	300			

Source: Same as Table 8.4.

9

AN INTEGRATED VIEW OF
POLICY EVOLUTION IN
TAIWAN

The thirty years, 1950–80, were a process of transition growth, the termination of colonialism, and the initiation of the epoch of modern economic growth. As the economy moved from the import substitution phase (1950–62) to the external orientation phase (1962–80), there was a conformable or accommodating evolution of economic policies. Since, by nearly all accounts, the development experience of Taiwan has been highly successful, the question naturally arises whether contemporary LDCs can learn from the policy experience of Taiwan. Are the policies transferable? Does the approach to policy formation apply to other cultures? My purpose in this chapter is therefore two-fold: to describe and analyze Taiwan's policy experience, and to consider how that experience can be helpful to other LDCs.

The art of economic policy making involves the use of a variety of market-related policy instruments (for example, foreign exchange rate, interest rate, monetary expansion rate). The exercise of these concrete policy instruments is predicated on the assumption that a social choice has already been made to accept at least the basic organizational features of the market mechanism. The policy experience of Taiwan becomes irrelevant when the market mechanism is rejected or neglected.

A clear-cut example is the contrast between Taiwan and mainland China. Both inherited the same traditional Chinese cultural heritage, and both claim Sun Yat-sen as a guiding force. Motivated·by different brands of political indoctrination, however, Taiwan and the mainland have employed institutions bearing drastically different organizational features. During the difficult years of the early 1950s, there was talk in certain circles of establishing a command economy in Taiwan, but such a move was resisted. Thus, while the mainland experimented with the collectivism of a planned (command) economy under Communism, Taiwan adopted a mixed economy, which, although tolerant of government interventions through a host of policy instruments, relies basically on private enterprise based on individual initiatives coordinated by a market mechanism.

The policy experience of Taiwan cannot be transferred easily to a command economy where overtly personalized political forces overwhelm the market forces. However, the policy experience of Taiwan can conceivably be transferred to the vast majority of contemporary LDCs, those that have not adopted a mixed economy in the transition process.

MIXED AND IDEALIZED MARKET ECONOMIES

Ideally, under free market institutions, the workers are motivated by higher wage income to work hard and to seek higher education, while the entrepreneurs are motivated by higher profits to take risks and to manage production efficiently. Through the rivalry of competition, the production potential of all market participants is fully unleashed while their greed and aggressiveness are curbed. They are all disciplined by market forces rather than by overtly personalized political forces.

An idealized market economy is thus a depoliticized system of organization, where the notion of an atomistic competition suggests the absence of any form of broadly defined collectivism (group-oriented actions)— be it a group of producers forming a monopoly, a group of workers forming a union, or, especially, a group of officials forming a government bureau that interferes with the operation of the market beyond the enforcement of competitiveness (for example, through anti-trust laws) to render the market fair and effective. An idealized market economy is not only an economic system regulating production, consumption, savings, and investment, but, intrinsically, it is also a welfare system based on the cardinal principle of "to each according to his production contribution" under "equality of opportunity" (the absence of any barrier, other than ability, to enter into any line of production, occupation, or educational institution).

Private property rights are an integral part of an idealized market economy. Given the universal desire for possession, the ownership of property is quite effective in inducing rivalry that is economically creative. Also, when individuals are busy minding their own business and tyrannical with respect to their own accounts, they are less likely to be tyrannical with respect to their fellow citizens in the political arena.

In the idealized (perfect) market economy, prices are the common language. In economic jargon, prices are the market signals, the market information, that perfectly illiterate farmers or workers can understand and can use to communicate with each other, allowing both to live a full economic life. Indeed, with this market language we can and do talk to strangers habitually and comfortably, just as foreign tourists use prices to talk to natives without much difficulty, as long as they can understand the price. Aside from an outright prohibition of exchange (in a trade embargo, for example), the destruction of this language — for example, through a distortion of the price system—by political force constitutes a major market imperfection.

A mixed economy is one that is neither a command economy, where prices are not explicitly used or are set by fiat, or an idealized market economy. This means that most non-Communist countries have mixed economies, with a wide range of nonmarket and market mixes. In a mixed economy, political force intervenes to distort at least some market prices, and an elimination of such distortions is a step in the liberalization process. By this criterion, the ROC government has taken major steps in the direction of liberalization.

LIBERALIZATION

Taiwan was not and is not a perfect market economy in the idealized sense just described. In fact, no country is, although Hong Kong has perhaps come closest. Indeed, it is true that, after over thirty years of moving toward a greater market orientation, the economy of Taiwan before the 1980s was still far from that of Japan or the United States, but it has changed since then.

What has been important in Taiwan's development has been the movement toward greater market orientation. From an evolutionary perspective, the policy experience of Taiwan shows that economic development benefits from a consistent and irrevocable trend of changes in the direction of a free market. This trend, ordinarily referred to as the liberalization of an economy, represents a process of depoliticizing the economic system, as the creative energies of the population are channeled increasingly through the market mechanism, and there is less and less political interference. A free market is not given in the social calculus. It must be constructed, slowly, through a process of changes in policy focus.

The economy of Taiwan has weathered the two oil crises of the 1970s and stabilized its structure with heavy dependence on trade. Total trade exceeded GNP. In the mid-1980s, gross national savings surpassed gross investment by a margin approaching 20%. The margin was a reflection of the trade surplus. Liberalization measures must be accelerated to ease the consequences, such as currency appreciation and inflationary pressure. As a result, the Taiwan economy would develop a greater dependence on the market mechanism.

In terms of methodology, the inductive evidence for our analysis of the liberalization movement is the set of policy measures adopted by the government in Taiwan since 1949. The major policies—over sixty of them—are presented, divided into ten areas, in the policy evolution chart in the appendix.

Liberalization as a Cumulative Process

Without exception, all major policy reforms converged on the path to a market-oriented economy, including the second rural land reform in 1981. The simultaneous depoliticizing of the economic system on all fronts should not be viewed as a sudden burst of the dam. Rather, it has been a slow but sure cumulative process that began with and accommodated the externally oriented growth phase that started in the early 1960s.

There must be good reasons for all this to have occurred in the short span of less than twenty years. It is one of my purposes to show that indeed there are good reasons, at least for a pragmatic people who attach a high value to gains in material well-being. It was this cultural pragmatism—an instinct to mind their own "economic business" and to survive—that historically has contributed to the growth of China's population into the largest single block of humans on earth.

Policy Areas

The policy evolution chart is divided into ten areas. Reforms in fiscal and monetary policies (the first four areas on the chart, including fiscal and trade policies, exchange rates, and interest rates) affect virtually all of the economy directly or indirectly, in terms of both the volume of transactions and the percentage of participants. These are the major policy areas.

Although these are not indicated on the chart, there have been two turning points: 1962, separating the import substitution and export orientation phases, and 1980, marking the initiation of a technology-oriented phase. The technology oriented phase is perhaps the last in the transition of an LDC into modern economic growth. It is always difficult to date turning points precisely, particularly in evolutionary transitions. The first, 1962, was chosen because a series of major policy reform measures had just been adopted, and a significant increase in exports followed.

For an LDC, the tax rate, interest rate, and foreign exchange rate—the three key instruments of policy in these areas—are intertwined with the money supply's growth rate. The power to create money is a monopoly of the government, and this prerogative is the most potent of all policy instruments. The relatedness of this quadruplet of rates in the liberalization experience of Taiwan will be the focal point of the economic analysis of this chapter.

Agricultural policies, human resources, and manpower policies deserve special mention because of the uniqueness of Taiwan's experience in these areas. Of all contemporary LDCs and NICS, Taiwan is exceptional in that considerable success was achieved early in the transition growth process—in the 1950s—with respect to agriculture's modernization, and this laid the foundation for later rapid growth. Taiwan's externally oriented growth after 1962 was based on the export of labor-intensive manufactured goods. Thus, both development and the utilization of human resources were important—in particular, the spread of fertility control practices and of vocational education.

Taiwan's experience in these two areas is instructive, although some of it was gained during the Japanese occupation. The government measures made the land more productive and promoted the building and improving of infrastructures over time. Such experiences are still useful for LDCs.

Taiwan, like Korea and Japan, has a cultural heritage that exalts education. This meant that it was relatively easy to develop economic agents, such as administrators and engineers, needed for modern economic growth. Such a heritage is not a sufficient condition for growth, since the mainland has the same tradition as Taiwan, and India has a large higher-education system. In India, the desire to go into white-collar work, particularly government service, has not been overcome, so the educational system is in some ways almost a drag on development. Taiwan faced this problem and found policies to overcome it.

Public enterprises, national construction, and international capital movements provide fertile grounds for government policy intrusions in countries with a colonial heritage. Liberalization in these areas involves a decreasing role for public enterprises and an increasing inflow of private, profit-seeking, foreign capital. In Taiwan, the government took over the island's major industries from the Japanese after the war. It sold the small and medium ones to the public because of the shortage of competent local managers and engineers during that time. Later, four big enterprises were transferred to private ownership under the land-to-the-tiller program. The government has always encouraged private investors to undertake the development of new industries. To the extent that public ownership is retained, the liberalizing trend is toward an approximation of the profit-motivated (or at least cost-based) provision of services. The ratio of private- to public-sector manufacturing grew from 43.6:56.6% in 1953, to 61.8:38.2% in 1966, to 79.8:20.2% in 1976, to 85.2:14.8% in 1986 and to 90:10% in 1991. Such a change is phenomenal.

Direct foreign investment includes not just capital but also management, technical, and marketing know-how. Openness to foreign capital is part of an international outlook, and goes beyond mere openness to foreign trade. Although the relative importance of a policy area is a matter of judgment, these two areas, public enterprises and international capital movements, are not as important as the four already discussed, as they do not affect as large a percentage of the population or volume of economic activity.

Science and technology are relatively new and undeveloped policy areas. This can be seen by the fact that the first entry on the chart is the creation in 1967 of a National Science Council, followed by the organization of the Chung Shan Institute of Science and Technology for the development of defense technology, also in 1967, and the merger of several applied industrial research institutes under the Ministry of Economic Affairs in 1970 into a semi-autonomous nonprofit corporate body, called the Industrial Technology Research Institute (ITRI), for research and development in applied technology to meet the needs of industrial development.

In 1976, under the leadership of Premier Chiang Ching-kuo, a committee at ministerial level was set up under myself, in my capacity as Minister of State, in order to coordinate the efforts of various ministries to develop applied science and technology not only in areas related to manufacturing and defense but also in areas related to transportation, communication, health, medicine, and the environment. In 1978, a national conference on science and technology, attended by representatives of government, academia, and industry, resulted in the formulation of a science and technology development program, which was approved by the Cabinet in May 1979; this was followed up by the Commission on Research, Development, and Evaluation and with government budget support.

Increasing attention has been paid to (1) the graduate programs in science and technology to provide high-level manpower, with emphasis on both quality and quantity; (2) the identification of major areas of technology, such as energy, material science, information science and technology, automation, electro-optics, biotechnology, hepatitis B prevention and control, and food technology; and (3) the need for ITRI to expand its research in electronics, mechanical engineering (automation), industrial materials, and energy. A new independent organization, the Institute for Information Industry, was organized in 1979 for the promotion of the information industry, the education and training of programmers and systems analysts, and applied software development. Since 1980, an "information week" has been held in the first week of December to carry out a series of activities that demonstrate how information is related to daily life, management, automation, and productivity. As part of the program, many activities are organized in principal cities from north to south of the island. The impact has been very great, particularly on the younger generation. As a result, the public has become more aware that the information age is coming and that they have to face the penetration of computers into every walk of life.

Of course, Taiwan has long sought to obtain technologies to improve productivity and profitability. In the early stages and less high-technology-oriented times, this was one reason for attracting foreign investment. In the early 1970s, the emphasis was laid on capital and technology-intensive industries. In the late 1970s, after two energy crises, more emphasis was placed on technology-intensive industries. In Hsinchu, a city fifty miles from Taipei where two technically oriented universities and ITRI are situated, a science-based industrial park was installed to attract new high-tech industries with an increasing research and development commitment. The park attracted foreign companies, and Chinese engineers and scientists trained abroad returned to set up their own businesses to produce new hi-tech products for marketing worldwide.

This area of science and technology has become important in its own right, both because of the worldwide stress on technology and because Taiwan has a vital need to attract back home those Chinese engineers who, having originally graduated from ROC universities, then went to the United States for advanced studies and settled there to work. The Science Park provides a natural opportunity for them to use their technical expertise in starting up their own businesses.

The area's late emergence also reflects the problem-oriented approach to policy formulation that has characterized the ROC government in Taiwan. Policies have appeared to solve visible problems or to resolve impending or actual conflicts. It was only in the late 1970s, as other countries with lower labor costs began to compete with Taiwan's traditional export products, that the need for Taiwan to upgrade the technological sophistication of its industrial structure became obvious. The promotion of technology-oriented science parks as a replacement for the more labor-intensive export processing zones, promotion of spending for research and development (including modest government expenditures), and the more rigorous enforcement of patent and trade-mark rights are all problem-solving policies. It is safe to predict that there will be many more policies in this area in the years ahead, as Taiwan's transition is completed and the economy moves into modern economic growth.

Liberalization in Taiwan

It is illuminating to look at the results of the liberalizing trend at the beginning of the 1980s, just after I became Minister without Portfolio. I shall discuss the events at the end for a pedagogical reason, namely to help demonstrate to the reader the extent to which liberalization has taken place. During the 1950s, 1960s, and 1970s, we did not always think of what we were doing as a liberalizing process. The main point is that there has been a long-term momentum toward liberalization.

Starting at the end of the policy evolution chart, for 1983 we saw the elimination of most quantitative import controls, the reduction of tariff protection, and the planned introduction of legislation to establish a value added tax (VAT), the form of taxation that least distorts prices. Taiwan's opening of its domestic market to foreign trade is another step in its integration into the world economy. The choice of VAT to replace the sales tax as a source of government revenue is consistent with openness to world prices. The VAT legislation was enacted and put into operation in April 1986. (The VAT is often attacked as regressive; in general, so are tariffs.)

The floating of the foreign exchange rate in 1978 was a major step in rationalizing Taiwan's foreign trade. In 1983, commercial banks were given the right to act as agents for buying and selling foreign exchange, ending the Central Bank's monopoly and making the exchange rate more fully reflective of market forces. In July 1987, foreign exchange was decontrolled. Capital movement was freed.

With regard to interest rates, the purpose of establishing a money market in 1976 was to promote the growth of a market for the demand and supply of loanable funds outside (that is, independent of) the commercial banking system, which was largely under government control. The new money market made it possible to have a rate of interest determined by the free play of market forces, a necessary prerequisite for liberalization of the controlled bank rates of interest. Bank rates were subsequently (in 1980) partially decontrolled, allowing banks some flexibility in determining interest rates when lending to bank customers.

The liberalization of these two crucial rates, the foreign exchange rate and the interest rate, was officially announced by the Central Bank to convey to the public the idea these rates would no longer be used as policy instruments and manipulated by political forces. This is not to deny the fact that, in practice, there has still been interference with the market mechanism in these areas, as, for example, when the oil crisis slowed growth significantly. It is safe to say, however, that the financial system is expected to move closer to a depoliticized system, characterized by a higher degree of Central Bank autonomy from government political pressure and by the automaticity of the market's adjustment mechanism.

In 1982, the Ministry of Economic Affairs, in the fact of continual losses by several government enterprises, decided to (1) merge the China Phosphate Company, the Taiwan Alkali Company, and the Caprolactam plant with the China Petrochemical Development Company; (2) shut down the Aluminum Company and transfer its newly installed sheet rolling mill to the well-managed China Steel Corporation; (3) shut down the Taiwan Metal Mining Corporation and transfer its newly installed copper melting furnace to the Taiwan Power Company, which is a consumer of copper cable. As a result of the merger, the China Petrochemical Development Company has turned out to be successful and profitable. The China Petrochemical Development Company has initiated new projects in the petrochemical field and has secured the necessary know-how by encouraging private foreign and domestic firms to acquire minority stakes in it.

The government has actively promoted joint ventures with foreign corporations. Earlier joint ventures were mostly between government enterprises and private foreign firms, for example, between the Taiwan Sugar Corporation and American Cyanamid to produce animal feeds and antibiotics, between the Chinese Petroleum Corporation and Allied Chemical and Mobil to manufacture urea, or between the Chinese Petroleum Corporation and Gulf Oil to produce lubricants and other oil products. In all of these, the foreign investor had a majority interest.

Still, for those with the mentality of the 1950s—glorification of public enterprise and resentment of the intrusion of private (former imperialist) Japanese capital—the events of the 1980s have been traumatic. All these policy innovations amounted to the abandonment of some highly treasured vested ideas, which were vaguely associated with a nationalism that could not withstand the onslaught of rationalism and the efficiency of an economy oriented toward a free market. This is, after all, consistent with the teachings of Dr. Sun Yat-sen that gave prominent recognition to individual initiative coordinated by the market mechanism.

MODERNIZATION OF THE AGRICULTURAL SECTOR

For LDCs with a large percentage of their population in agriculture, modernization of the agricultural sector is a prerequisite for successful industrialization. Positively, high agricultural productivity and farm income provide the industrial sector with a market for its production and with savings for investment. Negatively, as total population increases, a stagnant, traditional agricultural sector can no longer sustain additional labor on the land, which means that there is a rural-to-urban migration that aggravates the urban unemployment problem. Although the benefits of modernized agriculture are now quite clear, what is not so clear is how Taiwan managed to achieve considerable success in agricultural modernization in the early import-substituting years of the 1950s, a period when development planners and LDC governments were preoccupied with industrialization.

At least some of the credit for this early success must be given to Taiwan's colonial heritage. As a colony of food-deficient Japan, Taiwan benefited from an effort to promote the growth of farmers' organizations and to build an infrastructure, particularly irrigation systems. The geographic dispersion of the population and the high labor productivity of the colonial period provided Taiwan with a favorable foundation for its post-war modernization.

In particular, the large number of fairly good-sized urban areas spread over the island contributed to a spatially dispersed pattern of industrial location. This dispersal has meant that farmers have always been linked more firmly with the industrial sector in Taiwan than is the case for LDCs with large interior hinterlands (in this case, rural back-yards) lacking sizable cities. Farmers in the hinterland are isolated by distance and transportation costs from the forces of modernization, which are most observable in the large, usually coastal, urban centers. This situation changed when the economy moved toward export expansion, and industries had to be located closer to the harbor areas to accommodate international shipping routes. Taiwan's industries had been heavily concentrated in the north and the south until the construction of Taichung habor in central Taiwan and the completion of the North-South Expressway, then an industrial boom in the central Taiwan area began.

Taiwan initiated her transition growth process around 1950 with an agricultural background already quite conducive to the market orientation of small family farms. Given this favorable background, the government could launch agricultural modernization programs, with the cooperation of Chinese experts from the mainland and foreign experts, much more easily than other LDCs.

The much-heralded land reform of 1953 (especially the rent reduction and the land-to-the-tiller programs previously discussed) had a deep-rooted ideological origin in the teachings of Dr. Sun Yat-sen. In Taiwan, it was for a good, pragmatic reason—a circumstance entirely unanticipated more than thirty years earlier when Dr. Sun first presented his doctrine—that the program was finally carried out successfully.

In 1949 the mainland had been lost, and the government was faced with the responsibility of feeding an army as well as a rapidly expanding population. Food was in short supply. In 1950 the government adopted a rice-fertilizer barter program under which fertilizer produced in government-owned factories or imported from Japan was exchanged for rice. This approach killed two birds with one stone. On the one hand, modern inputs were injected into the farm sector without any commercial intermediation (such as the requirement of using cash or credit, or using a middle-man). On the other hand, the government, as a large buyer, solved a logistical problem—how to obtain rice for the army and civil servants—without legislating an agricultural tax system; the barter terms could be manipulated to achieve the same purpose more discretely during an inflationary period. Furthermore, by resorting to barter, the detrimental effects of highly volatile prices could be avoided. The system was abolished in 1973.

A land reform program motivated entirely by the political ideology of equity and fairness, as is often found in other LDCs, or of sympathy and hatred, as was the case in mainland China, can never be successful in the long run if population is stretching the land's capacity to provide employment and the goal is to increase agricultural well-being. Reform in Taiwan was a success for some twenty years, because it was based on the premise that giving the tiller title to the land was an incentive to produce more from it.

The Chinese peasant has a traditional lust for land; in that sense, Marx was right in thinking that peasants were the last bastion of the bourgeoisie. As land owners they were small-scale profit-seeking entrepreneurs. The land reform in Taiwan was a success because it appealed to the individual farmer's desire to improve his situation, motivating him to work as hard as possible on his land in order to earn the maximum amount of profit. This is, in reality, part of a process which might be described as making farmers into entrepreneurs or capitalists.

After farmers acquired their own land, they tilled it as intensively as possible. Because of the continuous improvement of irrigation systems, many paddyfields could yield two crops a year, each crop cycle requiring only 110 days. Farmers are now also able to grow one or two auxiliary crops, such as vegetables and beans. Some hardworking farmers even raise milk fish to the size of sardines in the paddy fields, becoming small entrepreneurs where abundant farm labor is available. In addition, the average multiple cropping index has increased substantially. The correctness of this interpretation has been demonstrated quite conclusively by the contrasting experience on the mainland. There, the damage done by ideologically-motivated collectivism and communization has belatedly been recognized by the Communist authorities, as can be seen by their current reliance on the *responsibility system*, as well as the downplaying of the role of large communes.

In Taiwan, the individualism of land reform has led to a flourishing agricultural sector, where the farmers are very sensitive to market signals (prices) and have responded to price incentives by diversifying products and increasing productivity with the help of various agricultural experiment stations. Indeed, the story of the early success of Taiwan's externally oriented drive, starting in 1962, can be told more in terms of a wave of new export cash crops (mushrooms and asparagus) for the canning industry in addition to the traditional canned pineapple than of manufactured products. The policy experience of Taiwan—

land reform followed by external orientation—has shown that when the "prices are right", farmers can take care of themselves, show flexibility and market sensitivity, and produce wave after wave of new products: for example, bananas, pineapple, pork, fish, and shrimp.

On the other hand, in the early 1950s, both Chinese land reformers, and their American advisors thought that improvement of the farmers' livelihood, both as a means of raising productivity and promoting fairness, should be a starting point in Taiwan's economic development. They were never concerned with the possibility that reform might turn farmers into capitalists, and probably few of them thought of this as a consequence.

Indeed, the notion of making farmers into small capitalists was probably an alien one to all those who advocated land reform on moralistic, ideological grounds in the early postwar years. The experience in Taiwan has shown, however, that this is precisely the source of success. The first key to agricultural modernization is making the farmers into modern economic agents, in effect making them responsive to market demand through price signals. The second key lies in the active interaction and linkage of the sector with the nonagricultural sector from which the farmers acquire not only modern fertilizers, insecticides, seeds, and tractors, but also a stream of consumer goods—particularly durables such as refrigerators, radios, television sets, bicycles, and motorcycles—and such notions as the use of bank accounts.

Efforts to transform farmers into small capitalists have been, in the end, strongly supported by policymakers for two reasons. First, the rationalization of farm operations has raised farm income; second, farmers have spent much of this extra income on domestic manufactures, helping to create a market for domestic industries. Indeed, this process has been shown to be one of the most important factors behind Taiwan's success.

It is by no means stretching the term to refer to farmers, in Taiwan or anywhere else, as capitalists. This was precisely the original meaning of the word as used by Adam Smith at the beginning of the Industrial Revolution in the late 18 Century. To Smith, a capitalist was a profit-seeking farmer, renting land from landlords and hiring laborers. This group played a crucial role in the modernization of the agricultural sector in England and helped start the Industrial Revolution. There is evidence that the agricultural sector in Taiwan is moving in the same direction: away from the family farming system.

Dr. Sun, who put so much emphasis in his teachings on the preservation of traditional Chinese cultural values, certainly would have been the last to deny that the time-honored Chinese virtue of land ownership is conducive to the requirement of modern economic growth. Indeed, although his teachings were not cast in terms of making farmers into small entrepreneurs, the terms in which they were cast would inevitably lead to the same end result, as can be seen from an evolutionary perspective. In particular, his teachings allow for the private ownership of property (land, capital, and consumer durable goods) that accommodates and accounts for a significant part of the drive to accumulate wealth. This drive encourages the use of human energy for something that is creative, rather than harmful as is the case when the energy is wasted in other dimension of social/political activity.

Technological evolution in agriculture during the early years consisted of an increase in such inputs as new fertilizers, seeds, insecticides, and irrigation. Also important were the improvement of services, the reorganization of farmers' associations to provide credit more efficiently, and the provision of agricultural extension services such as home economics, family planning, and training in cultivation methods. Technological evolution took a decided turn toward mechanization around 1970. "Tractor or no tractor" was an ideological issue on the mainland in the days of the Cultural Revolution; in Taiwan, the appearance of farm mechanization was a pragmatic response to a shortage of labor and concomitant higher wages due to industrialization. With the continued outflow of rural labor to the industrial and urban sector (primarily to produce labor-intensive manufactured exports), it became cheaper to use machines in agriculture, that is, to substitute capital for labor.

The experience of Taiwan shows that the timing of major reforms has its own evolutionary logic quite independent of ideology but not in conflict with it. A farm mechanization program launched too early can be as costly as one launched too late. The market mechanism provides the clearest guidance of when mechanization will increase efficiency. An ideologically oriented reform often makes timing mistakes because it ignores the signals or is motivated by goals considered larger than people's actual well-being. Such timing errors have proven costly economically and disruptive socially and politically.

The second land reform in late 1980 was necessitated by the success of the first and by the growth of the nonagricultural sector. In other words, the first land reform divided the land into smaller tracts allocated to the tillers. While the land was more productive, the farm family size also increased. As education became popular, most of the children of school age went to school and later on either continued their studies or became gainfully employed in industry, with earnings quite substantial compared with farmers' income. Mechanization was introduced, making it more economical to enlarge the tract size for each farmer. Some farm families whose children did very well left their farms but did not want to sell them. Nor could they lease the land to their neighbors for fear of violating the law. Thus, the second rural land reform was instituted to enlarge the landholding scale in conformity with mechanization needs. There was a hiatus of about ten years. I have suggested that some of the articles contained in the current Agricultural Development Statute be modified or new ones be added in order to better accommodate the changing conditions of rapid industrialization.

While the first land reform was aimed at the improvement of land productivity, the second reform was targeted specifically at improving efficiency or, in other words, at raising manpower productivity. The second reform was the direct outcome of a study I made in 1967 to compare farm productivity in Taiwan with that in the United States. The study showed that although land in Taiwan was eight times more productive than U.S. farmland, the American farmer was eight times more productive than his Taiwanese counterpart. The second reform has centered on promoting joint management and land consolidation by combining previously fragmented tracts so that they are more amenable to mechanized farming methods.

The second reform attempted to make farmers more productive within the context of rapid industrialization, a situation that Dr. Sun could hardly have imagined during his lifetime. The first land reform is rightly credited to Dr. Sun, the founding father of the Republic; the second reform could not happen in mainland China because industrialization there could not move as fast as in Taiwan in two decades. If anything, the second land reform appears somewhat contrary to the land-to-the-tiller tenet of Dr. Sun's teachings as interpreted in the early postwar years. Joint management and cultivation by machines of farms owned by several families implies that much of the cultivation (plowing, seeding, transplanting, harvesting, and marketing) can be divorced from the land owners and even from tenants. Sooner or later this will happen. Already, there are farmers organized to cultivate on a contractual basis even for resident owners. An evolutionary interpretation of Dr. Sun's teaching certainly emphasized efficiency orientation in this age of economic liberalization.

Taiwan's experience in agricultural has not, of course, been without problems and mistakes. The government started to guarantee rice prices in 1974, partly because of a rice shortage in 1973 and partly because of price inflation during the first oil crisis. This clearly constituted a counter-liberalizing move that has distorted prices and the balance between demand and supply, but it is a policy which has been practiced by almost all industrially advanced countries. This socialized program to narrow down the income gap between rural and urban workers has been costly, leading to the accumulation of surplus rice that fills warehouses and which has been sold on world markets at prices that other countries call dumping. This policy replaced the rice-fertilizer barter program, which initially had been a tax on agriculture but which had, through the years, become a subsidy for farmers. Price support programs for agriculture are normally considered a necessary evil in "mature" economies. Taiwan's drift toward price supports created a persistent surplus of rice and reached a turning point in 1984 with the introduction of a six-year program to encourage the conversion of paddyland to the growing of fruits and vegetables, corn, soybeans, and even fodder for dairy cows in order to alleviate the burgeoning rice surplus. In recent years, however, the appearance of a tendency for increasing agricultural protection testifies against the success of Taiwan's development in the past, leading to the emergence of social and economic problems typical of the advanced industrial countries.

It is expected, with a great possibility of being a full member of GATT in the early 1990s, that the ROC will liberalize its agricultural sector further.

KEY POLICY INSTRUMENTS

The import substitution approach to industrialization used by Taiwan and by other former overseas territories centered on the use of the quadruplet of major policy instruments—the money supply growth rate, the tax rate, the interest rate, and the foreign exchange rate—to achieve two purposes. First, they were used to promote industrialization, specifically, the growth of industries producing consumer goods that were previously imported. This was done through profit creation for domestic import-substituting businesses. Second, they were used to create revenue for the government. These two purposes, creating profits and creating revenues, are political acts. Indeed, the import substitution strategy represented an import political-economic decision to minimize our dependence on foreign assistance, create more jobs, and produce consumer goods for the market. Profits earned by the import substitution industries made possible the expansion of facilities to produce exports as well as intermediate goods, setting the wheel of capital formation turning smoothly.

Import substitution and export orientation properly are approaches to development that evolved more or less ad hoc, the former in the 1950s and the latter in the 1960s. They have come to be called strategies because they have been studied, formalized in models, and consciously applied. In this discussion, I have tried to use *approach* when talking about the actual process in Taiwan, and *strategy* when discussing the more formalized, generalized concepts, which generally postdate Taiwan's experience with them.

The key to understanding the economic and political aspects of the import substitution strategy is inflation. It was common to almost all the LDCs adopting import substitution. In the period 1950–70, while the industrially advanced countries (the major trading partners of most LDCs) enjoyed considerable price stability, the opposite was true for LDCs as a group. This is an important contrast. Although one can say, with justification, that the worldwide inflation of the 1970s was imported into the LDCs (that is, propagated and transmitted from outside), no such assertion can be made for the two earlier decades.

In the 1950s and 1960s, the monetary experiences in most LDCs, including Taiwan, demonstrated quite conclusively the fallacy of the so-called import cost-push thesis for domestic price inflation. Notwithstanding the blame heaped on the industrialized countries for their inflation, the LDCs created the problems of price inflation during this period themselves. Indeed, this internally-generated inflation was a crucial and integral part of the political aspect of the import substitution strategy.

The unique policy experience of Taiwan is that its government, with an almost single-minded dedication, directed its attention to bringing inflation under control in the early import substitution years (the 1950s). With several reforms in monetary and fiscal policies, and with the help of foreign aid, inflation was brought under control by the late 1950s, before the country launched its externally oriented drive. Taiwan enjoyed a period of considerable price stability through the early years of externally oriented growth (1962–71). Indeed, Taiwan's very rapid growth with low inflation during the 1960s has rarely been matched by any country at any time.

Even during the period of worldwide inflation in the 1970s, inflation in Taiwan occurred in short spurts, interspersed with longer periods of relative price stability. Taiwan was not an exception to overall inflation in the 1970s, the rate being greater than that of the 1960s (the average annual rate reached as high as 8.9%). Although greater than in the industrially advanced countries, price increases were not as sustained or as institutionalized as in some Latin American countries.

A truly valuable, transferable lesson from Taiwan's experience is the persistent effort on the part of policymakers to watch for every sign of impending price inflation and to stay alert to its danger. "Growth with stability", a slogan first popularized in the 1950s when these two considerations were equally important, became a rallying point for all citizens in the inflationary period of the 1970s. Many countries are haunted by memories of their own inflationary experiences. For Taiwan, this nightmare has been firmly associated with the even more painful memory of the loss of the mainland. In the absence of the disposition, acquired at the cost of bitter experience, to regard inflation as a prime social evil, inflation almost always creeps back as a political expedient. Taiwan's resistance to such temptation has been relatively strong, which differentiates it from other LDCs using import substitution as a development strategy. During the past thirty years of my involvement in government, I found out that rigid budgetary control has been observed by all the premiers I served under.

The Cause of Inflation During Import Substitution

It is difficult to analyze the import substitution strategy without a correct diagnosis of the cause of price inflation in LDCs. Although, in the short run, a cost-push explanation (be it a domestic wage push or an import cost push) may have some validity, the only feasible explanation of a sustained and severe long-term inflation is a monetary one. This is almost by definition. In the long run, a rate of growth in the money supply far in excess of the GNP growth rate is both a necessary and sufficient condition for price inflation, and this is recognized by most economists and policymakers whether or not they consider themselves monetarists.

Thus, to control inflation it is necessary to curb the money supply growth rate. This is difficult because of the popularity of an expansionary policy. Creating money is a convenient way to solve several types of social and economic problems, where the alternative remedies are more painful and thus are likely to be politically unpalatable. This means governments sensitive to public sentiment are particularly vulnerable.

From the politician's standpoint, the fact that inflation muddles the language of relative prices that allows people to communicate (to allocate goods and services rationally) is too often a desired outcome, a means of obscuring the effects of other policies. At the individual level, the popularity of an expansionary monetary policy can be traced in part to an erroneous generalization by society as a whole of the pleasantness of the personal experience of having a plentiful supply of money. How easy to accept a cost-push explanation, seemingly consistent with personal experience: my costs go up, I raise my prices. How easy to miss the effects of monetary expansion because of the time lag between the expansion and the impact on prices. If, with every pleasant puff of a cigarette, cancer cells appeared immediately in the lungs, fewer people would smoke. It is easy to be blinded by time lags.

With the appearance of Keynesian orthodoxy in the postwar world, the matter became much worse. Money creation has since been regarded, professionally and authoritatively, as a meritorious act. Something of value was being created: a liquid asset that lowered the rate of interest and thus the cost of investment. For a noneconomist, not baptized in Keynesianism, it was probably easier to recognize how ridiculous it is to believe that the real cost of borrowing could be kept artificially low for long simply because the government monopolized the power of the printing press. The total cost to society, if not to the specific borrower, includes more than the nominal interest paid when the borrowed money is manufactured by the monetary authorities rather than real savings.

For LDCs, it is not necessary to make a fine distinction between the two components of M1 (currency in circulation and demand deposits in commercial banks) because in most LDCs the central bank is not independent. When the central bank is not insulated from the rest of the government, M1 can be controlled through political pressure.

For the LDCs, the creation of money must be viewed directly and obviously as the manufacturing of purchasing power by the printing press. Few, including professional economists struggling with concepts such as medium of exchange and store of value, are willing to acknowledge that this purchasing power creation is singularly the most powerful instrument the government of a sovereign state possesses in the economic arena. With it, the government can acquire any amount of goods and services from the market, there being no need for exercising eminent domain. As long as the market participants must use money as a common language, as the medium of exchange for impersonal communication between strangers, a dollar printed is just as potent in acquiring goods and services as a dollar earned.

Monetary Expansion and Taxation

Any experience with hyperinflation during a long war, such as in China during the war against Japan and the Communists, demonstrates that total resource mobilization can be achieved without taxation by consent. When a government incurs a budget deficit, monetary creation and price inflation are parts of the mechanism for a covert form of taxation transferring income from those providing goods and services to the government. A government resorting to the expedient of the printing press because of a war emergency allows little time for the design of an equitable and efficient tax system where the burden of taxation can be assessed, negotiated, debated, and openly imposed by the legislature.

Although the implicit and ambiguous burden sharing of war inflation can be, and usually is, tolerated when national survival is at stake, it is amazing that many contemporary LDCs resort to the same convenience without a war emergency. There is simply an absence of desire to make the tax burden too explicit, to open it to debate, or to abandon the power and convenience of the government being able to create its own purchasing power. Thus we see that inflation in LDCs is generally symptomatic of the evasion and postponement of a vital responsibility of the government, an evasion typically tolerated by a social consensus. Fortunately, this was not the case in Taiwan.

For former colonies relying on primary exports, tariff revenue usually accounts for the largest share of total government revenue. This is because of the point specificity of the method of collection—tariffs are collected in a limited number of places (ports) on fairly identifiable items—which is a convenience for administration. Tariffs are also a basic policy instrument for excluding foreign products from the domestic market, thereby protecting the infant import substitution industries. There is thus a commonality of interest between the revenue-hungry government and the protection craving infant manufacturer in the use of a high tariff wall as a crucial component of import substitution.

Taiwan adopted a high protective tariff as well as import controls in 1952 as part of a strategy of initiating transition growth with an unmistakable import substitution strategy. Because governments face demands for spending that generally exceed easily raised revenue, tariff revenue is rarely adequate, and other means must be sought to deal with deficits. In Taiwan in the 1950s, the inflow of foreign aid mitigated the use of inflation. There has been an impressionistic, sometimes malicious, assertion that the success of Taiwan is all attributable to foreign aid. The underlying ideological conviction is that a long and steady injection of resources into the domestic economy through foreign aid is essential for rapid capital accumulation in LDCs. The experience of Taiwan, although cited as proof, is, in fact, a counter example of such a simplistic, almost romantic, notion. It nonetheless persists in the current, interminable, north-south dialogue. Quite simply, the foreign aid that flowed to Taiwan was not used for the kind of capital accumulation advocated today.

In the case of Taiwan, foreign aid played an important historical role by plugging the government budget gap and thus helping to combat inflation. The economic aid program included important agricultural commodities as raw material for processing industries, project-financed machinery and equipment such as power plants and fertilizer plants, and technical assistance for incoming specialists and outgoing trainees in different fields. All of the aid dollars (except those for technical assistance) were converted into local currency and deposited in a special account called a counterpart fund in the Bank of Taiwan. The funds were later used to finance local-currency projects, as grants for agriculture and education and loans to public and private enterprises. Thanks to cooperation between U.S. and ROC officials and the assistance of experts in different fields, the aid money was most efficiently used. In view of the ROC's huge military budget, it remains an open question just how much economic aid Taiwan received on a per capita basis. (The division of total aid into the military and economic sectors is not a straightforward calculation.) Initial aid came to Taiwan strictly as emergency aid, on a temporary basis. Such sustained programs as shipments of food under PL 480 had as much to do with domestic American farm policy as Taiwan's need. The role of aid declined steadily from the mid-1950s and was consciously phased out in the 1960s. In the late 1950s, the government, realizing that something had to be done to increase savings as the source of accelerated capital formation and committed to improving the investment climate and encouraging saving and investment, initiated such self-help measures as the nineteen-point economic reform. This paved the way for the eventual phasing out of U.S. economic aid. In 1965 Taiwan became one of the first graduates from the foreign aid program.

The lesson that can be learned from Taiwan is that—with the exception of an emergency, such as a destructive earthquake, flood, or drought—foreign aid in the sense of an open-ended, long-range commitment of resource transfer is not needed after a time. Such commitments violate the sound principle of self-help, which is, after all, a cardinal moral principle of the market-oriented economy. Moreover, the habit of dependence on hand-outs from foreigners violates the principle of self-respect just as much as the habitual dependence of manufacturers on protected markets and government subsidies. When C. K. Yen became Minister of Finance in 1950, he made every effort to compile a preliminary budget with the Controller General of the Budget, and he obtained the agreement of the Taiwan Provincial Government to provide tax revenues to the central government. These finances were supplemented with gold bars, some brought over from the mainland and some borrowed from the commercial banks. The aid-generated counterpart fund in local currency also provided a source of funding for construction projects, both civilian and military. The budget, once established, steadily improved because of the amendment of various tax laws.

With foreign aid and with self-help through the establishment of the consolidated income tax system in 1955, inflation was brought under control in Taiwan in the late 1950s. This led to another policy landmark, when, in 1961, the government deficit was brought under control. In 1964 there was a surplus. From that point on, a new era of fiscal responsibility began in Taiwan, as subsequent budget surpluses acted as inflation absorbers. A rationalization of the income tax system occurred in 1970. When a small budget deficit appeared in 1982, the government's immediate response was to curb expenditures and think in terms of another round of tax reform in the long run.

Rejection of the principle of relying on the printing press can be seen from another angle. When there is not a clear separation of power between the finance ministry and the central bank—that is, when there is little or no central bank autonomy, as was the case in most other LDCs and in Taiwan during its early post-war years—there is always the temptation and the possibility for the government to create purchasing power by what amounts to the printing of money. The government can simply order the central bank to buy government bonds. This was the method used in the 1940s to finance the war against Japan and then against the Communists. The Central Bank Governor could not say "no" to the Finance Minister, because frequently both positions were held by the same person and in each capacity subject to dismissal. Thus, development of an independent central bank is a virtual necessity for achieving fiscal responsibility. In Taiwan, this step was taken in 1974, when commercial banks were no longer required to cash government bonds held by the nonbank public prior to maturity. This meant that the banking system was no longer required to support the price of government bonds. Thus, since 1974 the Finance Ministry has had to borrow from savers rather than resort to the printing press if the budget is not in balance.

In reality, the current account of the government budget has always been in surplus. It was for capital-account purposes that borrowing was required. During my term as Minister of Finance, I presented a bill providing for the issuing of medium- and long-term bonds of up to 25% of the current budget, with interest and borrowing terms depending on market conditions, instead of promulgating an annual statute for the issuance of bonds. The Legislative Yuan still exercises the power of reviewing the annual budget and limiting the amount of borrowing during any given year.

Taiwan's experience shows that fiscal reforms (tax legislation) and monetary reforms (moving toward central bank autonomy) are major evolutionary steps toward government responsibility. What underlies both reforms is a rejection of the insanity of relying on the printing press to create purchasing power for the government to use in an effort to solve socioeconomic problems. The avoidance of the use of political power to create money signifies a depoliticizing of the economy in a most fundamental way.

Monetary Expansion and the Interest Rate

Even though an expansionary monetary policy is an unwarranted convenience for the government, it is a welcome blessing for big businesses that can borrow from the commercial banking system. Although these businessmen may not know the full theoretical implications of an expansionary monetary policy, they are aware of the advantage to themselves of a low interest rate. Rates can be suppressed to an artificially low level only by money creation or credit rationing. Money creation leads to inflation, which makes the debt cheaper to pay off. This is the main reason why an expansionary monetary policy is popular in powerful segments of the business community: they expect inflation to bail out their borrowing. The victims of the inflation often do not know they are being taken advantage of, and they may actually support an expansionist monetary policy.

In Taiwan, large enterprises with better book-keeping and accounting systems can more easily obtain credit from the commercial banks. To meet the needs of small and medium enterprises, I recommended that the government set up a Credit Guarantee Fund for small and medium enterprises to guarantee loans to them from the commercial banks, with the Fund compensating the banks if the enterprises failed to repay the loans. Thanks to Fund assistance, the volume of such loans has expanded dramatically.

Since 1980, the government has encouraged industries and investors to invest in high-technology products and to improve productivity by installing automation and pollution-control equipment. The government's Development Bank offers low-interest, medium-term credits as an instrument to promote further industrialization.

For the LDCs, it would have been far better for the interest rate to have been regarded as an integral part of the market mechanism and not as a policy instrument that could promote growth. When the government resorts to a suppression of the interest rate by monetary expansion, the supply of savings will not flow into the commercial banking system, as savers become wise to the fact that putting their money into time deposits usually implies an inflationary loss. When this occurs, the financial system will have to fund investment demand by monetary expansion; voluntary savings are not sufficient to meet the demand.

An artificially low interest rate is comparable to a narcotic: once started, however innocently, it inevitably is succeeded by ever-increasing doses. A remedy for high inflation rates is a high interest rate policy to restore equilibrium. This was what the U.S. Federal Reserve had come to realize under Chairman Volckev.

Although it is not widely known, even in the circles of professional economists and policymakers, Taiwan adopted a high interest rate policy in the early 1950s to combat inflation, and it demonstrated the policy's effectiveness. The experiment antedated the monetarist experiment in the United States by some twenty-five years. Haunted by the fear of price inflation, the government of Taiwan shifted to the high interest rate policy after listening to the advice of professional economists who were steeped in the pre-war monetary orthodoxy of the Swedish school, which meant that by contemporary Keynesian standards they were "conservative". This tradition holds that deviations of the politically allowed rate of interest from the natural rate (the equilibrating rate) are usually a direct cause of price inflation.

With monetary and fiscal conservatism and foreign aid, inflation was brought under control in Taiwan by the late 1950s, and the 1960s were a period of price stability (as they were in most industrially advanced countries, but not in most LDCs). The same high interest rate strategy was employed again in 1973–74 when, as in many other countries, inflation surged. The monetary authorities of most countries, industrially advanced and less developed, found the political pressure so unbearable or the Keynesian ideology so entrenched, that they resisted higher interest rates. Fearing factory shutdowns, unemployment, and bankruptcies, they succumbed to a policy of money creation. The policy, however, did not arrest the growth slowdown, did not solve the unemployment problem, and did not prevent factory shutdowns. But it did bring double-digit inflation.

The government of Taiwan did make a well-publicized concession to popular demand by temporarily lowering the interest rate. But even while continuing to mouth the low-interest rate orthodoxy and blaming the import-cost push for the inflation, the authorities quietly adopted a policy of tight money whenever inflationary pressures became intense. This is another example of the pragmatism of the policymakers, who say the "good" thing while doing the "right" thing. It was during the late 1970s that the central bank was gradually made autonomous, so that it could be insulated from political pressure to pursue monetary expansion. During the 1970s Taiwan did not escape inflation mainly due to two oil crises. In fact, prices increased at an average annual rate of up to 8.9%. But actions were taken to reduce the level of each surge, so that such high rates were not sustained.

Monetary Expansion and the Foreign Exchange Rate

In a primary-product exporting economy, inflation through monetary expansion is always intertwined with the foreign exchange rate, which is a crucial component of the import substitution strategy. This is because the exchange rate is almost universally regarded as a policy instrument rather than an equilibrating market price regulating the level of imports and exports. In such an economy, an overvaluation of the domestic currency by the official exchange rate benefits the import substitution manufacturing class, and amounts to an implicit tax on producers of exported products. Again, through the exercise of political power, windfall profits are transferred from the rural, primary-product producing sector and from consumers to the urban, manufacturing sector. The producer of import substitutes can buy imported raw materials and capital goods at artificially low prices and sell the finished product behind a tariff wall at artificially high prices.

The politically and artificially created cheapness of foreign exchange makes it so attractive to import at the official exchange rate that two types of problems are generated. First, available foreign currency must be rationed. This means it is allocated by a political process: import licenses, quantitative restrictions on imports, and the use of different exchange rates for different categories of goods. Second, the artificial prices lead to black marketing and smuggling. Although lawlessness cannot be condoned, here the propensity is politically created.

As domestic price inflation continues, the official foreign exchange rate is usually devalued periodically to correct partially for excessive overvaluation. The pace of devaluation, however, usually lags behind the domestic inflation rate, so that the external purchasing power of the domestic currency is always manipulated to be higher than its internal purchasing power. This clearly violates even crude versions of the theory of purchasing power parity.

With inflation in the background, the government is usually hesitant about deciding to devalue. If there is a devaluation, the government certainly would be accused of aggravating domestic inflation, because prices of imported products would immediately rise in terms of domestic currency. Such a directly visible consequence is politically unpalatable, particularly when the price increases will apply to many items of mass consumption, such as oil. If the government does not devalue, continued domestic inflation means an increasing degree of overvaluation, which makes imports ever more attractive. A temporary advantage in avoiding political unpopularity is obtained only at the cost of postponing the day of reckoning.

This very hesitancy over whether to devalue strengthens the false belief that domestic inflation is caused by the import-cost push.

Attention is diverted from the fundamental issue: it is excessive monetary expansion that is feeding the inflation. In this way, a controlled exchange rate goes hand in hand with monetary expansion. The government actually creates for itself a complicated set of problems requiring administrative controls that could have been avoided in the first place. Interfering with the market inevitably necessitates an administrative, inherently political, system to replace the market and correct or compensate for the problems created by the interference. The complexity of such policies usually comes at great cost to real development and efficient allocation of resources.

Even with an import substitution strategy with overvalued foreign exchange rates, there is a limit as to how hard primary producers (the earners of foreign exchange) can be squeezed. Depressed profits to the producers discourage production and thus decrease what is available for export. This can exacerbate problems in other areas, as the labor that otherwise would be producing export products is laid off and has to seek work in areas where its marginal productivity is less. It would be much simpler to control inflation directly by paying attention to its root causes and to let the exchange rate float.

Taiwan's shortage of natural resources proved to be a blessing. The exploitation of primary-product exports reached a limit in the late 1950s, necessitating an alternative approach. It was soon realized, that although there were limited natural resources to export, there was abundant labor whose output could be exported.

When the internally oriented import substitution growth phase gave way to the externally oriented growth phase, the exchange rate as a policy instrument went through a drastic change in orientation. Although it was consistently overvalued during import substitution, during the externally oriented phase it might occasionally be undervalued. This undervaluation contributed to the emergence of export surpluses in the 1970s. The undervaluation and the surplus were both the result of political interference with the economic system, with certain detrimental effects. The implication of the undervaluation and surplus is that domestic savings were not used to finance domestic capital accumulation, but were used instead for overseas investment (capital export) or the accumulation of foreign exchange reserves that have little growth effect. The appearance of export surpluses generated domestic monetary expansion, which then became a principal cause of inflation. In the 1980s, Taiwan is still in the process of formulating policies to neutralize monetary expansion from this source. Undervaluation and overvaluation of the exchange rate occurred in the decade of the 1970s and afterwards because of the two oil crises and the recovery from them.

Why the Republic of China maintains sizable foreign exchange reserves requires some explanation. Although Taiwan's burgeoning reserves may seem unnecessary from the economist's point of view, they appear otherwise in the light of unfavorable international political conditions, such as the withdrawal of the Republic of China from the United Nations in October 1971 and the breaking of diplomatic relations with a number of countries during the 1970s, including the United States in 1979. All these events served to isolate us from many international organizations, particularly financial institutions. As a consequence, we have been forced to become more conservative. If we are to secure international financing for major industrial and infrastructural projects, we must maintain a sound fiscal condition and a substantial cushion of international reserves.

We have adopted policies for the continuous expansion of trade to maintain steady growth of the economy and a low unemployment rate. These policies, in turn, have resulted in an expansion of substantive relations with Western European countries. The very fact that practically all developed countries in Europe have set up trade and cultural exchange offices in Taipei since 1980 attests to the international recognition that these policies have received.

In the early 1950s, there was indeed a serious shortage of foreign exchange. Thanks to import substitution, supplemented with U.S. aid, the foreign exchange situation gradually improved. However, the notion that foreign exchange is a precious commodity has been deeply rooted in the minds of the government and the public. Even with the continuous trade expansion, I still encounter newspaper articles mentioning the preciousness of foreign exchange. I have coined a new term for this phenomenon—"economic jet lag"—and its effects on an economy are similar to those of the more familiar jet lag on one's body clock. In the process of economic development, certain sectors always move more rapidly, while others may be slower. At their worst, conceptual lags of this type can distort the workings of an entire economic system.

Taiwan, like many other LDCs, used an import substitution approach in the initial stages of transitional growth. However, because of the island's scarcity of natural resources, the experiment was cut short and, judging from the way the four major policy instruments were employed, was not as extensive as in other LDCs. What determines the magnitude of the impact of government intervention is the rate of monetary expansion, intertwined with the interest rate, the tax rate, and the foreign exchange rate. On the positive side, the high interest rate policy adopted by the government in the early 1950s was a success and was recognized as such by international experts. On the negative side, since domestic prices were still rising rapidly during the first half of the 1950s, the authorities managed foreign exchange reserves so as to depreciate our currency. Under the regulations, imports enjoyed a fixed rate of NT$24 to US$1, and exports (mostly commodities like rice, sugar, and salt produced by government agencies and government enterprises) received a rate of between NT$15 and NT$18 to US$1, which was much lower than the rate paid by the importers. The difference in the rates used by importers and exporters had to be surrendered to the treasury as government revenue. This policy was actually unfavorable to both import substitution industries and export industries; the only beneficiaries were straight importers.

The renouncing of the exercise of political power to manufacture purchasing power through money creation lies behind the mild form of import substitution. This is the approach used in Taiwan, in sharp contrast to some Latin American countries. This renouncing was part of the liberalization movement—a trend toward the more restrained exercise of power. The depoliticizing of the economic system in Taiwan implies that the government gradually learned to be more responsible, and open, about what it was doing. Implicit taxes and covert transfers of income were replaced by explicit and overt ones that were more equitable and efficient.

For the government to abjure monetary expansion, it must forego certain powers and accept certain responsibilities. In fiscal (taxation) policy, it means rejecting the printing press as a source of revenue and adopting a more visible taxation system.

In monetary policy, ceasing to suppress the interest rate through monetary expansion reduces income transfers to the small number of firms able to borrow from the commercial banking system, and it opens up more opportunities for middle- and small-sized firms. Floating the exchange rate also eliminates a source of covert income transfer and increases the efficiency of resource allocation.

LIBERALIZATION THROUGH EXTERNAL ORIENTATION

The liberalization movement in Taiwan after 1962 has a domestic and a foreign dimension. Domestically, the movement implies a reduction of government controls to permit a greater play of market forces as well as to accelerate the growth of savings and investment. To the outside world, liberalization means an opening up of the economy with respect to trade and finance, with an orientation toward what can be called an internationalization of the market mechanism, an economic integration with the rest of the world. In both dimensions, liberalization implies a greater role for market forces and less resort to government fiat, with government providing the proper climate for growth.

It is well known that an external orientation includes efficiency orientation in a dynamic sense. When domestic entrepreneurs are subject to the rigors of international competition—that is, when they compete in world markets that recognize only the merits of quality and price— they become more efficient as production managers and risk takers in the context of a learning-by-doing process.

This dynamism warrants being stressed for several reasons. First, international competition is characterized by less government control than is found in most domestic economies. A situation in which one producer dominates the local market may warrant watching by domestic antitrust agencies but is much more likely to be competitive in the international arena. The more open an economy is to world trade, the more foreign competition helps control domestic antitrust problems attributable to sheer size and market share.

Under the import substitution strategy, the sheltering of domestic manufacturers by political means helped instill an intense fear of competition. It is one of those vicious circles of underdevelopment that the fear generated under political protection in turn generates demand for the very political patronage that created the fear in the first place. Thus, to open an economy to international competition can only be a slow process, because it must work against the intertwining of vested ideas (including deep-rooted fear) and vested interests.

Initially, the fear is of competition in both the domestic and international markets. With experience in world markets during the external orientation phase, the latter fear is allayed. Success of domestic producers following the opening of the domestic market ultimately allays the former fear as well. This is not to say that producers like the competition, only that they cease to be afraid of it.

Tariff Rebates and Export Processing Zones

The general principle of trade liberalization aims at the creation of an environment in which international prices prevail in the domestic market and guide the free flow of goods and services across national geographic boundaries. This ideal state of affairs is desirable not only for its consistency with static optimum resource allocation, but also for its conduciveness to progress through competition, that is, dynamic efficiency. Because tariff protection and trade embargoes are the major barriers to trade erected during the import substituting years, policies promoting free trade take shape primarily in the field of fiscal (tax) policy. This relates to the need to replace tariff revenue.

Tariff protection and import quantity controls were instituted in Taiwan in 1952. As a member of the Industrial Development

Commission of the Economic Stabilization Board, I made a first study on how to encourage exports by a rebate system for customs duty paid on imported material. The proposal was discussed by Committee A, which was responsible for taxation and monetary matters. It was finally approved in 1955 by the Cabinet and then implemented. In 1966, an export processing zone was opened, into which goods and equipment could be imported duty free without a complicated rebate system; output had to be exported. In 1970, investors outside the EPZs were allowed to file an application with the general customs office to set up a bonded factory under the supervision of customs officers.

In historical perspective, these were export promotion programs that encouraged the growth of labor-intensive exports. The Taiwan experience has shown that when entrepreneurs gain access to the world market, they will select the best combination of inputs and outputs according to the principle of comparative advantage. Moreover, they will learn over time. If they do not, they are driven out of the market.

The market solution to economic development also contributes to the elimination of the unemployment problem. After the external orientation drive has been successful for six to seven years, the concern for unemployment gives way to a palpable fear that a labor shortage is imminent, which would bring growth to a halt. This expansion of employment opportunities is a principal factor in the growth with increased equity in income distribution that Taiwan enjoyed in the 1960s and 1970s. Actually, in 1972–73 the economy reached full employment before the first oil crisis.

For the first time in the transition growth process a way had been found to provide those seeking jobs with factory employment that brought them not only wage income but also a sense of participation and dignity. Indeed, an important lesson to be learned from Taiwan's experience is that it is beneficial to open up the economy to competition and the world market. Not only did domestic labor and entrepreneurs take care of themselves, their well-being increased through their exploitation of new opportunities.

After a decade of externally oriented growth, the advantages of openness were widely recognized in the island, and the slogan "everything for export" was heard frequently. Such a dramatic psychological transformation can be traced to policy innovations in the late import substitution years, particularly the 1956 adoption of the customs rebate system, followed by the adoption of a rebate excise tax system and a local sales tax, and the policy reforms of the late 1950s when a unitary foreign exchange rate system was introduced and inflation was brought under control. An important point here is how the ground for the 1960s transformation to export orientation was broken some five to six years earlier—that is, before it could be realized how beneficial the transformation of policy together with the customs rebate would prove to be.

When the initial liberalization efforts were made, no one had any inkling that a more prosperous growth epoch was in the making. The early efforts were not ideologically motivated by any clear vision of the advantages of externally oriented growth, and there was only a vague awareness of the benefits of comparative advantage. The late 1950s reform measures were adopted for a pragmatic reason, namely, to reduce the reliance on American aid and to solve the problems of unemployment and foreign exchange shortages. Most important of all was recognition by government leaders of the traditional Chinese value of self-help, a practical consequence of which was an acceleration in the growth of domestic capital formation. In those days, the anticipated expansion of exports was interpreted more modestly as simply a vent for surplus for domestic production and a source of employment. Indeed, the term externally oriented growth was coined by economists only after its epochal significance became apparent.

From Partial to Full Trade Liberalization

In Taiwan, the erection of a high tariff wall with tariff rebates and export processing zones amounted to a partial liberalization of trade. Protected industries, that is, those whose costs were such that they could only sell in the domestic market, remained isolated from international competition, and thus had little incentive to increase efficiency. The consuming public was coerced by political forces not only to pay import duties but also to pay for the inefficiency of those protected companies. On the other hand, export-oriented companies are efficient because the ROC government does not possess the political power needed to coerce a housewife in New York to pay for the inefficiency of a Chinese producer in Taiwan.

In the partially liberalized production structure of the 1960s, there appeared the slogan "foster exports through the internal market". This was an application of the infant industry argument in disguise: inefficient enterprises should enjoy the benefit of high domestic prices to help them gain the strength to compete in world markets. The subsidy of high local prices would be a source of investment. The premise is that the infant wants to and will grow up. But why should it?

Businessmen usually put a good deal of effort into keeping their subsidies, claiming that they are not ready to face the outside world. That at least was true: they were not. But if the effort to keep their protective tariff wall had gone into finding products with strong demand and more efficient ways to produce them, they undoubtedly would have been ready earlier.

In a partially liberalized economy, the next major step in policy evolution with regard to trade is to eliminate the direct quantitative controls and to dismantle the protective tariffs. This does not, of course, mean that the productive activity of every firm or every household must be directed to the export market, or that it will face foreign competition. In fact, when the matter is viewed from an evolutionary perspective, the slogan of "everything for export" is the wrong one—it is not a correct characterization of the secret of success of Taiwan. The true meaning of a fuller liberalization is to expose the production behavior of all—including those operating only in the domestic market—to competitive market forces that will induce them to operate more efficiently.

A movement toward full liberalization has indeed taken place in Taiwan during the course of the externally oriented period. The protective wall was partly dismantled in 1971 with the easing of quantitative restrictions on imports. The executive branch of the government was granted the authority, without additional legislative approval, to adjust tariffs up and down by 50%, which I proposed in case of a sudden change in the international economy.

Since the early 1980s, economic liberalization has been accelerated through such measures as the decontrol of foreign exchange, larger tariff cuts, and easier access for imports to the domestic market. With the lifting of foreign-exchange controls on July 15, 1987, private enterprises have been exposed to a riskier and more competitive international financial environment. Such openness, in line with the principle of comparative advantage, is expected to give a healthy stimulus to the local economy and prompt improvements in productivity and efficiency since major industries have grown strong enough to compete successfully in the world market.

With a further step-up in the pace of liberalization in prospect, Taiwan is making every effort to strengthen the functioning of the market mechanism and to improve the welfare of its own citizens and other people throughout the world.

The Investment Incentive Program

The Statute for the Encouragement of Investment, promulgated in 1960, exempted businesses from the obligation to pay corporate income tax for a certain period of time after a new investment project started production. This program must be interpreted with care, particularly as far as the movement toward liberalization is concerned.

On the negative side, such programs contain strong elements of government intervention in the market mechanism. This happens when the new investment projects are broadly categorized, and because some industries are eligible for tax relief, but some are not. Those eligible are supposedly "pioneering", externally oriented, technologically innovative, or some similar description. These industries were selected in accordance with regulations specifying a minimum production scale and other requirements. Their status is viewed from time to time by relevant economic and financial agencies, with final approval given by the Executive Yuan. In assessing the impact of the tax holiday program in Taiwan (and in general) it is important to remember that the political decision to categorize some as eligible and others as not is a reallocation of the tax burden as well as of investment.

Official encouragement of "pioneering" industries through tax breaks was a practice used in Taiwan as well as in many other contemporary LDCs, especially in Korea, Singapore, and other Southeast Asian countries. In Taiwan, in particular, incentives have been targeted mainly at capital- and technology-intensive industries, most of whose production is for export. The tax incentives offered to eligible industries under the Statute for the Encouragement of Investment reflect the government's views on the priority of industrial development, taking into consideration suggestions from industry. Such eligible industries changed from time to time to lead the structural change of industries. In the technology-oriented phase of development, the government's discretionary encouragement of investment is expected to shift increasingly to those areas where external economies can be manifested in crucial technological breakthroughs.[1]

The Statute for the Encouragement of Investment was repealed at the end of 1990, replaced by the Statute for Industrial Upgrading. The latter Statute, which is function-oriented, offers tax benefits primarily for investments and expenditures promoting industrial modernization. The prominent features in the Statute include:

- Accelerated depreciation of facilities for R & D energy conservation and restructuring;
- 5–20% tax credit for investments in automation, pollution control, R & D training, and enhancement of product image;
- tax credit of up to 20% for shareholders of high-tech industries and venture capital firms;

---

[1]The ROC government has set up an Industrial Technology Research Institute (ITRI) which, as a nonprofit corporate body, is entrusted with the role of financing technology development and transfer in Taiwan. It has so far sponsored major projects in the development of integrated circuits, automation, CAD/CAM, energy research, materials research, and computers and computer peripherals. At the appropriate time, ITRI transfers its technology to start-up ventures producing new, innovative products, and to long-established firms as well. Moreover, it serves as a bridge between academia and industry, providing advanced technical training and hands-on experience for graduates fresh from the university. All these government undertakings are quite consistent with the liberalization trend because of their emphasis on the principle of external economy.

- income tax exemption earnings from intellectual property rights (IPR); and
- tax relief for mergers and relocation and factories.

Long-Tem Capital Movements

The evolution of events in the area of long-term international capital movements involving Taiwan during the period 1950–80 had political as well as economic aspects. Politically, the evolution was away from an immature nationalism, under which foreign intrusions in the domestic market were resented, toward a mature nationalism, possessing of self-confidence and thus a willingness to accept foreign capital and companies. Economically, the evolution moved in the direction of an integration of the financial market of Taiwan into that of the rest of the world, with a gradual reduction in the role of the government.

Before U.S. aid was phased out in June 1965, the government had already created a favorable climate to attract private investment, both domestic and foreign. In the early 1960s, the World Bank sent a team to study our economy and identify projects to be financed with long-term and interest-free loans from its sister institution, the International Development Association. The visiting team was received by the Ministry of Finance of the Republic of China, a member of the World Bank. Before U.S. aid was phased out in June 1965, I secured one line of credit from the Japanese Overseas Economic Cooperation Fund and the Export-Import Bank of Japan amounting to the equivalent of US$150 million, and another line of credit from the U.S. Export-Import Bank to finance two electric power generators, each with an output of 300,000 kilowatts. While relations with these banks were maintained, the Asian Development Bank offered additional credit to us as a founding member.

The first foreign private investment was made by Allied Chemical Corporation and Mobil Oil Corporation in a big fertilizer plant, following our discovery of natural gas. After 1964, U.S. electronics companies flocked in to make consumer electronic products and important parts and components. Our own private industries also expanded their facilities, mainly for the export market, and so it was very easy to obtain supplier credit on five-year terms without guarantee.

In spite of dwindling diplomatic recognition of the ROC after its withdrawal from the United Nations in 1971, a steady growth in foreign investment in Taiwan has been viewed as a vote of confidence in the country's future. Taiwan today trades with over 150 countries and areas, and enjoys substantive relations with many with whom it does not have formal diplomatic ties. By the 1980s, foreign investment was no longer viewed simply as a means of gaining employment for a growing labor force seeking a rise in living standards. Instead, it came to be viewed as a vehicle for transferring more advanced technologies to Taiwan.

The Government's Ongoing Role

In the transition growth process of a developing country, liberalization of the economic system does not imply complete laissez-faire or a complete abandonment by the government of all economic roles. What is to be emphasized is the positive construction of the market mechanism. Liberalization does imply that the government should gradually abandon quantitative restrictions on trade and interference with the price mechanism. In particular, the interest rate, the foreign exchange rate, and, above all, the money supply growth rate that constitute the core of the market mechanism should be used less and less as policy instruments to promote growth. The government can play useful roles using other policy instruments, such as the tax rate, that constitute the least interference with the market mechanism.

Even in a perfectly functioning market economy, there are at least two types of roles that can be played safely by the government. One of these is the enforcement of competition. Even though infant industries may need to be protected, such protection should be given only with a view to their early termination. But they should grow up in a reasonable period. So the opening up of a small economy is not unconditional. Otherwise, how can infant industries ever get a chance to stand up?

The best way to promote competitiveness in most small (relative to the world economy) LDCs is to open the economy and subject domestic businesses to international competition. Enactment and enforcement of antitrust laws is not essential when the economy is open.

A second role that government can usefully play is to seek out those areas of production characterized by the existence of conspicuous external economies—that is, activities where the provider of the goods or services cannot easily charge those who benefit. Such areas can best, indeed often only, be exploited collectively.

It is important to remember that what constitutes such collective goods will evolve as the economy matures. Many things that are appropriately government-operated in the early stages of growth can become less so as the economy matures and grows, with the exception of the public utilities, transportation systems, and the like, which enjoy a natural monopoly because of economies of scale. As with the government directing investment through incentive programs, deciding what is appropriately collectively provided because of external economies is a difficult and ongoing task.

At the present point of development in Taiwan, the initiation of the technology-oriented phase, the spotlight is on a broad area of production, the exploration of the potential of science and technology. When the patent and trademark laws were changed in 1983 and the copyright law in 1986, it was an indication that the promotion of science and technology was to be primarily the responsibility of private inventors and entrepreneurs. However, the government does have a positive role to play that can go beyond the enforcement of these laws. Many kinds of research have external economies of sufficient magnitude that, given the expense involved, makes it unlikely that they will be undertaken by private parties. This is a worldwide issue, and how it will be handled within each country and among transnational firms remains open to debate.

PRAGMATISM AND TIMING

One important lesson from Taiwan's experience is that policy innovations should be based on the anticipation of impending problems and conflicts, rather than be purely ideologically motivated. The adoption of a whole set of science and technology programs in 1979 was really designed in an effort to promote a new wave of industrialization. New industries were needed because labor-intensive industries were becoming less competitive owing to rising wage scales and some capital-intensive industries were becoming uneconomical due to heavy energy consumption. The policy innovations on the chart were, in every case, induced by some preceding events.

The very notion of an evolution of policy suggests that the timing (or timely appearance) of a particular policy is important, and a good policy innovation is one that does not arrive prematurely. Ideological considerations often get in the way of appropriate timing as, for example, with so-called welfare state legislation that the economy simply cannot support. What can almost be called a rejection of ideology lies at the heart of a healthy pragmatism that has guided policymakers in Taiwan and has supported a social consensus for growth and economic liberalization.

As regards cultural pragmatism, it can be noted in evaluating the policy experience of Taiwan that what is seen on the policy evolution chart may not even be as important as what is not found. Moreover, in the past, minimum wage and similar legislation and the intrusion of unionism have not been such as to deter the expansion of labor intensive manufactured exports to the world market. The government concentrated its effort on welfare as traditionally defined—basic health and education—but not on the trappings of the modern welfare state found in Western Europe and North America.[2]

---

[2]There are modest welfare programs providing benefits to workers, government employees and their dependents, teachers, service men and women, the needy, the handicapped, and the aged. Social insurance, the mainstay of Taiwan's social-welfare system, currently provides payments to almost one-quarter of the population in such cases as childbirth, injury, illness, old age, death, and disability.

The absence in Taiwan of a combative labor movement, so evident in some Latin American countries, is not due so much to active suppression (although there has been some) as to the universality of a demand by all social classes for something other than unionism to represent labor dignity. That something else has been the opportunity to send their sons and daughters to a university. Chinese workers have sought vocational training for themselves and higher education and better job opportunities for their children. So far, the system has been able to deliver. All levels of education are open virtually to everyone on the basis of merit.

The accountability of the government in this respect can be seen from the sequence of integrated manpower policy measures in education, training, and employment. By 1968, there was in place nine years of compulsory education, and capacity at higher levels was continuing to expand, particularly at schools providing technical skills. Although the Chinese are often thought of as being very group-oriented, almost inherently collectivist, there is a strong streak of individualism centered on developing one's skills, or at least those of one's children—what is called, in today's parlance, exploiting (one's own) human resources.

A basic reason for rapid growth in Taiwan is that human energy was used productively and creatively for economic growth rather than wasted ideologically. To those who argue that the government merely encouraged growth to buy political quiescence, it is possible to say that the improvement of economic well-being should certainly receive the highest national priority in the modernization process. After all, human dignity is often measured in this way. Economic development preceded political liberalization in Europe and even in the United States. Why should contemporary developing countries, which have already telescoped into decades economic growth that took centuries in the Old World, be expected simultaneously and quickly to achieve the Western standard of constitutional democracy?

To many economists and political scientists, it is logical to see a depoliticizing of the economy as being not just concomitant with, but necessary for, real political liberalization. Just as the trend in Taiwan has been toward economic liberalization, so has there been a trend (albeit a slower trend) toward political liberalization. As the writing of this book draws to a close, the time is ripe for political modernization in Taiwan. The effects of such modernization on future economic growth remain to be seen. But that is not the topic of this book; I leave that to others to chronicle and analyze.

Nationalism has been an element that has worked against the market mechanism in most LDCs, as it has justified collective (that is, government) involvement and ownership in diverse areas of the economy. Rallying round the government to promote economic growth through government-led industrialization has been a way of asserting independence. The experience of Taiwan has shown that with self-confidence generated by the success of development, a country will sooner or later adopt a course of liberalized policy on its march toward economic maturity.

The notion of an evolution of policies suggests that two types of issues must be analyzed. On the one hand, there is the issue of the impact of policies in the narrow economic sense. Popular understanding of what policy is all about invariably focuses on this issue. On the other hand, there is the issue of causation—the reason a particular policy appears at a particular time in an evolutionary perspective. The question here is why a particular policy was adopted? This is a difficult political, sometimes ideological, issue that Taiwan solved in a particularly pragmatic way. Whether or not Taiwan's policy experience can be transferred to contemporary LDCs depends, unfortunately, very much on whether their cultures can allow pragmatism to overcome ideology as well as on how strongly they are dedicated to political and economic freedom.

My personal experience over the past thirty-odd years convinces me that, while our policy experiences cannot be transferred to LDCs as a whole package, individual measures (such as EPZs and investment incentives) that I introduced have, from time to time, been adopted successfully by neighboring countries. In the 1960s and 1970s, I strongly advocated bilateral cooperation with countries such as the Republic of South Vietnam (1960), the Republic of Korea (1966), the

Kingdom of Thailand (1968), the Republic of the Philippines (1966), the Commonwealth of Australia (1968), and the Kingdom of Saudi Arabia (1973–74), mainly to exchange development experiences and promote mutually beneficial projects. I firmly believe that what our people can accomplish under a given set of policy measures can be achieved by the people of other countries as well.

In the course of the past three decades, many epoch-making policy innovations were adopted and later modified or abandoned by the government of Taiwan. What are some of the factors that may be regarded as the cause of the timely appearance, and later disappearance, of a particular policy? The underlying question raised here is, "What is the heart of a theory of policy evolution?"

To say that policy changes are caused by changes in ideology is both incorrect (or, at least, an oversimplification) and harmful. To attribute the cause of a policy change entirely to ideology only begs the question of what caused the ideological position.

It appears that the evolution of ideology, policies, and economic conditions go hand in hand. Indeed, particularly in historical perspective, policy is more likely to be a handmaiden of the other two than in the driver's seat. This is not to say that policy is unimportant, only that the more important issues are the economic environment in which the policy is made and the limits ideology places on policies considered acceptable to deal with that environment. Throughout this book I have stressed that each of these modifies the other with the passage of time.

This philosophical issue has some bearing on the transferability of the policy experience of Taiwan to other LDCs. If an experience is transferable at all, the key question concerns the circumstances under which the policy was instituted. If the circumstances are too different, it is not likely that the policy will lead to the same result. The question of a policy's results is an economic issue, but the way policy is formulated is a political issue. Good economics can be rejected by bad politics.

In Taiwan, economic policy innovations were made to solve impending economic problems that were visible and were abandoned, usually quietly, when the problems disappeared. In this way, policy changes in Taiwan seem to have been guided by the invisible hand of the market mechanism that was being constructed, or allowed to operate, by the liberalization trend of successive policies. There has been a pragmatism in Chinese policy formulation that has deep cultural roots, and ideological considerations have generally been kept subordinate to it.

Depoliticizing the Market

Economic development in Taiwan, although not ideologically committed to policies designed to achieve this specific end, has achieved an equity in income distribution almost unique at such an early stage of development experience. This result destroys the twin myths that there is a necessary conflict between growth and equity and that market solutions are doomed to failure in LDCs, particularly as regards the distribution of the benefits of growth.[3]

The alleged failure of the market in some other LDCs may, in fact, be due precisely to the opposite reason: the failure of political intervention in the market. Although the market structure was far from perfect at the beginning of transition growth in the 1950s, the overall trend has been for a strengthening of the market mechanism—a depoliticizing of the market. Taiwan's experience shows that reduced intervention can work.

The withdrawal of political forces from the market system does not mean laissez-faire, with the government playing no role. It must help enforce competition, provide collective goods (such as defense or the legal system), and explore areas where external economies are such that its active involvement (at least for a time) is beneficial to society. But the government's most important role is in building a social consensus that will support growth with equity.

---

[3]While in 1952 the income of the wealthiest 20% of Taiwan's households was some fifteen times that of the poorest 20%, the gap is now four to five times. Land reform, ample opportunities for education and training, a high degree of social mobility, and an early emphasis on labor-intensive employment have been cited as major reasons for this outstanding example of growth with equity.

At conferences on the comparative historical development of Latin American and non-Communist Asian countries one generally finds that the Asian papers are more oriented toward economics, while the Latin American ones are more political, that is, punctuated with the upheavals of experiments with socialist reforms and military interventions. The contrast is, perhaps, not an accident. Policy evolution in Asian countries has been characterized by a continuity, an almost irreversible linearity, that almost inherently implies a lack of excitement, less ideological oscillation between left and right.

The process of depoliticizing the market mechanism became less and less difficult in Taiwan as both the economy and the political system evolved and matured. Political activity shifted from the economic forum to other areas. It may take a great cultural revolution in Latin America to generate an awareness and a social consensus that politics and the market should be separated if the economy is really to provide for the people. That this is so may be the most important lesson of the policy experience in Taiwan.

The rapid growth of the East Asian NICs may be due to their economic pragmatism, with its roots in traditional Chinese culture. Although the movement was sometimes gradual and sporadic, this problem-oriented approach has led to a decided shift over time toward greater reliance on the market mechanism. The evolutionary transformation of their economies has, moreover, proven to be conducive to the realization of other cultural values and aspirations.

10

FINAL REFLECTIONS

What can contemporary LDCs learn from Taiwan's unquestioned economic success? More specifically, given this book's emphasis, what can other countries learn from Taiwan's policy experience? There are obviously some experiences that are transferable and some that are not. What is transferable is the determination to control inflation by adopting high interest rates to absorb savings and the policy of *growth with stability*; maintaining realistic exchange rates; establishment of the export processing zones (already emulated by a large number of developing countries); promoting automation and technology as the labor surplus disappears and wages go up; government provision of adequate infrastructure and government initiative in investment in industry once private capital does come forward. What is not likely to be transferable is the availability of a large pool of trained and experienced personnel evacuated from mainland China to Taiwan after World War II; the effective functioning of JCRR/CUSA with their very strong professional staffs to make the best use of U.S. economic aid, relatively free of political and bureaucratic interference; and land reform carried out by government leaders who were evacuated from the mainland and therefore had no vested interest in land ownership in Taiwan. Thus, the transferability of even "transferable" experience depends upon the political environment of the countries concerned and the availability of their hardworking populations.

The development experience of the Republic of China on Taiwan would be useful to many LDCs within a wide range of per capita GNP below US$3,000. Our experience would be applicable even to large countries with a substantial farming sector, as demonstrated by the Agricultural Technical Missions that we sent to many countries in

Asia, Africa, and Latin America. As a matter of fact, the latest techniques we have developed in agriculture are right now being transferred to Southeast Asian countries, particularly Thailand and the Philippines.

In the industrial sector, EPZs were established in Korea, India, Malaysia, the Philippines, and other countries. In larger countries, lacking transport facilities, it would be better to build plants of a size sufficient to meet the needs of far-flung consumption centers, assuming the availability of raw materials and markets. To all free developing countries, those who enjoy diplomatic relations with us and those who do not, we are ready to provide help upon request.

Economic growth was something the government and people of Taiwan wanted. This is important, because in many countries, development is not necessarily in the interest of the ruling elite or even the desire of the general population. Their indifference, sometimes even opposition, can be a major barrier. Taiwan had the will, and that is probably a necessary (though by no means sufficient) condition for economic growth.

What, then, is the way? The contention is that Taiwan's growth has been propelled in part by government policies that progressively increased the openness of the economy to market forces and reduced direct government involvement—a process of depoliticizing the economic system. This evolution was not itself an explicit, *ex ante* policy; there was no timetable for reforms and liberalization. But there was, from the beginning of Taiwan's post-war development, at least a nominal commitment to the market economy by those charged with running the government. To the extent that contemporary LDCs are unwilling to allow the emergence of free markets, the relevance of Taiwan's experience is reduced.

It is not my purpose here to compare market and planned economies. The reader will recognize, however, that Taiwan's development is consistent with the assertion that market economies can be conducive to growth with equity, while most developing countries with planned economies have been less successful. I would go so far as to suggest that the experience of Taiwan and the other NICs strongly suggests that a key transferable element of successful economic growth policy is allowing the development of free markets.

This is not to say that a developing country should begin (or end) with completely free markets or that Taiwan did. Taiwan's is a mixed economy. Countries with a Chinese cultural tradition are often perceived as having entrenched, powerful bureaucracies and central governments, and this not only is historically true but is still true for Taiwan. Nonetheless, what we as policymakers did in Taiwan was to help various parts of the economy first to stand and then to walk; and then we let go. In other words, a major trend in Taiwan's policy evolution has been toward greater and greater freedom in the market as the economy has maintained a steady and sustained growth to strengthen its confidence.

This overview of what can be termed the government-encouraged emergence of a market economy is analogous at the macro level to the concept of task-relevant maturity (TRM) in business management. When the economy (an employee) has only limited experience and capability (low task-relevant maturity), direct government (management) involvement may be the most effective way to achieve results. When a sector of the economy gains experience and confidence, the emphasis shifts to support; too much supervision and involvement can be counterproductive. As the economy continues to advance, the government, like a good manager, will have only minimal involvement in day-to-day activities, instead of monitoring and setting overall objectives.[1]

Taiwan's experience is thus most directly relevant to countries willing to accept the social and political consequences of growth and willing to allow an economy that, while mixed, is primarily market-oriented. Policymakers in developing countries and aid providers in developed countries may find, and I hope have found, applicable policy approaches in this account of Taiwan's development. But beyond those specifics, there is something more universally applicable. I feel that three factors have been fundamental in shaping Taiwan's development:

---

[1]For a concise discussion of TRM in business, see Andrew S. Grove, *High Output Management* (New York: Random House, 1983), chap. 20.

(1) Sun Yat-sen's teachings;
(2) the government's commitment to fulfilling social expectations; and
(3) the pragmatic approach adopted in policy formulation.

Although Taiwan's economic policies have been more problem-oriented than ideology oriented, the guideline has been Dr. Sun's Principle of the People's Livelihood, namely, that Taiwan's economic development should get started with land reform and the promotion of industries that provide for the basic needs of life—food, clothing, housing, and transportation. Thus, although it was important in Taiwan that we had Dr. Sun's teachings, in other countries a similar outlook under another name would serve the same purpose: a consensus ideology, if you will, favoring growth and a generally agreed framework to achieve it.

Dr. Sun's basic principle accepts private ownership of the means of production, the market mechanism, and free enterprise, while allowing for government ownership of monopolistic key enterprises (the definition of these has changed through time), and government regulation of economic activities. The principle intends to take the advantages of capitalism — individual incentives and the market economy's allocation through prices—and to avoid the disadvantages — inequitable distribution of wealth and income and excessive monopoly power. And of course it avoids Communism's total controls.

Arthur Okun wrote that a "democratic capitalist society will keep searching for better ways of drawing the boundary lines between the domain of rights and the domain of dollars. And it can make progress. To be sure, it will never solve the problem, for the conflict between equality and economic efficiency is inescapable. In that sense, capitalism and democracy are really a most improbable mixture".[2]

Dr. Sun's principle may be considered an approach to reconciling the conflict. His teaching provided Taiwan with more than the framework; it also charged the government with a goal: improving "the people's livelihood". As an operational goal, this translated into

[2]Arthur Okun, *Equality and Efficiency* (Washington, D.C.: The Brookings Institution, 1975), p.120.

striving for growth with equity. The government's commitment to satisfying the desire for a rising living standard has been unyielding. We also have striven to achieve equity in Taiwan, first through concentrating on improving the agricultural sector in which most people lived, then through promoting industries that were open to large numbers of people (that is, required little skill), all the while increasing education opportunities for everybody.

At the same time, as the economy improved steadily Taiwan moved gradually to implement welfare programs and safety nets. In more advanced, wealthier nations, society may expect or accept these. In a country still poor, or striving not to be, it can be argued that those not immediately benefiting from growth are as well off as they would be otherwise and that the increased level of well-being will soon reach them. Life can be harsh in poor countries; to put the main emphasis on everyone immediately rising together too often can be tantamount to denying an improved life to anyone. Taiwan's experience with income distribution was one of dramatic improvements associated with rapid growth, hardly a case of "trickle down". Those who try too hard to avoid trickle down end up with less to "trickle", that is, less growth and a worse distribution to boot.

This relates to the third, perhaps decisive, factor: pragmatism. Professor Fei ended his introduction on this theme, and it runs throughout the book. Ideology is fine, but a lot of good is lost and damage done by means justified by dogmatic ends that are then never achieved. Based on my experience in Taiwan and observing other countries, I feel that a generally free-market orientation is far more likely to achieve general welfare than any other system, but that it is not an end in itself.

Appendix
POLICY MATRIX
AND STATISTICAL
TABLES

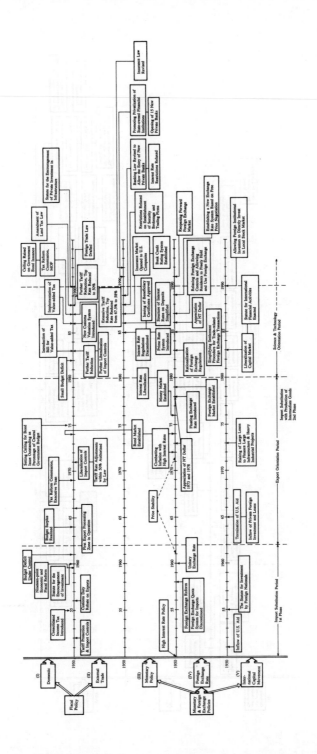

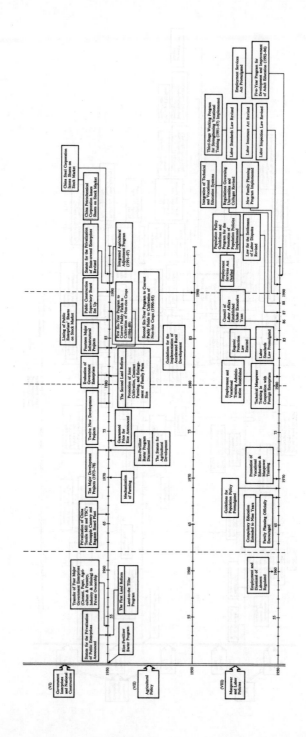

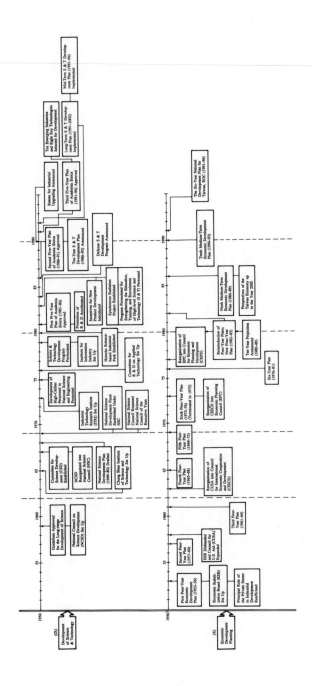

1. Major Indicators of Taiwan Economy

Period	Growth rate of population	Unemploy-ment rate	Real growth rate of gross national product	Gross national product	Per capita GNP	Growth rate of index of agricultural production	Growth rate of index of industrial production	Increase rate of money supply (M_{IB})
	(%)	(%)	(%)	US$million	(US$)	(%)	(%)	(%)
1951	4.2	4.5		1,196	145	2.5	18.4	
1952	3.3	4.4	12.0	1,674	196	11.2	25.2	
1953	3.8	4.2	9.3	1,476	167	15.4	25.4	
1954	3.7	4.0	9.5	1,621	177	0	5.7	
1955	3.8	3.8	8.1	1,928	203	2.9	13.0	
1956	3.4	3.6	5.5	1,388	141	5.2	3.6	
1957	3.2	3.7	7.3	1,619	160	7.9	12.6	
1958	3.6	3.8	6.6	1,807	173	7.3	8.5	
1959	3.9	3.9	7.7	1,420	131	1.7	11.9	
1960	3.5	4.0	6.4	1,717	154	0.6	14.2	
1961	3.3	4.1	6.8	1,749	152	7.3	15.6	
1962	3.3	4.2	7.9	1,926	162	3.1	8.0	5.0
1963	3.2	4.3	9.4	2,178	178	1.8	9.2	28.1
1964	3.1	4.3	12.3	2,550	203	9.5	21.1	35.0
1965	3.0	3.3	11.0	2,811	217	6.6	16.3	15.8
1966	2.9	3.0	9.0	3,148	237	3.6	15.6	12.2
1967	2.3	2.3	10.6	3,637	267	7.1	16.7	30.1
1968	2.7	1.7	9.1	4,236	304	7.7	22.3	11.5
1969	5.0	1.9	9.1	4,915	345	−1.2	19.9	15.6
1970	2.4	1.7	11.3	5,660	389	6.9	20.1	15.0
1971	2.2	1.7	13.0	6,589	443	2.8	23.6	30.6
1972	2.0	1.5	13.4	7,906	522	4.6	21.2	34.1
1973	1.8	1.3	12.8	10,727	695	7.0	16.2	50.4
1974	1.8	1.5	1.2	14,458	920	−0.4	−4.5	10.5
1975	1.9	2.4	4.4	15,429	964	−1.4	9.5	28.8
1976	2.2	1.8	13.7	18,492	1,132	12.7	23.3	25.1
1977	1.8	1.8	10.3	21,681	1,301	5.5	13.3	33.6
1978	1.9	1.7	14.0	26,773	1,577	0.3	22.5	37.0
1979	2.0	1.3	8.5	33,229	1,920	7.9	6.4	7.7
1980	1.9	1.2	7.1	41,360	2,344	1.1	6.8	22.7
1981	1.9	1.4	5.8	47,955	2,669	−1.4	3.5	13.8
1982	1.8	2.1	4.1	48,550	2,653	1.8	−0.9	14.6
1983	1.5	2.7	8.7	52,503	2,823	4.0	12.7	18.4
1984	1.5	2.4	11.6	59,780	3,167	3.1	11.8	9.3
1985	1.3	2.9	5.6	63,097	3,297	3.1	2.7	12.2
1986	1.0	2.7	12.6	77,299	3,993	−0.3	13.9	51.4
1987	1.1	2.0	11.9	103,200	5,275	8.0	10.7	37.8
1988	1.2	1.7	7.8	125,316	6,333	1.5	4.4	24.4
1989	1.0	1.6	7.3	150,283	7,512	−0.2	3.4	6.1
1990	1.2	1.7	5.0	160,913	7,954	2.1	−1.2	−6.6
1991	1.0	1.5	7.2	179,763	8,788	1.0	7.2	12.1

Note: Money supply (M_{IB}) includes currency in circulation and deposit money (including checking accounts, passbook deposits, and passbook savings deposits held by enterprises and individuals with monetary institutions).

Source: Complied from concerning government agency statistics.

Appendix

1. Major Indicators of Taiwan Economy (*Continued*)

Period	Growth rate of consumer prices	Growth rate of wholesale prices	Merchandise trade (customs statistics)			Foreign exchange holdings of Central Bank of China (year-end)	Outstanding public debt (year-end)
			Exports (fob)	Imports (cif)	Surplus (+) Deficit (−)		
	(%)	(%)	US$million			(US$ billion)	
1951		65.5	102	149	−47		
1952		23.0	119	205	−86		
1953	18.8	8.8	128	192	−64		
1954	1.7	2.4	93	211	−118		
1955	9.9	14.1	123	201	−78		
1956	10.5	12.7	118	193	−75		
1957	7.5	7.2	148	212	−64		
1958	1.3	1.4	156	226	−70		
1959	10.6	10.3	157	231	−74		
1960	18.5	14.2	164	297	−133		
1961	7.8	3.2	195	322	−127		
1962	2.4	3.0	218	304	−86		
1963	2.2	6.5	332	362	−30		
1964	−0.2	2.5	433	428	+5	0.24	
1965	−0.1	−4.6	450	556	−106	0.25	
1966	2.0	1.5	536	622	−86	0.28	
1967	3.4	2.5	641	806	−165	0.34	
1968	7.9	3.0	789	903	−114	0.30	
1969	5.1	−0.3	1,049	1,212	−163	0.36	
1970	3.6	2.7	1,481	1,524	−43	0.54	
1971	2.8	0	2,060	1,844	+216	0.62	
1972	3.0	4.4	2,988	2,513	+475	0.95	0.55
1973	8.2	22.9	4,483	3,792	+691	1.03	0.72
1974	47.5	40.6	5,639	6,966	−1,327	1.09	0.93
1975	5.2	−5.1	5,309	5,952	−643	1.07	1.14
1976	2.5	2.8	8,166	7,599	+567	1.52	1.95
1977	7.0	2.8	9,361	8,511	0	1.35	2.32
1978	5.8	3.5	12,687	11,027	+1,660	1.41	2.69
1979	9.8	13.8	16,103	14,774	+1,329	1.47	2.88
1980	19.0	21.5	19,811	19,733	+78	2.21	4.36
1981	16.3	7.6	22,611	21,199	+1,412	7.24	5.94
1982	3.0	−0.2	22,204	18,888	+3,316	8.53	6.04
1983	1.4	−1.2	25,123	20,287	+4,836	11.86	6.14
1984	0	0.5	30,456	21,959	+8,497	15.66	5.64
1985	−0.2	−2.6	30,726	20,102	+10,624	22.56	4.90
1986	0.7	−3.3	39,862	24,182	+15,680	46.31	3.41
1987	0.5	−3.3	53,679	34,983	+18,695	76.75	1.83
1988	1.3	−1.6	60,667	49,673	+10,994	73.90	1.51
1989	4.4	−0.4	66,304	52,265	+14,039	73.22	1.06
1990	4.1	−0.6	67,214	54,716	+12,498	72.44	0.81
1991	3.6	0.2	76,178	62,861	+13,317	82.41	0.72

1. Major Indicators of Taiwan Economy (*Continued*)

Period	Rediscount rate of Central Bank of China (year-end)	Exchange rate of NT$ to US$ (year-end)	Composition of GDP			Household income distribution
			Agriculture	Industry	Services	Folds of 5th group to 1st group
	(% per annum)		(%)			
1951			32.3	21.3	46.4	
1952			32.2	19.7	48.1	
1953	21.60		34.5	19.4	46.1	
1954	21.60		28.0	23.9	48.1	
1955	21.60		29.1	23.2	47.7	
1956	18.00		27.5	24.4	48.1	
1957	18.00		27.3	25.3	47.4	
1958	14.40		26.8	24.8	48.4	
1959	18.00		26.4	27.1	46.6	
1960	18.00–21.96	40.05	28.5	26.9	44.6	
1961	14.40	40.05	27.4	26.6	46.0	
1962	12.96	40.05	25.0	28.2	46.8	
1963	11.52	40.05	23.2	29.9	46.8	
1964	11.52	40.05	24.5	30.4	45.1	5.33
1965	11.52	40.05	23.6	30.2	46.2	—
1966	11.52	40.05	22.5	30.5	46.9	5.25
1967	10.80	40.05	20.6	33.0	46.4	—
1968	11.88	40.05	19.0	34.4	46.5	5.28
1969	10.80	40.05	15.9	36.9	47.2	—
1970	9.80	40.05	15.5	36.8	47.7	4.58
1971	9.25	40.05	13.1	38.9	48.0	—
1972	8.50	40.05	12.2	41.6	46.1	4.49
1973	10.75	38.00	12.1	43.8	44.1	—
1974	12.00	38.00	12.4	40.7	46.9	4.37
1975	10.75	38.00	12.7	39.9	47.4	—
1976	9.50	38.00	11.4	43.2	45.5	4.18
1977	8.25	38.00	10.6	44.0	45.4	4.21
1978	8.25	36.00	9.4	45.2	45.4	4.18
1979	11.00	36.03	8.6	45.3	46.1	4.34
1980	11.00	36.01	7.7	45.7	46.6	4.17
1981	11.75	37.84	7.3	45.5	47.2	4.21
1982	7.75	39.91	7.7	44.4	47.9	4.29
1983	7.25	40.27	7.3	45.0	47.7	4.36
1984	6.75	39.47	6.3	46.2	47.5	4.40
1985	5.25	39.85	5.8	46.3	47.9	4.50
1986	4.50	35.50	5.5	47.6	46.8	4.60
1987	4.50	28.55	5.3	47.4	47.3	4.69
1988	4.50	28.17	5.0	45.7	49.3	4.85
1989	7.75	26.16	4.9	43.6	51.5	4.94
1990	7.75	27.1075	4.1	42.5	53.4	5.18
1991	6.25	25.7475	3.7	42.5	53.8	4.97

2. Population Density and Vital Statistics

Period	Population Density[1] per sq. km	Population Density[1] per sq. km of cultivated land	Birth Number (1,000)	Birth Rate (%)
1952	226.03	927.7	373	4.66
1953	234.64	966.9	375	4.52
1954	243.29	1,000.9	384	4.46
1955	252.43	1,039.9	404	4.53
1956	261.13	1,072.2	414	4.48
1957	269.47	1,109.6	395	4.14
1958	279.18	1,136.3	411	4.17
1959	290.07	1,188.3	421	4.12
1960	300.11	1,241.6	419	3.95
1961	310.03	1,278.8	420	3.83
1962	320.12	1,320.3	423	3.74
1963	330.45	1,362.5	424	3.63
1964	340.83	1,389.4	417	3.45
1965	351.17	1,419.5	407	3.27
1966	361.30	1,449.6	415	3.24
1967	369.75	1,473.5	374	2.85
1968	379.59	1,516.8	394	2.93
1969	398.62	1,564.3	391	2.79
1970	408.11	1,621.1	394	2.72
1971	416.74	1,661.3	380	2.56
1972	424.92	1,701.4	366	2.41
1973	432.58	1,737.9	367	2.38
1974	440.57	1,727.7	368	2.34
1975	448.83	1,761.0	368	2.30
1976	458.79	1,794.9	423	2.59
1977	467.16	1,822.0	396	2.38
1978	476.13	1,866.5	409	2.41
1979	485.53	1,909.4	423	2.44
1980	494.58	1,962.3	413	2.34
1981	503.76	2,015.1	413	2.30
1982	512.62	2,071.6	404	2.21
1983	520.36	2,094.6	382	2.06
1984	528.12	2,132.3	370	1.96
1985	534.95	2,180.7	345	1.80
1986	540.40	2,192.1	308	1.59
1987	546.46	2,219.7	313	1.60
1988	552.88	2,224.0	341	1.72
1989	558.54	2,247.6	315	1.57
1990	565.36	2,286.6	335	1.66
1991	571.02	2,326.6	321	1.57

Note: [1]End of year. Including servicemen since 1969.

Source: Ministry of the Interior(MOI), *Taiwan-Fukien Demographic Fact Book, Republic of China*, various issues.

2. Population Density and Vital Statistics (*Continued*)

Period	Death Number (1,000)	Death Rate (%)	Natural increase Number (1,000)	Natural increase Rate (%)
1952	79	0.99	294	3.67
1953	78	0.94	297	3.58
1954	70	0.82	314	3.64
1955	77	0.86	327	3.67
1956	74	0.80	340	3.68
1957	81	0.85	314	3.29
1958	75	0.76	336	3.41
1959	74	0.72	347	3.40
1960	74	0.70	345	3.25
1961	74	0.67	346	3.16
1962	73	0.64	350	3.10
1963	72	0.61	352	3.02
1964	69	0.57	348	2.88
1965	68	0.55	339	2.72
1966	70	0.55	345	2.69
1967	72	0.55	302	2.30
1968	74	0.55	320	2.38
1969	71	0.50	320	2.29
1970	71	0.49	323	2.23
1971	71	0.48	309	2.08
1972	71	0.47	295	1.94
1973	73	0.48	294	1.90
1974	75	0.48	293	1.86
1975	75	0.47	293	1.83
1976	77	0.47	346	2.12
1977	79	0.48	317	1.90
1978	79	0.47	330	1.94
1979	82	0.47	341	1.97
1980	84	0.48	329	1.86
1981	87	0.48	326	1.81
1982	87	0.48	317	1.73
1983	91	0.49	291	1.57
1984	90	0.48	280	1.48
1985	92	0.48	253	1.32
1986	95	0.49	213	1.10
1987	96	0.49	217	1.11
1988	102	0.51	239	1.21
1989	103	0.51	212	1.06
1990	105	0.52	230	1.13
1991	106	0.52	215	1.05

Appendix

3. Labor Force Statistics[1]

Period	Population Aged 15 & Over	In labor force			Not in labor force
		Total	Employed	Unemployed	
I. Number (1,000 persons)					
1951 Average	4,485	3,030	2,893	137	1,455
1952 Average	4,609	3,063	2,929	134	1,546
1953 Average	4,736	3,094	2,964	130	1,642
1954 Average	4,870	3,152	3,026	126	1,718
1955 Average	5,022	3,231	3,108	123	1,791
1956 Average	5,179	3,268	3,149	119	1,911
1957 Average	5,338	3,354	3,229	125	1,984
1958 Average	5,503	3,472	3,340	132	2,031
1959 Average	5,659	3,560	3,422	138	2,099
1960 Average	5,795	3,617	3,473	144	2,178
1961 Average	5,919	3,655	3,505	150	2,264
1962 Average	6,065	3,695	3,541	154	2,370
1963 Average	6,244	3,752	3,592	160	2,492
1964 Average	6,455	3,824	3,658	166	2,632
1965 Average	6,689	3,891	3,763	128	2,798
1966 Average	6,948	3,976	3,856	120	2,972
1967 Average	7,212	4,145	4,050	95	3,067
1968 Average	7,482	4,298	4,225	74	3,185
1969 Average	7,787	4,474	4,390	84	3,314
1970 Average	8,115	4,654	4,576	79	3,461
1971 Average	8,444	4,819	4,738	80	3,625
1972 Average	8,763	5,022	4,948	75	3,742
1973 Average	9,070	5,395	5,327	68	3,675
1974 Average	9,383	5,571	5,486	85	3,812
1975 Average	9,712	5,656	5,521	136	4,056
1976 Average	10,043	5,772	5,669	103	4,271
1977 Average	10,375	6,087	5,980	107	4,288
1978 Average	10,777	6,333	6,228	106	4,444
1979 Average	11,084	6,507	6,424	83	4,577
1980 Average	11,378	6,629	6,547	82	4,749
1981 Average	11,698	6,764	6,672	92	4,934
1982 Average	12,013	6,959	6,811	149	5,053
1983 Average	12,263	7,266	7,070	197	4,997
1984 Average	12,544	7,491	7,308	183	5,053
1985 Average	12,860	7,651	7,428	222	5,210
1986 Average	13,161	7,945	7,733	212	5,216
1987 Average	13,432	8,183	8,022	161	5,248
1988 Average	13,696	8,247	8,108	139	5,449
1989 Average	13,955	8,390	8,258	132	5,565
1990 Average	14,219	8,423	8,283	140	5,795
1991 Average	14,496	8,569	8,439	130	5,927

Note: [1]Referring to civilian labor force only.

Source: Directorate-General of Budget, Accounting & Statistics, (DGBAS), R.O.C., *Monthly Bulletin of Manpower Statistics, Taiwan Area, Republic of China*, various issues.

3. Labor Force Statistics[1] (*Continued*)

Period	Population Aged 15 & Over	In labor force			Not in labor force
		Total	Employed	Unemployed	
II. Percentage (%)					
1951 Average	100.0	67.6	64.5	3.1	32.4
1952 Average	100.0	66.5	63.6	2.9	33.5
1953 Average	100.0	65.3	62.6	2.7	34.7
1954 Average	100.0	64.7	62.1	2.6	35.3
1955 Average	100.0	64.3	61.9	2.4	35.7
1956 Average	100.0	63.1	60.8	2.3	36.9
1957 Average	100.0	62.8	60.5	2.3	37.2
1958 Average	100.0	63.1	60.7	2.4	36.9
1959 Average	100.0	62.9	60.5	2.4	37.1
1960 Average	100.0	62.4	59.9	2.5	37.6
1961 Average	100.0	61.8	59.2	2.6	38.2
1962 Average	100.0	60.9	58.4	2.5	39.1
1963 Average	100.0	60.1	57.5	2.6	39.9
1964 Average	100.0	59.2	56.7	2.5	40.8
1965 Average	100.0	58.2	56.3	1.9	41.8
1966 Average	100.0	57.2	55.5	1.7	42.8
1967 Average	100.0	57.5	56.2	1.3	42.5
1968 Average	100.0	57.5	56.5	1.0	42.5
1969 Average	100.0	57.5	56.4	1.1	42.5
1970 Average	100.0	57.4	56.4	1.0	42.6
1971 Average	100.0	57.1	56.1	1.0	42.9
1972 Average	100.0	57.3	56.5	0.8	42.7
1973 Average	100.0	59.5	58.7	0.8	40.5
1974 Average	100.0	59.4	58.5	0.9	40.6
1975 Average	100.0	58.2	56.8	1.4	41.8
1976 Average	100.0	57.5	56.5	1.0	42.5
1977 Average	100.0	58.7	57.6	1.1	41.3
1978 Average	100.0	58.8	57.8	1.0	41.2
1979 Average	100.0	58.7	58.0	0.7	41.3
1980 Average	100.0	58.3	57.6	0.7	41.7
1981 Average	100.0	57.8	57.0	0.8	42.2
1982 Average	100.0	57.9	56.7	1.2	42.1
1983 Average	100.0	59.3	57.7	1.6	40.7
1984 Average	100.0	59.7	58.3	1.4	40.3
1985 Average	100.0	59.5	57.8	1.7	40.5
1986 Average	100.0	60.4	58.8	1.6	39.6
1987 Average	100.0	60.9	59.7	1.2	39.1
1988 Average	100.0	60.2	59.2	1.0	39.8
1989 Average	100.0	60.1	59.2	0.9	39.9
1990 Average	100.0	59.2	58.3	1.0	40.8
1991 Average	100.0	59.1	58.2	0.9	40.9

Appendix

4. Employment by Industry

Period	Total	Agriculture	Industry			
			Subtotal	Mining	Mfg.	Const.

I. Number (1,000 persons)

Period	Total	Agriculture	Subtotal	Mining	Mfg.	Const.
1951 Average	2,893	1,640	472	54	347	65
1952 Average	2,929	1,642	495	56	362	70
1953 Average	2,964	1,647	522	59	381	74
1954 Average	3,026	1,657	536	58	392	78
1955 Average	3,108	1,667	560	57	411	84
1956 Average	3,149	1,675	577	64	415	89
1957 Average	3,229	1,689	612	75	433	95
1958 Average	3,340	1,707	659	78	471	100
1959 Average	3,422	1,722	695	79	500	105
1960 Average	3,473	1,742	713	80	514	107
1961 Average	3,505	1,747	732	83	525	111
1962 Average	3,541	1,760	745	83	534	114
1963 Average	3,592	1,775	764	81	551	117
1964 Average	3,659	1,810	779	82	563	119
1965 Average	3,764	1,748	840	83	612	130
1966 Average	3,856	1,735	871	83	633	139
1967 Average	4,051	1,723	996	85	736	158
1968 Average	4,225	1,725	1,072	84	785	186
1969 Average	4,391	1,726	1,156	80	841	218
1970 Average	4,575	1,680	1,278	72	958	231
1971 Average	4,738	1,665	1,417	65	1,053	281
1972 Average	4,949	1,632	1,576	61	1,218	277
1973 Average	5,327	1,624	1,795	59	1,419	296
1974 Average	5,486	1,697	1,882	62	1,479	319
1975 Average	5,522	1,681	1,928	62	1,518	325
1976 Average	5,670	1,641	2,065	65	1,628	348
1977 Average	5,981	1,597	2,251	61	1,767	398
1978 Average	6,228	1,553	2,447	60	1,892	470
1979 Average	6,424	1,380	2,684	57	2,084	517
1980 Average	6,547	1,277	2,774	56	2,138	553
1981 Average	6,672	1,257	2,814	54	2,146	585
1982 Average	6,811	1,284	2,808	51	2,169	557
1983 Average	7,070	1,317	2,907	46	2,305	523
1984 Average	7,308	1,286	3,090	41	2,494	521
1985 Average	7,428	1,297	3,078	35	2,488	521
1986 Average	7,733	1,317	3,207	33	2,614	525
1987 Average	8,022	1,226	3,430	31	2,810	554
1988 Average	8,108	1,112	3,450	28	2,798	588
1989 Average	8,258	1,065	3,488	24	2,803	625
1990 Average	8,283	1,064	3,385	20	2,647	682
1991 Average	8,439	1,092	3,386	19	2,611	719

Source: See Table 3.

4. Employment by Industry (*Continued*)

Period	Industry Utilities	Subtotal	Services Comm.	Trans.	Other services

I. Number (1,000 persons)

Period	Utilities	Subtotal	Comm.	Trans.	Other services
1951 Average	6	781	312	89	380
1952 Average	7	792	310	100	382
1953 Average	8	795	309	107	379
1954 Average	8	833	309	115	409
1955 Average	8	881	313	124	444
1956 Average	9	897	315	129	453
1957 Average	9	928	324	134	470
1958 Average	10	974	334	143	497
1959 Average	11	1,005	343	150	512
1960 Average	12	1,018	346	154	518
1961 Average	13	1,026	347	156	523
1962 Average	14	1,036	347	159	530
1963 Average	15	1,053	348	165	540
1964 Average	15	1,070	350	170	550
1965 Average	15	1,176	389	179	608
1966 Average	16	1,250	417	180	653
1967 Average	17	1,332	472	194	666
1968 Average	17	1,428	548	201	679
1969 Average	17	1,509	585	211	713
1970 Average	17	1,617	623	248	746
1971 Average	18	1,656	632	250	774
1972 Average	20	1,741	691	257	793
1973 Average	21	1,908	767	296	845
1974 Average	22	1,907	782	293	832
1975 Average	23	1,913	775	314	824
1976 Average	24	1,964	777	326	861
1977 Average	25	2,133	869	337	927
1978 Average	25	2,227	918	343	966
1979 Average	26	2,360	986	378	996
1980 Average	27	2,497	1,046	387	1,064
1981 Average	29	2,601	1,107	387	1,107
1982 Average	31	2,718	1,158	389	1,171
1983 Average	33	2,845	1,229	384	1,232
1984 Average	34	2,932	1,280	378	1,274
1985 Average	34	3,054	1,336	388	1,330
1986 Average	34	3,209	1,382	407	1,420
1987 Average	35	3,367	1,435	429	1,504
1988 Average	35	3,546	1,539	431	1,577
1989 Average	35	3,705	1,613	450	1,642
1990 Average	36	3,834	1,630	459	1,745
1991 Average	37	3,960	1,725	457	1,778

Appendix

4. Employment by Industry (*Continued*)

Period	Total	Agriculture	Industry			
			Subtotal	Mining	Mfg.	Const.
II. Percentage (%)						
1951 Average	100.0	56.7	16.3	1.9	12.0	2.2
1952 Average	100.0	56.1	16.9	1.9	12.4	2.4
1953 Average	100.0	55.6	17.6	2.0	12.8	2.5
1954 Average	100.0	54.8	17.7	1.9	12.9	2.6
1955 Average	100.0	53.6	18.0	1.8	13.2	2.7
1956 Average	100.0	53.2	18.3	2.0	13.2	2.8
1957 Average	100.0	52.3	19.0	2.3	13.4	3.0
1958 Average	100.0	51.1	19.7	2.3	14.1	3.0
1959 Average	100.0	50.3	20.3	2.3	14.6	3.1
1960 Average	100.0	50.2	20.5	2.3	14.8	3.1
1961 Average	100.0	49.8	20.9	2.4	15.0	3.1
1962 Average	100.0	49.7	21.0	2.3	15.1	3.2
1963 Average	100.0	49.4	21.3	2.3	15.3	3.3
1964 Average	100.0	49.5	21.3	2.2	15.4	3.3
1965 Average	100.0	46.5	22.3	2.2	16.3	3.4
1966 Average	100.0	45.0	22.6	2.2	16.4	3.6
1967 Average	100.0	42.5	24.6	2.1	18.2	3.9
1968 Average	100.0	40.8	25.4	2.0	18.6	4.4
1969 Average	100.0	39.3	26.3	1.8	19.1	5.0
1970 Average	100.0	36.7	28.0	1.6	20.9	5.1
1971 Average	100.0	35.1	29.9	1.4	22.2	5.9
1972 Average	100.0	33.0	31.8	1.2	24.6	5.6
1973 Average	100.0	30.5	33.7	1.1	26.6	5.6
1974 Average	100.0	30.9	34.3	1.1	27.0	5.8
1975 Average	100.0	30.4	34.9	1.1	27.5	5.9
1976 Average	100.0	29.0	36.4	1.2	28.7	6.1
1977 Average	100.0	26.7	37.6	1.0	29.5	6.7
1978 Average	100.0	24.9	39.3	1.0	30.4	7.5
1979 Average	100.0	21.5	41.8	0.9	32.5	8.0
1980 Average	100.0	19.5	42.4	0.9	32.6	8.5
1981 Average	100.0	18.8	42.2	0.8	32.2	8.8
1982 Average	100.0	18.9	41.2	0.8	31.8	8.2
1983 Average	100.0	18.6	41.1	0.6	32.6	7.4
1984 Average	100.0	17.6	42.3	0.6	34.1	7.1
1985 Average	100.0	17.5	41.4	0.5	33.5	7.0
1986 Average	100.0	17.0	41.5	0.4	33.8	6.8
1987 Average	100.0	15.3	42.8	0.4	35.0	6.9
1988 Average	100.0	13.7	42.6	0.3	34.5	7.3
1989 Average	100.0	12.9	42.2	0.3	33.9	7.6
1990 Average	100.0	12.8	40.9	0.2	32.0	8.2
1991 Average	100.0	12.9	40.1	0.2	30.9	8.5

4. Employment by Industry (*Continued*)

Period	Industry Utilities	Services Subtotal	Comm.	Trans.	Other services
II. Percentage (%)					
1951 Average	0.2	27.0	10.8	3.1	13.1
1952 Average	0.2	27.0	10.6	3.4	13.0
1953 Average	0.3	26.8	10.4	3.6	12.8
1954 Average	0.3	27.5	10.2	3.8	13.5
1955 Average	0.3	28.4	10.1	4.0	14.3
1956 Average	0.3	28.5	10.0	4.1	14.4
1957 Average	0.3	28.7	10.0	4.1	14.6
1958 Average	0.3	29.2	10.0	4.3	14.9
1959 Average	0.3	29.4	10.0	4.4	15.0
1960 Average	0.3	29.3	10.0	4.4	14.9
1961 Average	0.4	29.3	9.9	4.5	14.9
1962 Average	0.4	29.3	9.8	4.5	15.0
1963 Average	0.4	29.3	9.7	4.6	15.0
1964 Average	0.4	29.2	9.6	4.6	15.0
1965 Average	0.4	31.2	10.3	4.8	16.1
1966 Average	0.4	32.4	10.8	4.7	16.9
1967 Average	0.4	32.9	11.7	4.8	16.4
1968 Average	0.4	33.8	13.0	4.8	16.0
1969 Average	0.4	34.4	13.3	4.8	16.3
1970 Average	0.4	35.3	13.6	5.4	16.3
1971 Average	0.4	35.0	13.3	5.3	16.4
1972 Average	0.4	35.2	14.0	5.2	16.0
1973 Average	0.4	35.8	14.4	5.6	15.8
1974 Average	0.4	34.8	14.3	5.3	15.2
1975 Average	0.4	34.7	14.1	5.7	14.9
1976 Average	0.4	34.6	13.7	5.7	15.2
1977 Average	0.4	35.7	14.5	5.7	15.5
1978 Average	0.4	35.8	14.8	5.5	15.5
1979 Average	0.4	36.7	15.3	5.9	15.5
1980 Average	0.4	38.1	16.0	5.9	16.2
1981 Average	0.4	39.0	16.6	5.8	16.6
1982 Average	0.4	39.9	17.0	5.7	17.2
1983 Average	0.5	40.3	17.4	5.4	17.5
1984 Average	0.5	40.1	17.5	5.2	17.4
1985 Average	0.5	41.1	18.0	5.2	17.9
1986 Average	0.4	41.5	17.9	5.3	18.3
1987 Average	0.4	42.0	17.9	5.3	18.7
1988 Average	0.4	43.7	19.0	5.3	19.4
1989 Average	0.4	44.9	19.5	5.4	19.9
1990 Average	0.4	46.3	19.7	5.5	21.1
1991 Average	0.4	46.9	20.4	5.4	21.1

Appendix

5. Expenditure on Gross Domestic Product
(At current prices)

Period	Gross domestic product	National consumption Subtotal	Private	Government	Subtotal
I. Amount (NT$ million)					
1951 Average	12,328	11,128	8,928	2,200	1,779
1952 Average	17,251	15,661	12,728	2,933	2,643
1953 Average	22,955	20,917	17,353	3,564	3,224
1954 Average	25,204	23,270	18,664	4,606	4,041
1955 Average	29,981	27,278	21,623	5,655	3,998
1956 Average	34,410	31,245	24,235	7,010	5,524
1957 Average	40,173	35,874	27,773	8,101	6,355
1958 Average	44,966	40,374	31,035	9,339	7,458
1959 Average	51,833	46,382	35,638	10,744	9,732
1960 Average	62,507	54,591	42,559	12,032	12,618
1961 Average	70,043	61,025	47,541	13,484	13,983
1962 Average	77,159	67,543	52,103	15,440	13,733
1963 Average	87,252	72,301	55,912	16,389	15,950
1964 Average	101,966	82,102	64,315	17,787	19,089
1965 Average	112,627	90,454	71,452	19,002	25,546
1966 Average	126,022	98,937	77,066	21,871	26,736
1967 Average	145,817	112,920	87,407	25,513	35,882
1968 Average	169,904	132,112	101,789	30,323	42,624
1969 Average	196,845	150,050	113,861	36,189	48,219
1970 Average	226,805	169,033	127,636	41,397	57,886
1971 Average	263,676	188,009	142,531	45,478	69,179
1972 Average	316,172	215,347	164,580	50,767	81,082
1973 Average	410,405	269,268	206,919	62,349	119,373
1974 Average	549,577	376,835	299,346	77,489	215,325
1975 Average	589,651	429,910	336,846	93,064	179,047
1976 Average	707,710	476,217	368,690	107,527	216,231
1977 Average	828,995	555,629	426,802	128,827	232,950
1978 Average	991,602	647,975	497,649	150,326	279,671
1979 Average	1,195,838	788,940	604,473	184,467	393,379
1980 Average	1,491,059	1,004,902	767,742	237,160	503,911
1981 Average	1,773,931	1,207,881	922,154	285,727	529,833
1982 Average	1,899,971	1,322,950	1,002,305	320,645	479,224
1983 Average	2,100,005	1,425,719	1,085,429	340,290	492,861
1984 Average	2,343,078	1,561,277	1,189,459	371,818	519,371
1985 Average	2,473,786	1,660,944	1,261,580	399,364	471,359
1986 Average	2,855,180	1,789,348	1,366,466	422,882	500,656
1987 Average	3,222,993	2,001,702	1,537,782	463,920	659,848
1988 Average	3,496,951	2,295,173	1,765,247	529,926	816,052
1989 Average	3,878,547	2,689,764	2,070,811	618,953	885,164
1990 Average	4,222,004	3,045,782	2,302,009	743,773	945,839
1991 Average	4,704,137	3,394,525	2,554,494	840,031	1,071,802

Source: Directorate-General of Budget, Accounting & Statistics, (DGBAS), R.O.C., *Monthly Income the Republic of China*, various issues.

5. Expenditure on Gross Domestic Product (*Continued*)
(At current prices)

Period	Gross capital formation		National expenditure	Exports of goods & services	Less: imports of goods & services
	Gross fixed capital formation	Increase in inventory			
I. Amount (NT$ million)					
1951 Average	1,328	451	12,907	1,257	1,836
1952 Average	1,940	703	18,304	1,386	2,439
1953 Average	2,678	546	24,141	1,984	3,170
1954 Average	3,337	704	27,311	1,634	3,741
1955 Average	3,401	597	31,276	2,475	3,770
1956 Average	4,591	933	36,769	3,110	5,469
1957 Average	5,283	1,072	42,229	3,889	5,945
1958 Average	6,765	693	47,832	4,689	7,555
1959 Average	8,595	1,137	56,114	6,573	10,854
1960 Average	10,361	2,257	67,209	7,192	11,894
1961 Average	11,349	2,634	75,008	9,803	14,768
1962 Average	11,623	2,110	81,276	10,498	14,615
1963 Average	13,335	2,615	88,251	15,637	16,636
1964 Average	14,872	4,217	101,191	20,371	19,596
1965 Average	19,090	6,456	116,000	21,771	25,144
1966 Average	24,031	2,705	125,673	27,522	27,173
1967 Average	30,022	5,860	148,802	32,286	35,271
1968 Average	37,319	5,305	174,736	41,268	46,100
1969 Average	43,564	4,655	198,269	52,909	54,333
1970 Average	49,054	8,832	226,919	68,746	68,860
1971 Average	61,282	7,897	257,188	93,776	87,288
1972 Average	74,978	6,104	296,429	133,610	113,867
1973 Average	102,301	17,072	388,641	193,755	171,991
1974 Average	156,712	58,613	592,160	241,395	283,978
1975 Average	183,312	−4,265	608,957	233,701	253,007
1976 Average	195,724	20,507	692,448	336,228	320,966
1977 Average	212,590	20,360	788,579	405,534	365,118
1978 Average	255,597	24,074	927,646	519,372	455,416
1979 Average	335,916	57,463	1,182,319	637,586	624,067
1980 Average	456,446	47,465	1,508,813	783,272	801,026
1981 Average	494,043	35,790	1,737,714	920,920	884,703
1982 Average	490,923	−11,699	1,802,174	952,471	854,674
1983 Average	478,430	14,431	1,918,580	1,114,298	932,873
1984 Average	496,281	23,090	2,080,648	1,317,482	1,055,052
1985 Average	466,341	5,018	2,132,303	1,341,253	999,770
1986 Average	517,461	−16,805	2,290,004	1,658,744	1,093,568
1987 Average	620,098	39,750	2,661,550	1,855,409	1,293,966
1988 Average	724,904	91,148	3,111,225	1,914,488	1,528,762
1989 Average	855,292	29,872	3,574,928	1,953,257	1,649,638
1990 Average	947,477	−1,638	3,991,621	2,013,953	1,783,570
1991 Average	1,042,983	28,819	4,466,327	2,280,505	2,042,695

5. Expenditure on Gross Domestic Product (*Continued*)
(At current prices)

Period	Gross domestic product	National consumption			Subtotal
		Subtotal	Private	Government	
II. Percentage (%)					
1951	100.0	90.2	72.4	17.8	14.5
1952	100.0	90.8	73.8	17.0	15.3
1953	100.0	91.1	75.6	15.5	14.1
1954	100.0	92.4	74.1	18.3	16.0
1955	100.0	91.0	72.1	18.9	13.3
1956	100.0	90.8	70.4	20.4	16.0
1957	100.0	89.3	69.1	20.2	15.9
1958	100.0	89.8	69.0	20.8	16.5
1959	100.0	89.5	68.8	20.7	18.8
1960	100.0	87.3	68.1	19.2	20.2
1961	100.0	87.2	67.9	19.3	20.0
1962	100.0	87.5	67.5	20.0	17.8
1963	100.0	82.9	64.1	18.8	18.3
1964	100.0	80.5	63.1	17.4	18.7
1965	100.0	80.3	63.4	16.9	22.6
1966	100.0	78.6	61.2	17.4	21.2
1967	100.0	77.4	59.9	17.5	24.6
1968	100.0	77.7	59.9	17.8	25.1
1969	100.0	76.2	57.8	18.4	24.5
1970	100.0	74.6	56.3	18.3	25.5
1971	100.0	71.3	54.1	17.2	26.2
1972	100.0	68.2	52.1	16.1	25.6
1973	100.0	65.6	50.4	15.2	29.1
1974	100.0	68.6	54.5	14.1	39.2
1975	100.0	72.9	57.1	15.8	30.4
1976	100.0	67.3	52.1	15.2	30.6
1977	100.0	67.0	51.5	15.5	28.1
1978	100.0	65.4	50.2	15.2	28.2
1979	100.0	65.9	50.5	15.4	32.9
1980	100.0	67.4	51.5	15.9	33.8
1981	100.0	68.1	52.0	16.1	29.9
1982	100.0	69.7	52.8	16.9	25.2
1983	100.0	67.9	51.7	16.2	23.5
1984	100.0	66.7	50.8	15.9	22.2
1985	100.0	67.1	51.0	16.1	19.1
1986	100.0	62.7	47.9	14.8	17.5
1987	100.0	62.1	47.7	14.4	20.4
1988	100.0	65.7	50.5	15.2	23.3
1989	100.0	69.4	53.4	16.0	22.8
1990	100.0	72.1	54.5	17.6	22.4
1991	100.0	72.2	54.3	17.9	22.8

5. Expenditure on Gross Domestic Product (*Continued*)
(At current prices)

Period	Gross capital formation		National expenditure	Exports of goods & services	Less: imports of goods & services
	Gross fixed capital formation	Increase in inventory			
II. Percentage (%)					
1951	10.8	3.7	104.7	10.2	14.9
1952	11.2	4.1	106.1	8.0	14.1
1953	11.7	2.4	105.2	8.6	13.8
1954	13.2	2.8	108.4	6.5	14.8
1955	11.3	2.0	104.3	8.3	12.6
1956	13.3	2.7	106.9	9.0	15.9
1957	13.2	2.7	105.1	9.7	14.8
1958	15.0	1.5	106.4	10.4	16.8
1959	16.6	2.2	108.3	12.7	20.9
1960	16.6	3.6	107.5	11.5	19.0
1961	16.2	3.8	107.1	14.0	21.1
1962	15.1	2.7	105.3	13.6	18.9
1963	15.3	3.0	101.1	17.9	19.1
1964	14.6	4.1	99.2	20.0	19.2
1965	16.9	5.7	103.0	19.3	22.3
1966	19.1	2.1	99.7	21.8	21.6
1967	20.6	4.0	102.0	22.1	24.2
1968	22.0	3.1	102.8	24.3	27.1
1969	22.1	2.4	100.7	26.9	27.6
1970	21.6	3.9	100.1	30.3	30.4
1971	23.2	3.0	97.5	35.6	33.1
1972	23.7	1.9	93.8	42.3	36.0
1973	24.9	4.2	94.7	47.2	41.9
1974	28.5	10.7	107.7	43.9	51.7
1975	31.1	−0.7	103.3	39.6	42.9
1976	27.7	2.9	97.8	47.5	45.4
1977	25.6	2.5	95.1	48.9	44.0
1978	25.8	2.4	93.6	52.4	45.9
1979	28.1	4.8	98.9	53.3	52.2
1980	30.6	3.2	101.2	52.5	53.7
1981	27.9	2.0	98.0	51.9	49.9
1982	25.8	−0.6	94.9	50.1	45.0
1983	22.8	0.7	91.4	53.1	44.4
1984	21.2	1.0	88.8	56.2	45.0
1985	18.9	0.2	86.2	54.2	40.4
1986	18.1	−0.6	80.2	58.1	38.3
1987	19.2	1.2	82.6	57.6	40.1
1988	20.7	2.6	89.0	54.7	43.7
1989	22.1	0.8	92.2	50.4	42.5
1990	22.4	0.0	94.5	47.7	42.2
1991	22.2	0.6	94.9	48.5	43.4

6. Finances of Gross Domestic Capital Formation

Period	Gross domestic capital formation	Gross national savings			
		Total	Provisions for capital consumption		
			Subtotal	Public enterprises	Private sector
I. Amount (NT$ million)					
1951	1,779	1,931	641	236	405
1952	2,643	2,639	827	292	535
1953	3,224	3,316	1,063	305	758
1954	4,041	3,371	1,259	439	820
1955	3,998	4,364	1,504	448	1,056
1956	5,524	4,583	1,835	604	1,231
1957	6,355	5,524	2,346	821	1,525
1958	7,458	6,830	2,622	865	1,757
1959	9,732	8,069	3,239	1,093	2,146
1960	12,618	11,100	4,037	1,379	2,658
1961	13,983	12,872	4,380	1,426	2,954
1962	13,733	11,700	4,846	1,623	3,223
1963	15,950	16,627	5,422	1,927	3,495
1964	19,089	20,685	6,419	2,175	4,244
1965	25,546	23,294	7,051	2,218	4,833
1966	26,736	27,935	7,817	2,372	5,445
1967	35,882	33,549	9,252	2,847	6,405
1968	42,624	37,978	10,899	3,163	7,736
1969	48,219	46,861	13,052	3,924	9,128
1970	57,886	57,917	15,298	4,669	10,629
1971	69,179	76,001	18,236	5,679	12,557
1972	81,082	101,591	22,557	6,756	15,801
1973	119,373	141,031	28,872	6,761	22,111
1974	215,325	173,046	36,611	9,369	27,242
1975	179,047	156,685	41,153	11,292	29,861
1976	216,231	227,250	51,746	14,936	36,810
1977	232,950	268,408	62,455	17,908	44,547
1978	279,671	340,220	77,210	22,446	54,764
1979	393,379	399,307	92,043	27,282	64,761
1980	503,911	480,628	109,343	31,154	78,189
1981	529,833	553,005	138,055	41,998	96,057
1982	479,224	571,055	154,988	50,174	104,814
1983	492,861	675,850	172,484	56,700	115,784
1984	519,371	800,487	192,765	65,549	127,216
1985	471,359	844,192	216,676	79,009	137,667
1986	500,656	1,125,196	237,485	81,589	155,896
1987	659,848	1,265,081	261,005	86,414	174,591
1988	816,052	1,235,080	281,639	90,156	191,483
1989	885,164	1,223,090	305,686	94,615	211,071
1990	945,839	1,261,409	337,451	101,685	235,766
1991	1,071,802	1,419,976	405,007	—	—

Source: See Table 5.

6. Finances of Gross Domestic Capital Formation (*Continued*)

Period	Gross national savings				Net borrowing from rest of the world
	Subtotal	Government	Public enterprises	Private sector	
I. Amount (NT$ million)					
1951	1,290	458	59	773	−152
1952	1,812	939	64	809	4
1953	2,253	1,134	144	975	−92
1954	2,112	1,185	139	788	670
1955	2,860	1,515	231	1,114	−366
1956	2,748	1,076	351	1,321	941
1957	3,178	1,059	429	1,690	831
1958	4,208	1,781	542	1,885	628
1959	4,830	1,932	694	2,204	1,663
1960	7,063	2,492	1,155	3,416	1,518
1961	8,492	2,456	1,138	4,898	1,111
1962	6,854	1,245	592	5,017	2,033
1963	11,205	1,287	1,420	8,498	−677
1964	14,266	1,701	2,069	10,496	−1,596
1965	16,243	2,945	1,929	11,369	2,252
1966	20,118	3,121	1,668	15,329	−1,199
1967	24,297	3,545	2,693	18,059	2,333
1968	27,079	6,494	4,502	16,083	4,646
1969	33,809	9,400	6,323	18,086	1,358
1970	42,619	8,075	5,770	28,774	−31
1971	57,765	10,954	5,469	41,342	−6,822
1972	79,034	20,404	6,048	52,582	−20,509
1973	112,159	25,423	5,359	81,377	−21,658
1974	136,435	45,851	9,687	80,897	42,279
1975	115,532	41,338	12,404	61,790	22,362
1976	175,504	58,107	16,797	100,600	−11,019
1977	205,953	68,822	17,728	124,403	−35,458
1978	263,010	85,071	20,658	157,281	−60,549
1979	307,264	112,162	23,536	171,566	−5,928
1980	371,285	117,712	41,727	211,846	23,283
1981	414,950	116,879	41,029	257,042	−23,172
1982	416,067	96,950	46,312	272,805	−91,831
1983	503,366	118,118	56,838	328,410	−182,989
1984	607,722	135,846	77,391	394,485	−281,116
1985	627,516	131,075	60,129	436,312	−372,833
1986	887,711	126,883	61,863	698,965	−624,540
1987	1,004,076	207,175	54,485	742,416	−605,233
1988	953,441	259,515	65,769	628,157	−419,028
1989	917,404	310,728	50,861	555,815	−337,926
1990	923,958	250,913	53,616	619,429	−315,570
1991	1,014,969	—	—	—	−348,174

Source: See Table 5.

6. Finances of Gross Domestic Capital Formation (*Continued*)

Period	Gross domestic capital formation	Gross domestic savings			
		Total	Provisions for capital consumption		
			Subtotal	Public enterprises	Private sector

II. Percentage (%)

Period	Gross domestic capital formation	Total	Subtotal	Public enterprises	Private sector
1951	100.0	108.5	36.0	13.3	22.8
1952	100.0	99.8	31.3	11.0	20.2
1953	100.0	102.9	33.0	9.5	23.5
1954	100.0	83.4	31.2	10.9	20.3
1955	100.0	109.2	37.6	11.2	26.4
1956	100.0	83.0	33.2	10.9	22.3
1957	100.0	86.9	36.9	12.9	24.0
1958	100.0	91.6	35.2	11.6	23.6
1959	100.0	82.9	33.3	11.2	22.1
1960	100.0	88.0	32.0	10.9	21.1
1961	100.0	92.1	31.3	10.2	21.1
1962	100.0	85.2	35.3	11.8	23.5
1963	100.0	104.2	34.0	12.1	21.9
1964	100.0	108.4	33.6	11.4	22.2
1965	100.0	91.2	27.6	8.7	18.9
1966	100.0	104.5	29.2	8.9	20.4
1967	100.0	93.5	25.8	7.9	17.9
1968	100.0	89.1	25.6	7.4	18.1
1969	100.0	97.2	27.1	8.1	18.9
1970	100.0	100.1	26.4	8.1	18.4
1971	100.0	109.9	26.4	8.2	18.2
1972	100.0	125.3	27.8	8.3	19.5
1973	100.0	118.1	24.2	5.7	18.5
1974	100.0	80.4	17.0	4.4	12.7
1975	100.0	87.5	23.0	6.3	16.7
1976	100.0	105.1	23.9	6.9	17.0
1977	100.0	115.2	26.8	7.7	19.1
1978	100.0	121.7	27.6	8.0	19.6
1979	100.0	101.5	23.4	6.9	16.5
1980	100.0	95.4	21.7	6.2	15.5
1981	100.0	104.4	26.1	7.9	18.1
1982	100.0	119.2	32.3	10.5	21.9
1983	100.0	137.1	35.0	11.5	23.5
1984	100.0	154.1	37.1	12.6	24.5
1985	100.0	179.1	46.0	16.8	29.2
1986	100.0	224.7	47.4	16.3	31.1
1987	100.0	191.7	39.6	13.1	26.5
1988	100.0	151.3	34.5	11.0	23.5
1989	100.0	138.2	34.5	10.7	23.8
1990	100.0	133.4	35.7	10.8	24.9
1991	100.0	132.5	37.8	—	—

6. Finances of Gross Domestic Capital Formation (*Continued*)

Period	Gross national savings				Net borrowing from rest of the world
	Subtotal	Government	Public enterprises	Private sector	
II. Percentage					
1951	72.5	25.7	3.3	43.5	−8.5
1952	68.6	35.5	2.4	30.6	0.2
1953	69.9	35.2	4.5	30.2	−2.9
1954	52.3	29.3	3.4	19.5	16.6
1955	71.5	37.9	5.8	27.9	−9.2
1956	49.7	19.5	6.4	23.9	17.0
1957	50.0	16.7	6.8	26.6	13.1
1958	56.4	23.9	7.3	25.3	8.4
1959	49.6	19.9	7.1	22.6	17.1
1960	56.0	19.7	9.2	27.1	12.0
1961	60.7	17.6	8.1	35.0	7.9
1962	49.9	9.1	4.3	36.5	14.8
1963	70.3	8.1	8.9	53.3	−4.2
1964	74.7	8.9	10.8	55.0	−8.4
1965	63.6	11.5	7.6	44.5	8.8
1966	75.2	11.7	6.2	57.3	−4.5
1967	67.7	9.9	7.5	50.3	6.5
1968	63.5	15.2	10.6	37.7	10.9
1969	70.1	19.5	13.1	37.5	2.8
1970	73.6	13.9	10.0	49.7	−0.1
1971	83.5	15.8	7.9	59.8	−9.9
1972	97.5	25.2	7.5	64.9	−25.3
1973	94.0	21.3	4.5	68.2	−18.1
1974	63.4	21.3	4.5	37.6	19.6
1975	64.5	23.1	6.9	34.5	12.5
1976	81.2	26.9	7.8	46.5	−5.1
1977	88.4	27.4	7.6	53.4	−15.2
1978	94.0	30.4	7.4	56.2	−21.7
1979	78.1	28.5	6.0	43.6	−1.5
1980	73.7	23.4	8.3	42.0	4.6
1981	78.3	22.1	7.7	48.5	−4.4
1982	86.8	20.2	9.7	56.9	−19.2
1983	102.1	24.0	11.5	66.6	−37.1
1984	117.0	26.2	14.9	76.0	−54.1
1985	133.1	27.8	12.8	92.6	−79.1
1986	177.3	25.3	12.4	139.6	−124.7
1987	152.2	31.4	8.3	112.5	−91.7
1988	116.8	31.8	8.1	77.0	−51.3
1989	103.6	35.1	5.7	62.8	−38.2
1990	97.7	26.5	5.7	65.5	−33.4
1991	94.7	—	—	—	−32.5

Appendix

7. Foreign & Overseas Chinese Investment in Approvals

Amount unit: US$1,000

	Total		Overseas Chinese		Foreign Nationals	
	Number of Cases	Amount	Number of Cases	Amount	Number of Cases	Amount
1952	5	1,067	5	1,067	—	—
1953	14	3,695	12	1,654	2	2,041
1954	8	2,220	3	128	5	2,092
1955	5	4,599	3	176	2	4,423
1956	15	3,593	13	2,484	2	1,009
1957	14	1,622	10	1,574	4	48
1958	9	2,518	6	1,402	3	1,116
1959	2	965	—	820	2	145
1960	14	15,473	6	1,135	8	14,338
1961	29	14,304	24	8,340	5	5,964
1962	36	5,203	10	1,660	26	3,543
1963	38	18,050	22	7,703	16	10,347
1964	41	19,897	28	8,007	13	11,890
1965	66	41,610	30	6,470	36	35,140
1966	103	29,281	51	8,377	52	20,904
1967	212	57,006	105	18,340	107	38,666
1968	325	89,894	203	36,449	122	53,445
1969	201	109,437	90	27,499	111	81,938
1970	151	138,896	80	29,731	71	109,165
1971	130	162,956	86	37,808	44	125,148
1972	166	126,656	114	26,466	52	100,190
1973	351	248,854	201	55,166	150	193,688
1974	168	189,376	85	80,640	83	108,736
1975	85	118,175	44	47,235	41	70,940
1976	98	141,519	53	39,487	45	102,032
1977	102	163,909	52	68,723	50	95,186
1978	116	212,929	50	76,210	66	136,719
1979	123	328,835	50	147,352	73	181,483
1980	110	465,964	39	222,584	71	243,380
1981	105	395,757	32	39,463	73	356,294
1982	132	380,006	50	59,720	82	320,286
1983	149	404,468	49	29,086	100	375,382
1984	174	558,741	74	39,770	100	518,971
1985	174	702,460	67	41,757	107	660,703
1986	286	770,380	80	64,806	206	705,574
1987	480	1,418,796	117	195,727	363	1,223,069
1988	527	1,182,538	89	121,377	438	1,061,161
1989	548	2,418,299	70	177,273	478	2,241,026
1990	461	2,301,772	85	220,115	376	2,081,657
1991	389	1,778,419	65	219,462	324	1,558,957
Total	6,162	15,030,035	2,253	2,173,242	3,909	12,856,793

Source: Ministry of Economic Affairs, R.O.C., *Statistics on Overseas Chinese and Foreign Investment, Technical Cooperation, Outward Investment, Outward Technical Cooperation, R.O.C.*, various issues.

8. Per Capita Gross National Product in Comparison with Other Major Countries

Unit: US$

Period	Republic of China	U.S.A.	Japan	Germany	France	U.K.
1971	443	5,310	2,195	3,514	3,113	2,561
1972	522	5,778	2,847	4,196	3,784	2,903
1973	695	6,415	3,814	5,548	4,862	3,300
1974	920	6,887	4,161	6,140	5,156	3,584
1975	964	7,401	4,471	6,767	6,496	4,262
1976	1,132	8,176	4,984	7,271	6,726	4,145
1977	1,301	9,038	6,117	8,411	7,343	4,569
1978	1,577	10,107	8,592	10,488	9,060	5,818
1979	1,920	11,145	8,730	12,401	10,878	7,530
1980	2,344	11,996	9,137	13,273	12,335	9,605
1981	2,669	13,264	9,925	11,086	10,748	9,214
1982	2,653	13,616	9,168	10,678	10,127	8,670
1983	2,823	14,505	9,963	10,716	9,605	8,235
1984	3,167	16,926	10,544	10,166	9,083	7,779
1985	3,297	16,779	11,322	10,266	9,481	8,216
1986	3,993	17,513	16,552	14,863	13,214	10,039
1987	5,275	18,714	19,847	18,253	15,960	12,233
1988	6,333	20,029	23,786	19,531	17,190	14,742
1989	7,512	21,219	23,493	19,258	17,189	14,770
1990	7,954	22,105	23,965	23,775	21,016	17,180
1991	8,788	22,501	27,323	24,622	21,188	—

Note: Figures for France and Italy are per capita GDP.
Source: IMF, *International Financial Statistics*; the Bank of Korea, *Statistical Yearbook*.

8. Per Capita Gross National Product in Comparison
with Other Major Countries (*Continued*)

Unit: US$

Period	Singapore	Italy	Republic of Korea	Portugal	Spain
1971	1,058	2,046	289	810	1,223
1972	1,345	2,367	319	997	1,537
1973	1,855	2,809	396	1,341	2,033
1974	2,255	3,090	542	1,511	2,477
1975	2,490	3,467	594	1,560	2,935
1976	2,575	3,379	803	1,586	2,989
1977	2,789	3,852	1,012	1,656	3,301
1978	3,329	4,666	1,396	1,778	3,987
1979	3,950	5,777	1,644	2,021	5,239
1980	4,688	7,010	1,592	2,424	5,600
1981	5,469	6,253	1,734	2,314	4,907
1982	6,012	6,142	1,824	2,210	4,699
1983	6,921	6,243	2,002	1,948	4,099
1984	7,563	6,114	2,158	1,786	4,147
1985	7,160	7,429	2,194	1,972	4,261
1986	7,022	10,544	2,505	2,882	5,925
1987	7,688	13,238	3,101	3,616	7,496
1988	9,350	14,603	4,112	4,128	8,793
1989	10,595	15,122	4,983	4,535	9,697
1990	11,856	18,986	5,552	6,024	12,497
1991	14,818	—	6,493	—	13,380

INDEX